MW01643577

Klee/Kandinsky

HARCOURT BRACE JOVANOVICH MASTERS OF ART SERIES

Harcourt Brace Jovanovich, Inc. New York

Text and design by the staff of Tokyo International Publishers, Ltd.

ISBN 0-15-147280-7
Library of Congress Catalog Card Number: 79-161095
Printed in Japan

CONTENTS

Photographed by

Felix Klee (1) Kunstmuseum Bern—Paul Klee-Stiftung (2, 6, 9, 10, 12, 21, 25, 32, 38, 43) The Solomon R. Guggenheim Museum (7, 59, 61) Philadelphia Museum of Art (19, 55) The Phillips Collection—Henry B. Beville (30, 36) The Baltimore Museum of Art (35) Kunstmuseum der Stadt Düsseldorf—Walter Klein (48) The Art Institute of Chicago (52) René Roland (54, 58, 70, 71) Kunst-und Museumsbibliothek der Stadt Köln (57) Bousch-Reisinger Museum, Harvard University—James Ufford (62) Galerie Maeght (63, 68, 69, 73, 74) San Francisco Museum of Art (64) Hans Hinz SWB (3, 4, 5, 8, 13, 15, 17, 22, 24, 26, 29, 37, 39, 40, 41, 42, 45, 47, 53, 56, 60, 66) Photographie Giraudon (11, 14, 18, 51, 67, 72) André Held (16, 20, 23, 27, 28, 31, 33, 34, 44, 46, 49, 50, 65)

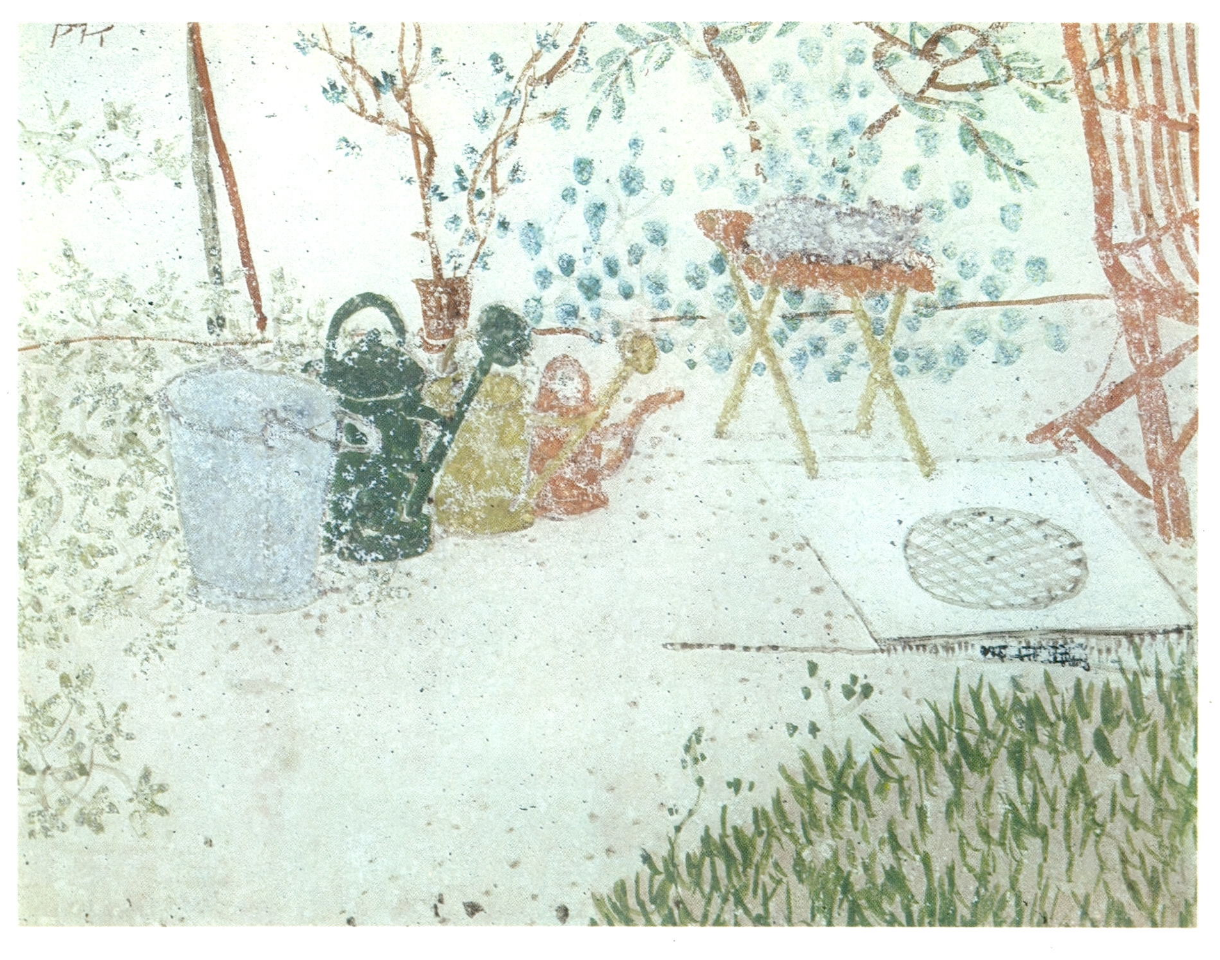

1 Klee *Garden Scene with a Watering Can* 1905 Felix Klee Bern

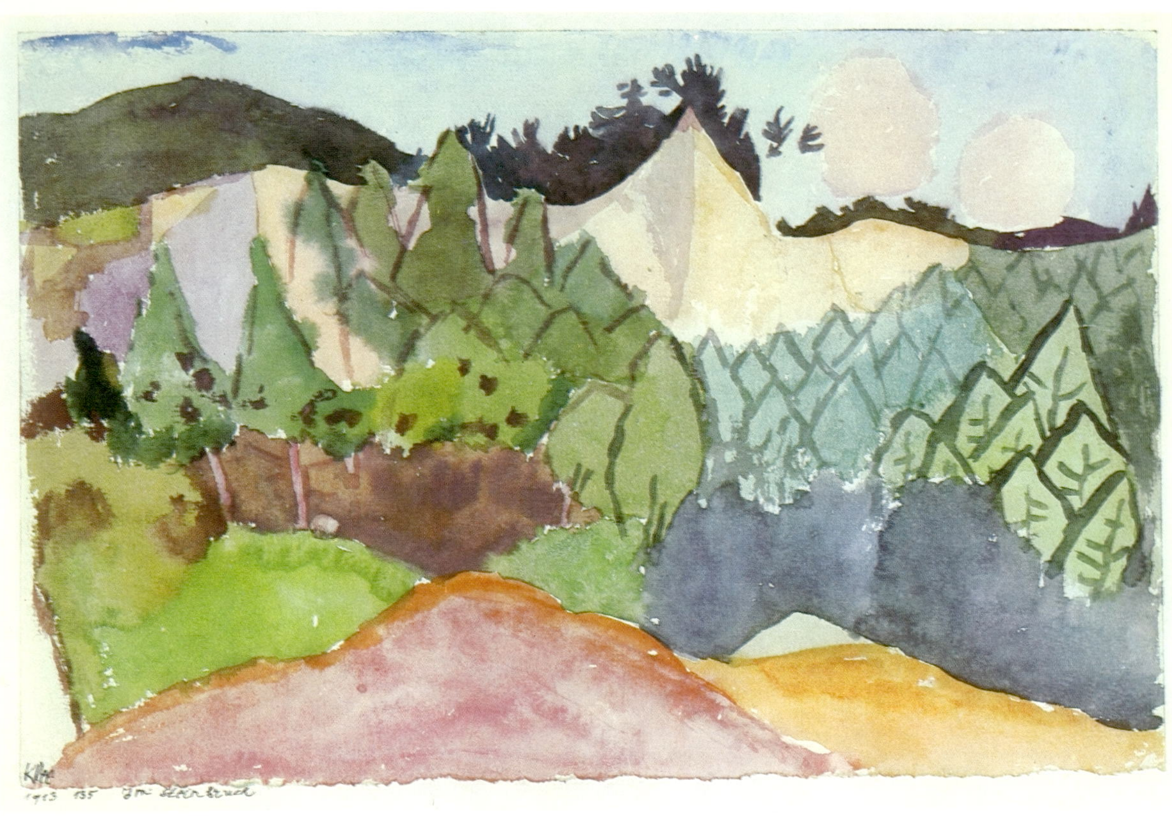

2 Klee *In the Quarry* 1913 Klee Foundation Bern

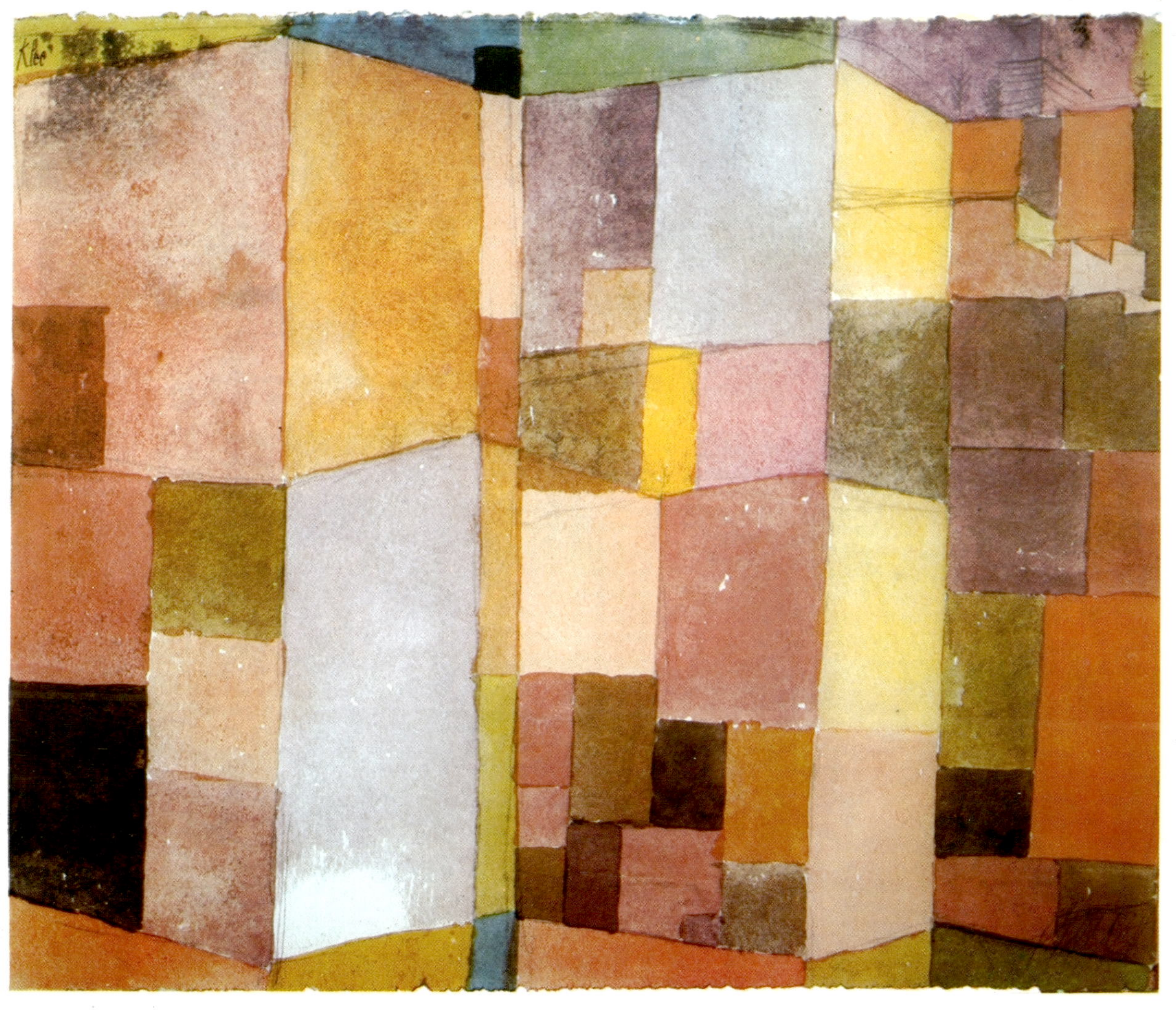

3 Klee *The Quarry at Ostermundigen* 1915 Klee Foundation Bern

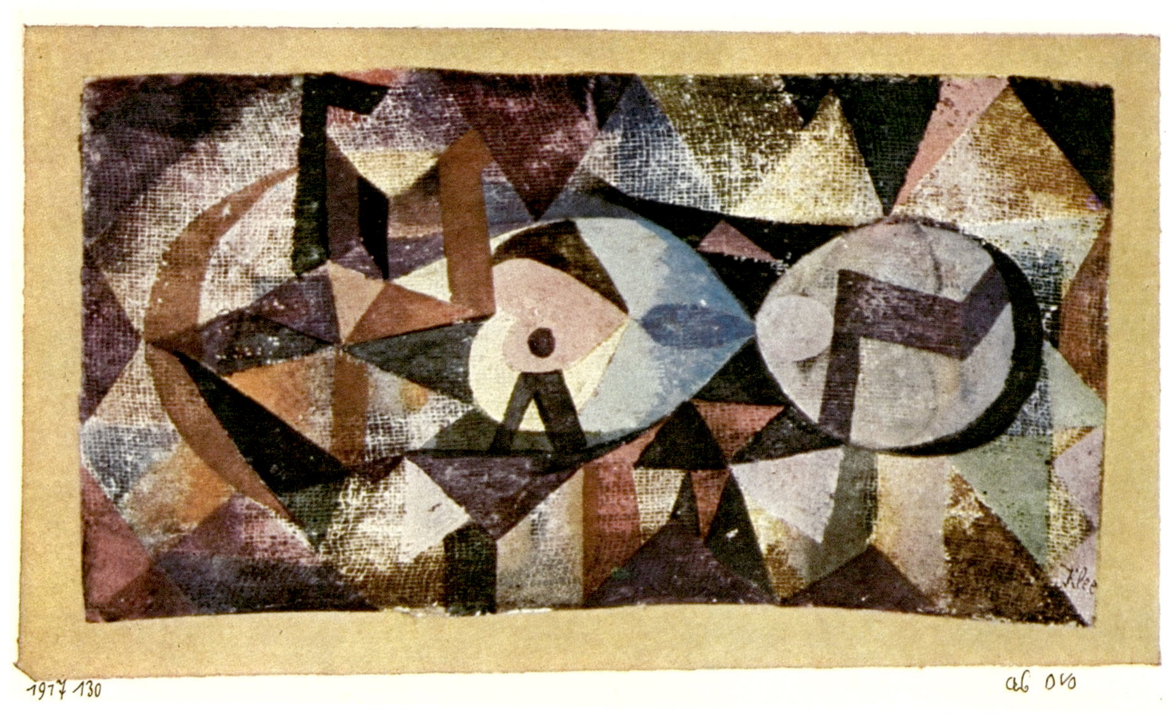

4 Klee *Ab Ovo* 1917 Klee Foundation Bern

5 Klee *Once Emerged from the Gray of Night* 1918 Klee Foundation Bern→

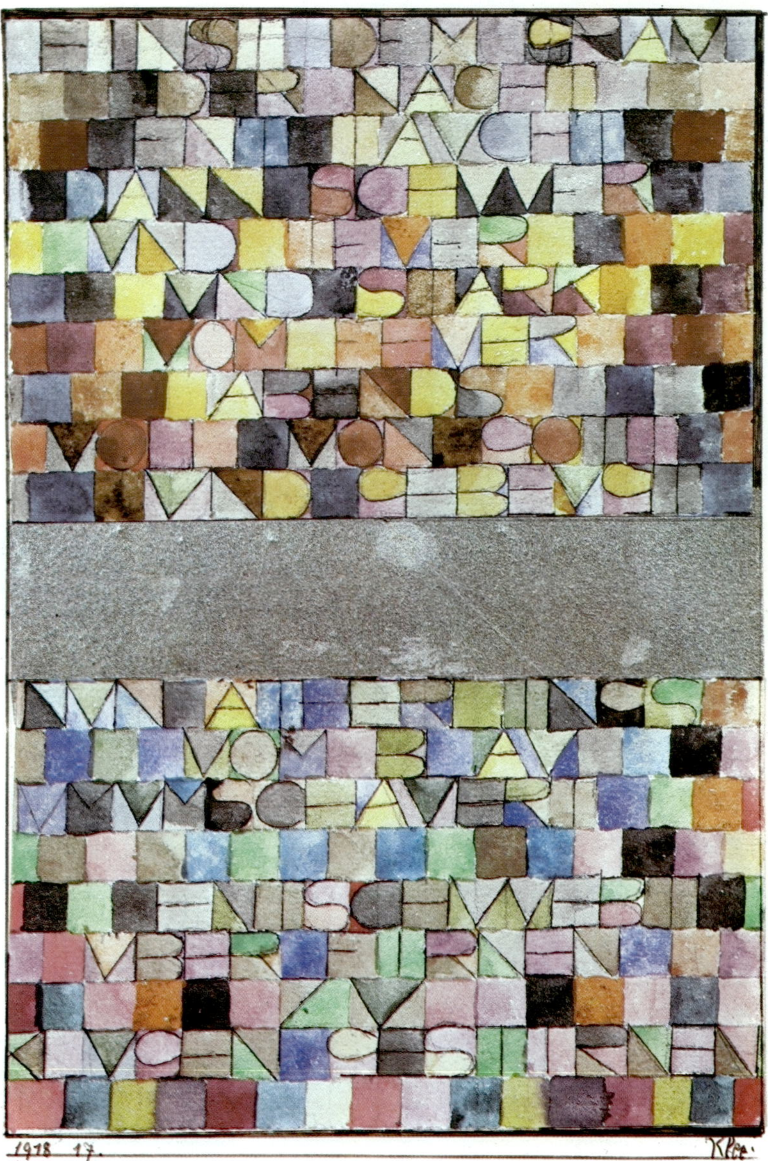
Einst dem Grau der Nacht enttaucht / Dann schwer und teuer / und stark vom Feuer /
Abends voll von Gott und gebeugt / Nun ätherlings vom Blau umschauert, / entschwebt
über Firnen, / zu klugen Gestirnen.
1918 17.
Klee.

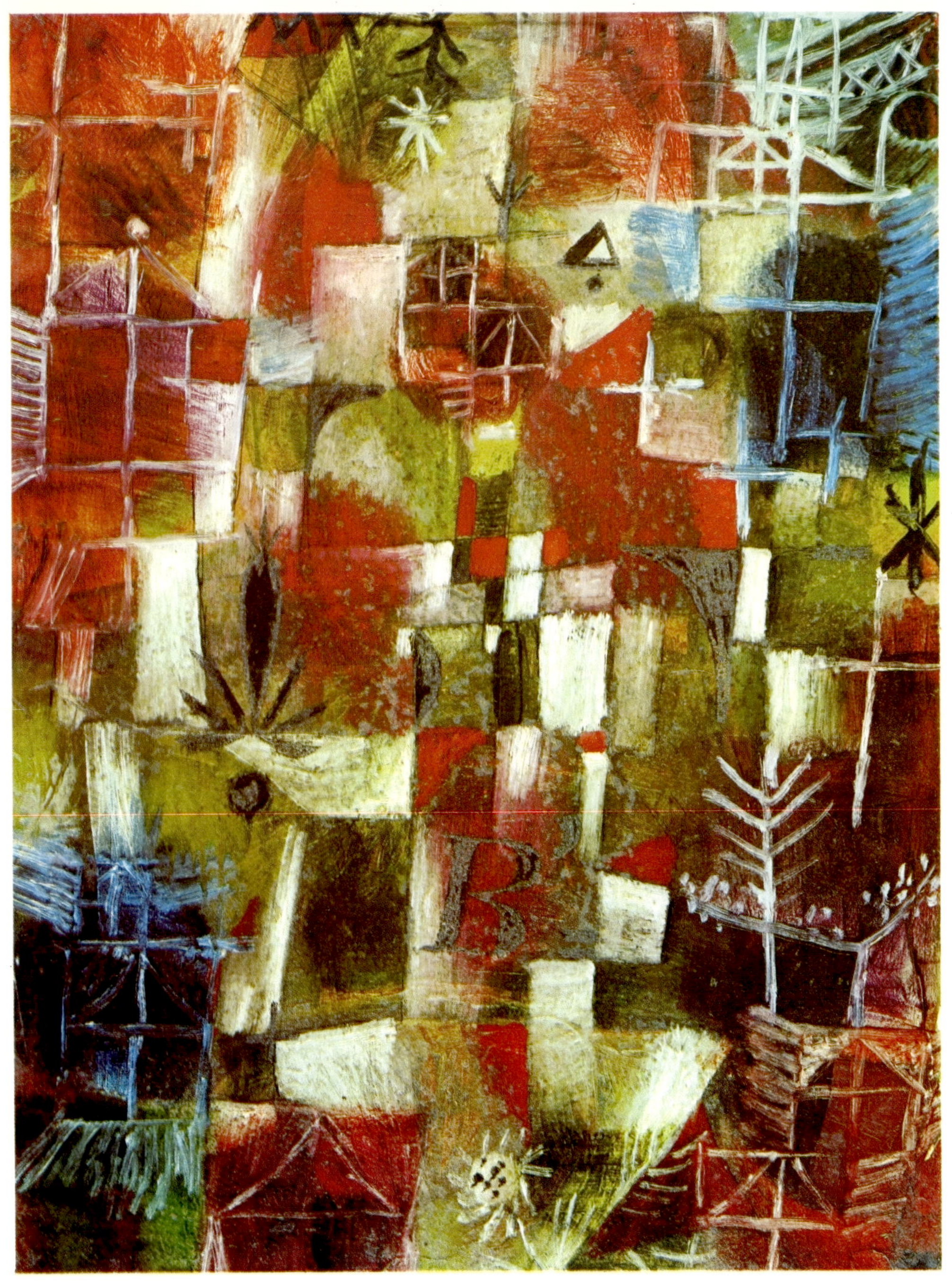

6 Klee *Composition with a B* 1919 Klee Foundation Bern

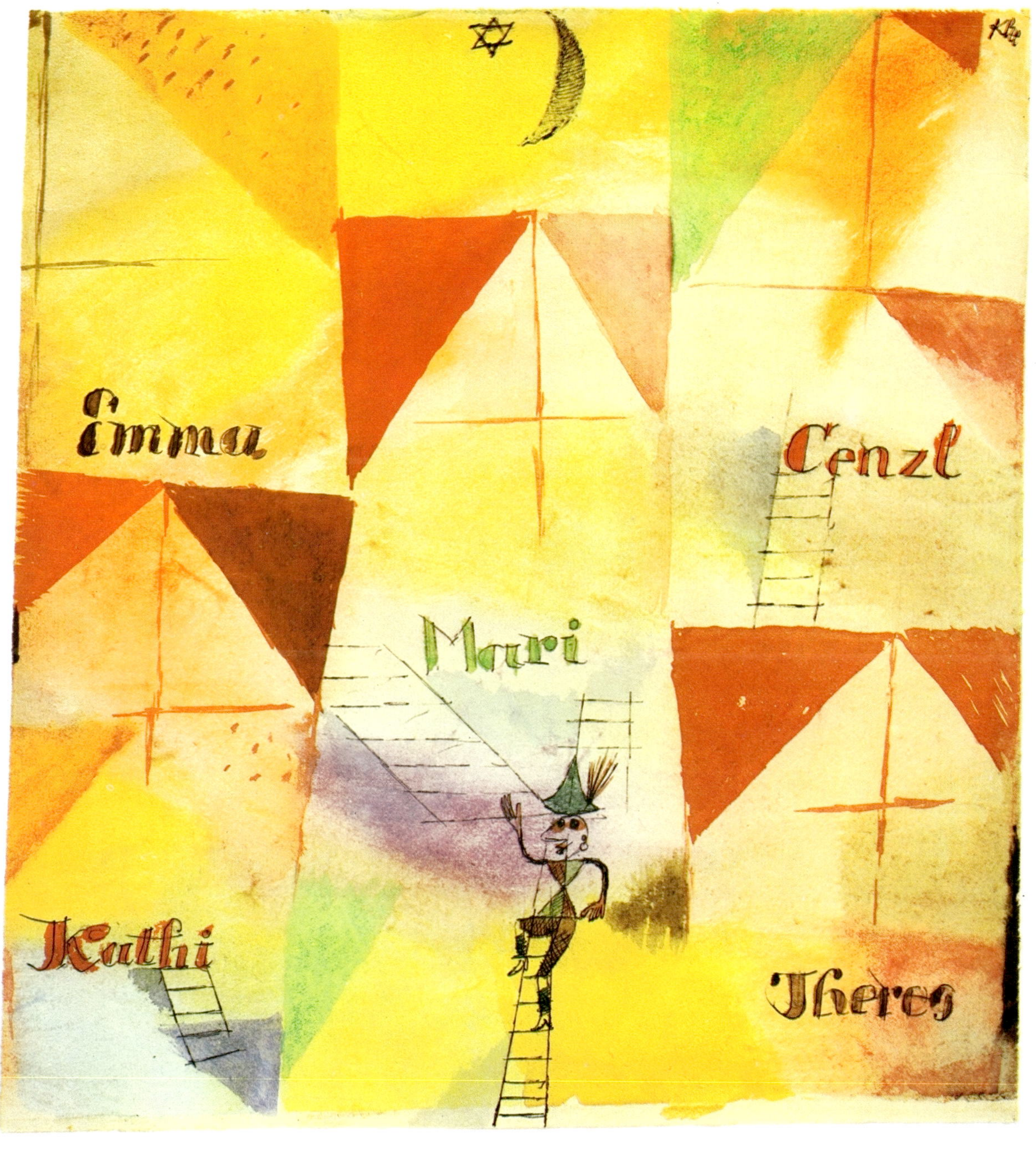

7 Klee *The Bavarian Don Giovanni* 1919 Guggenheim Museum New York

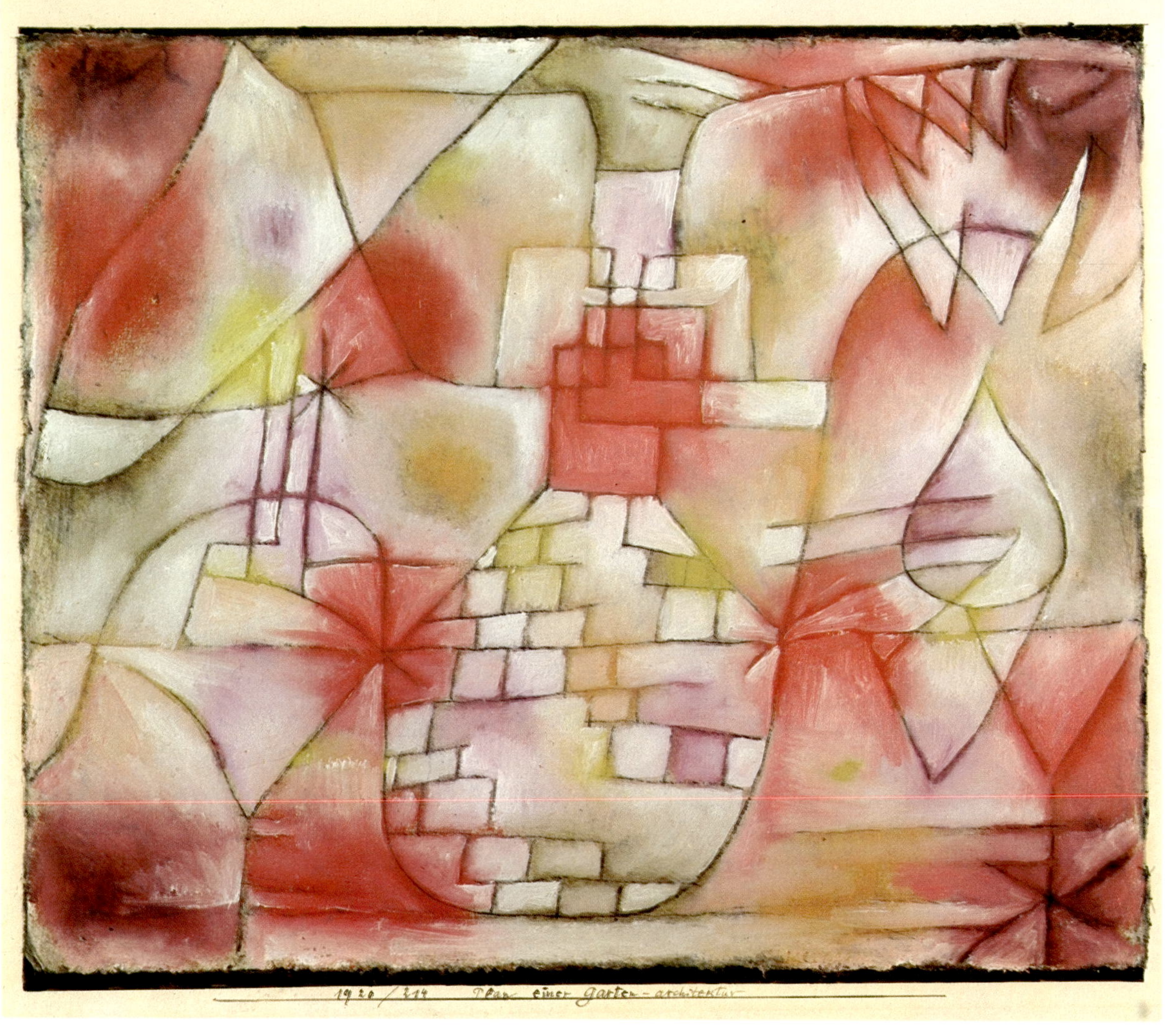

8 Klee *Ground Plan for Garden Architecture* 1920 Klee Foundation Bern

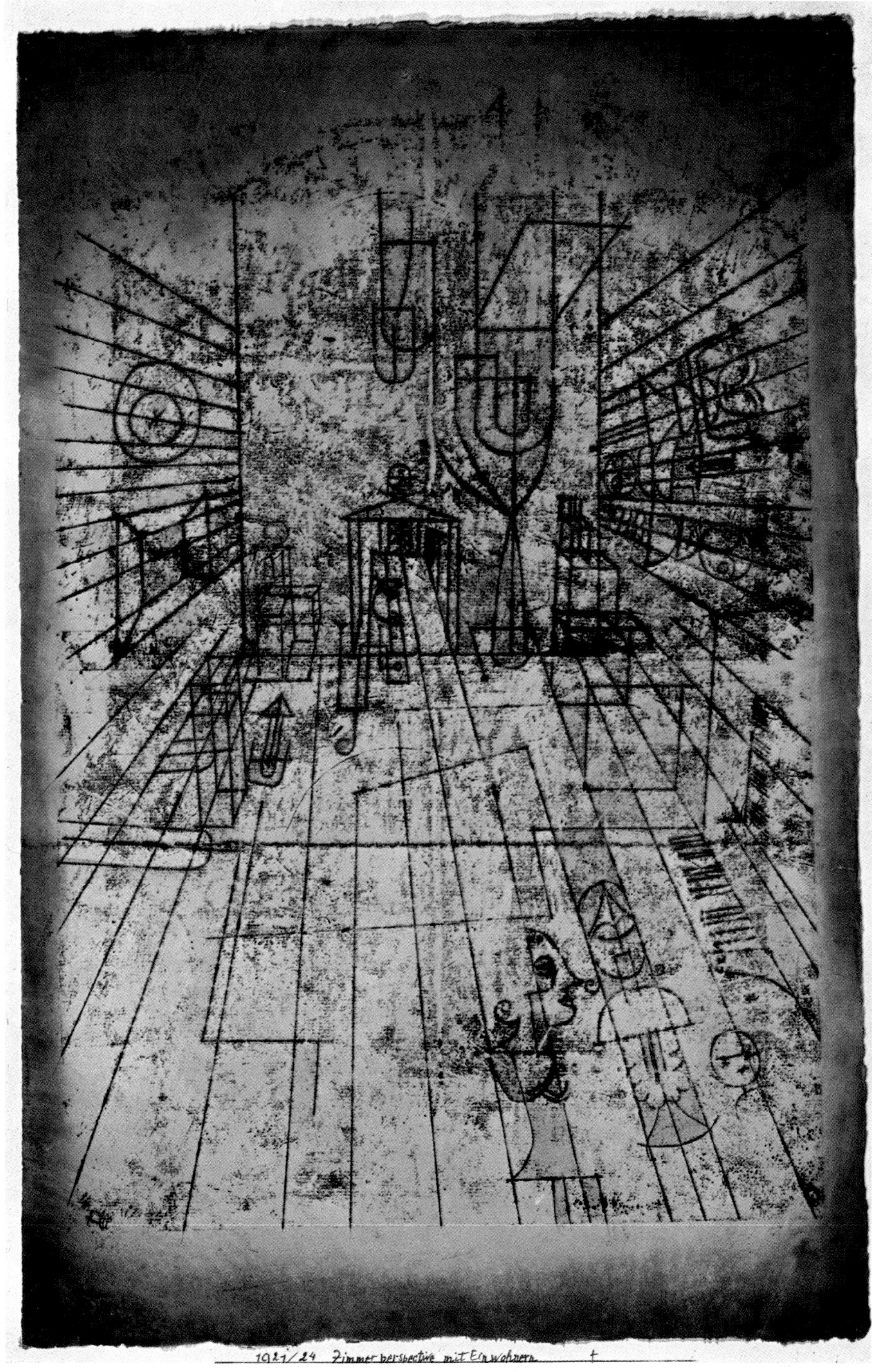

9
Klee *Perspective of a Room with Occupants* 1921 Klee Foundation Bern

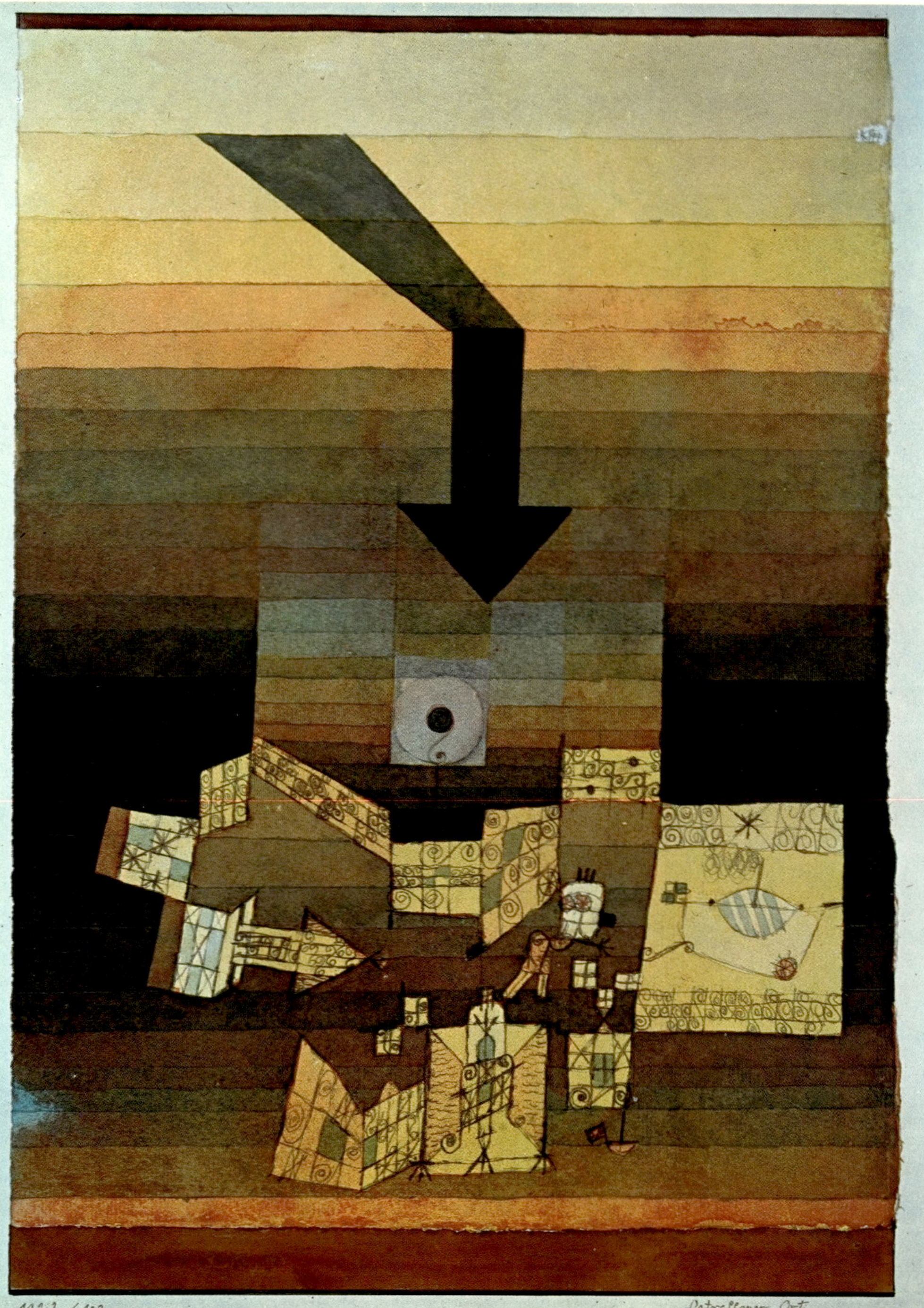

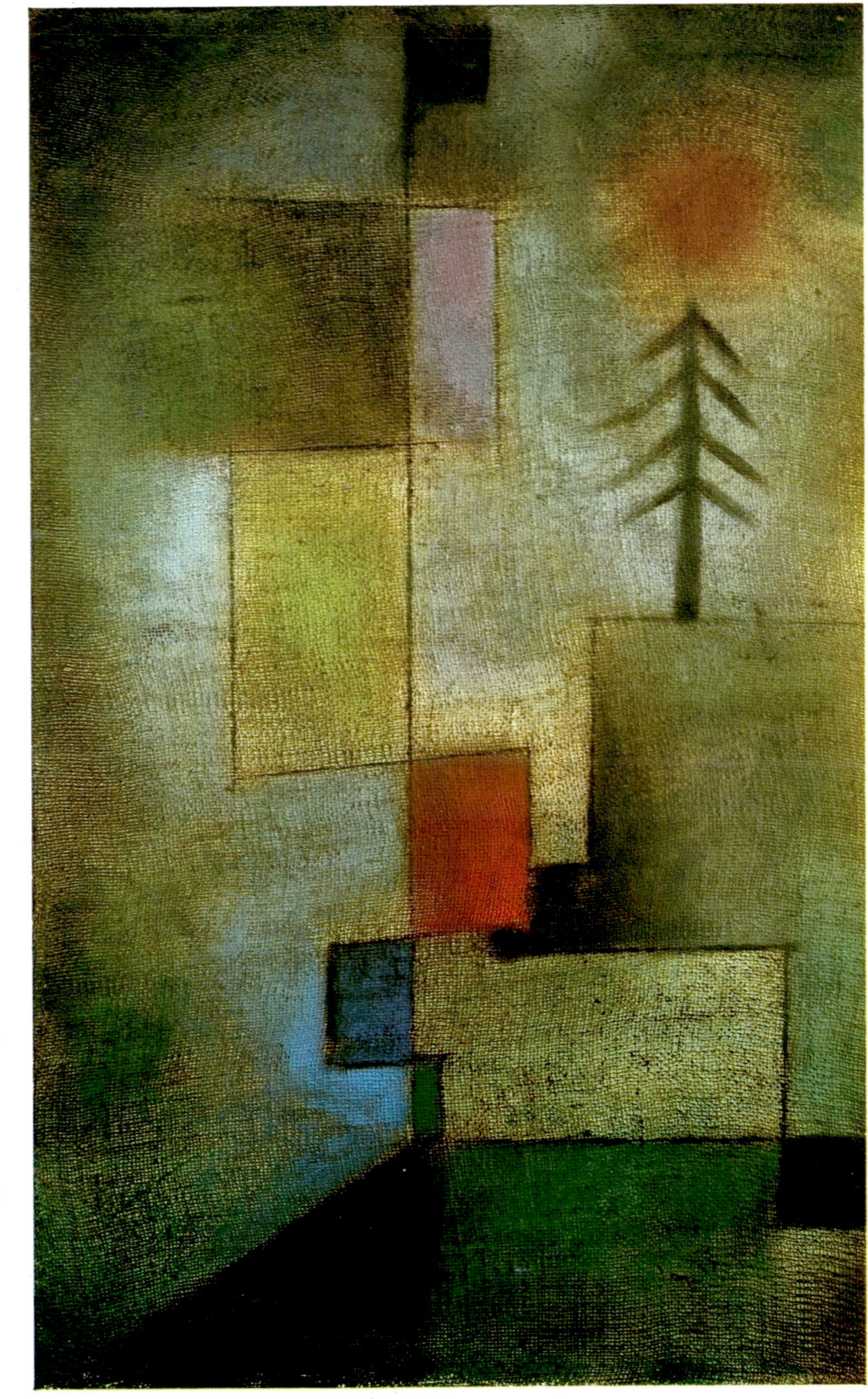

←10
Klee *Stricken Place*
1922 Klee Foundation
Bern

11
Klee *Little Fir Tree*
1922 Kunstmuseum
Basel

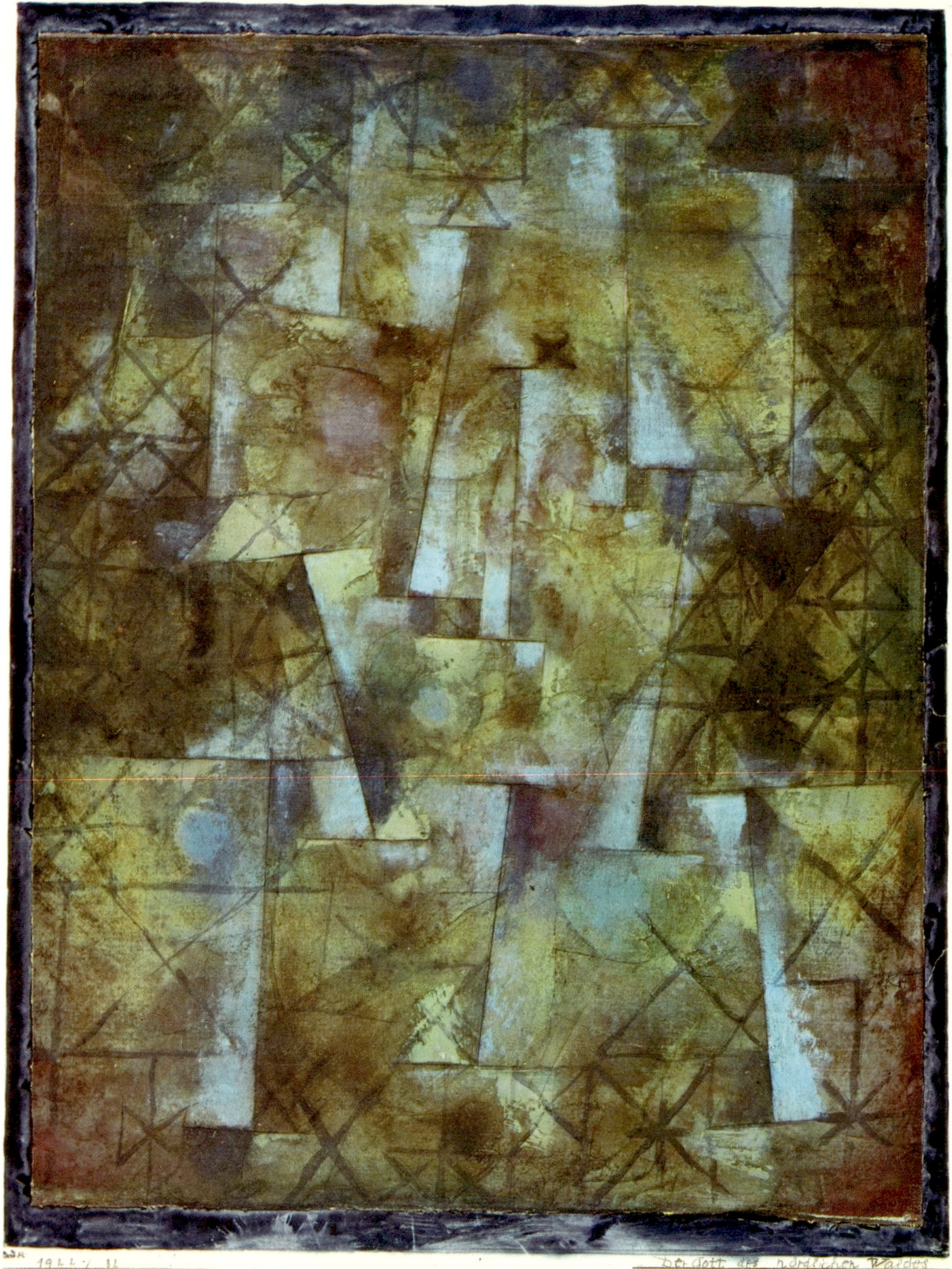
Der Gott des nördlichen Waldes

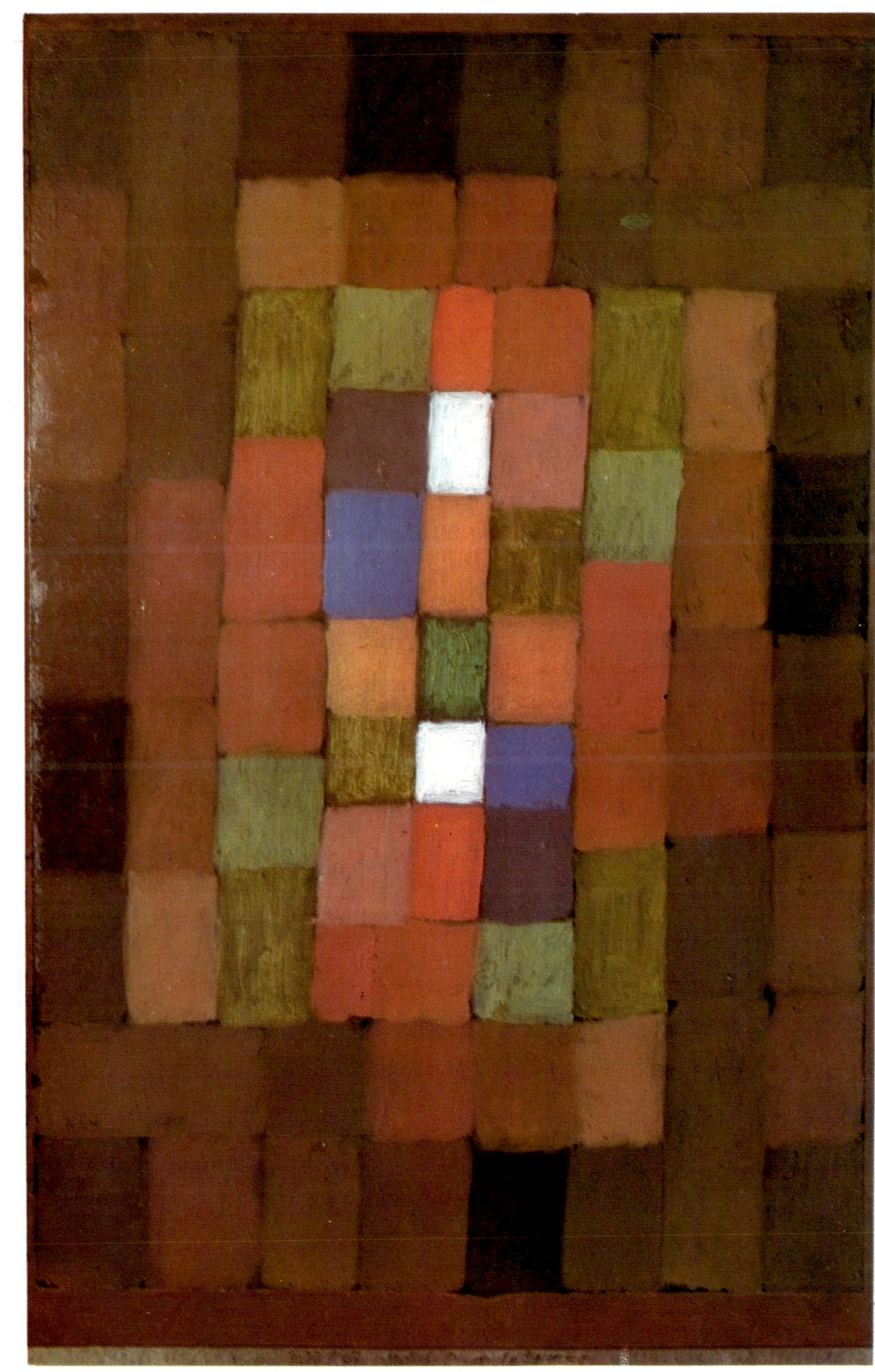

-12
Klee *God of the Northern Forests* 1922 Klee Foundation Bern

13
Klee *Intensification of Color from the Static to the Dynamic* 1923 Private Collection Berlin

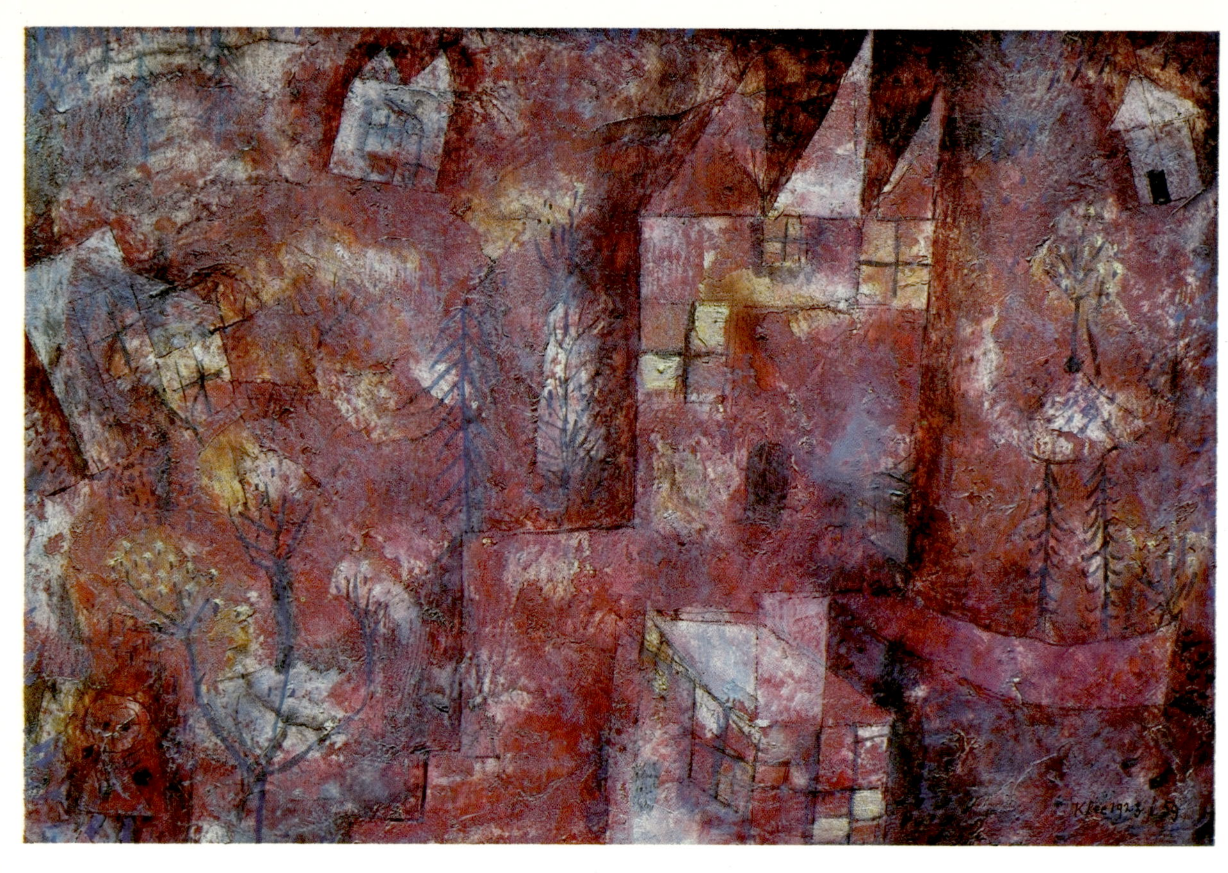

14 Klee *Child in Landscape* 1923 Museum of Art Grenoble

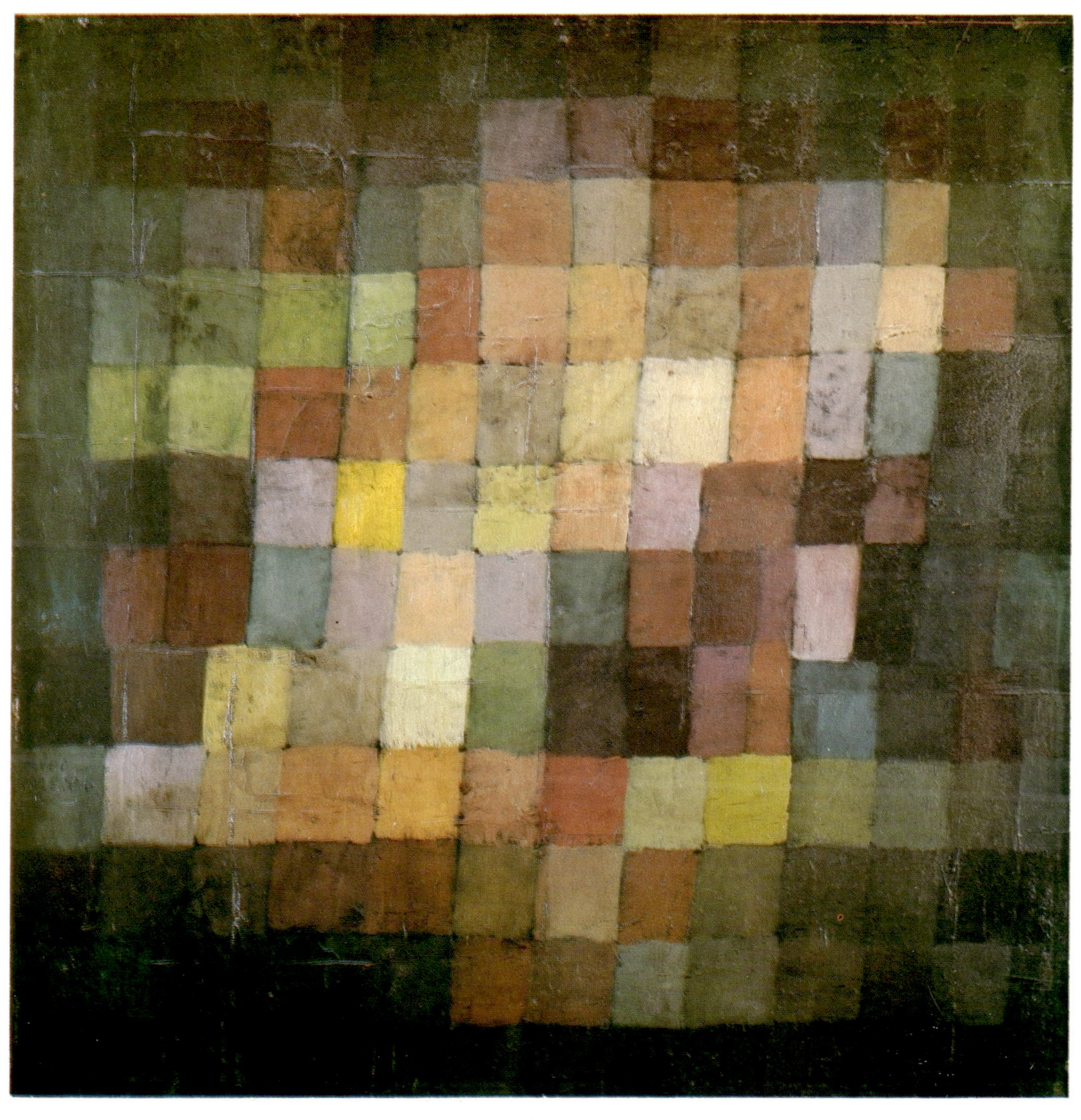

18 Klee *Ancient Sound* 1925 Kunstmuseum Basel

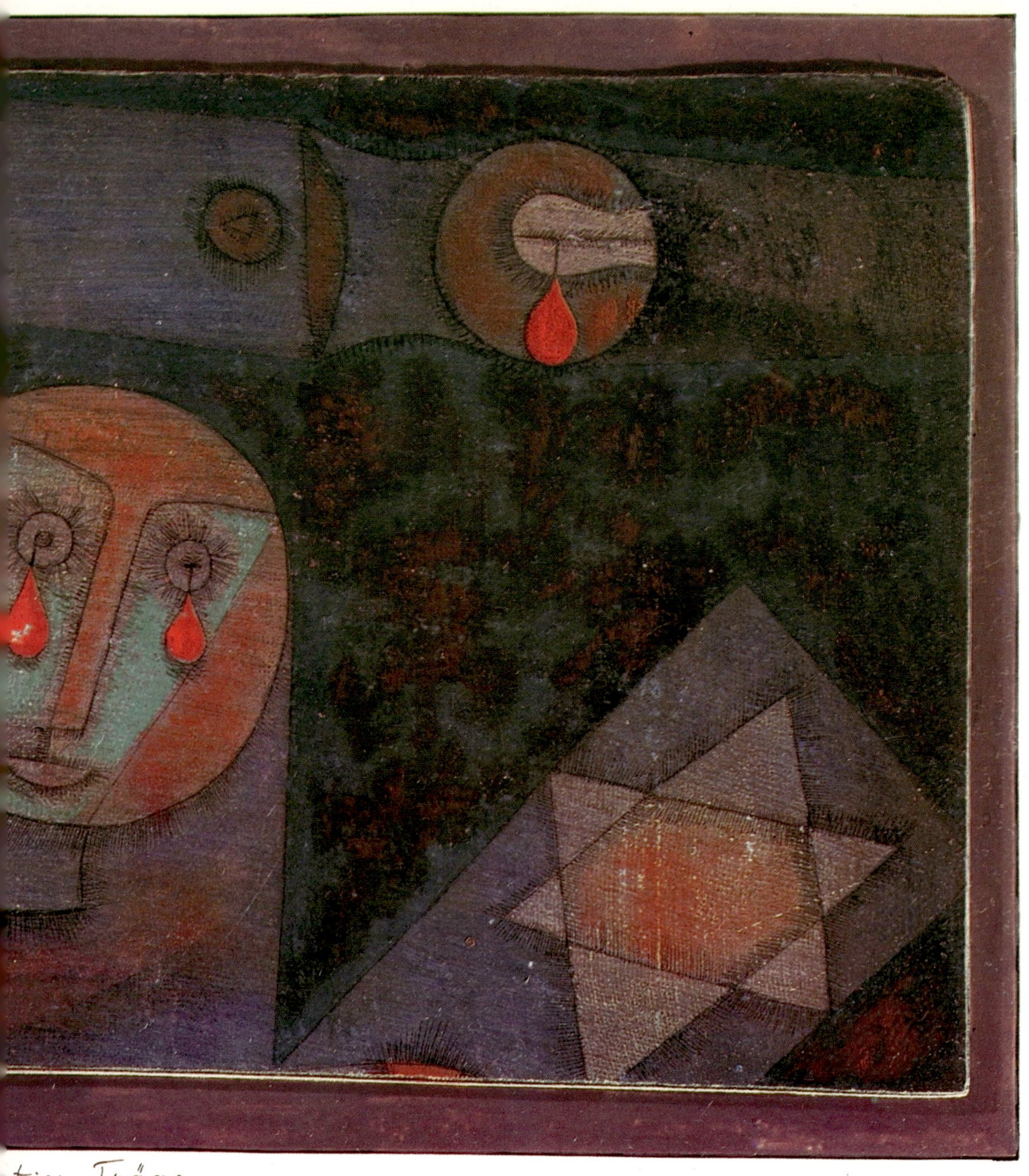

17 Klee *Tears of Blood* 1923 Klee Foundation Bern

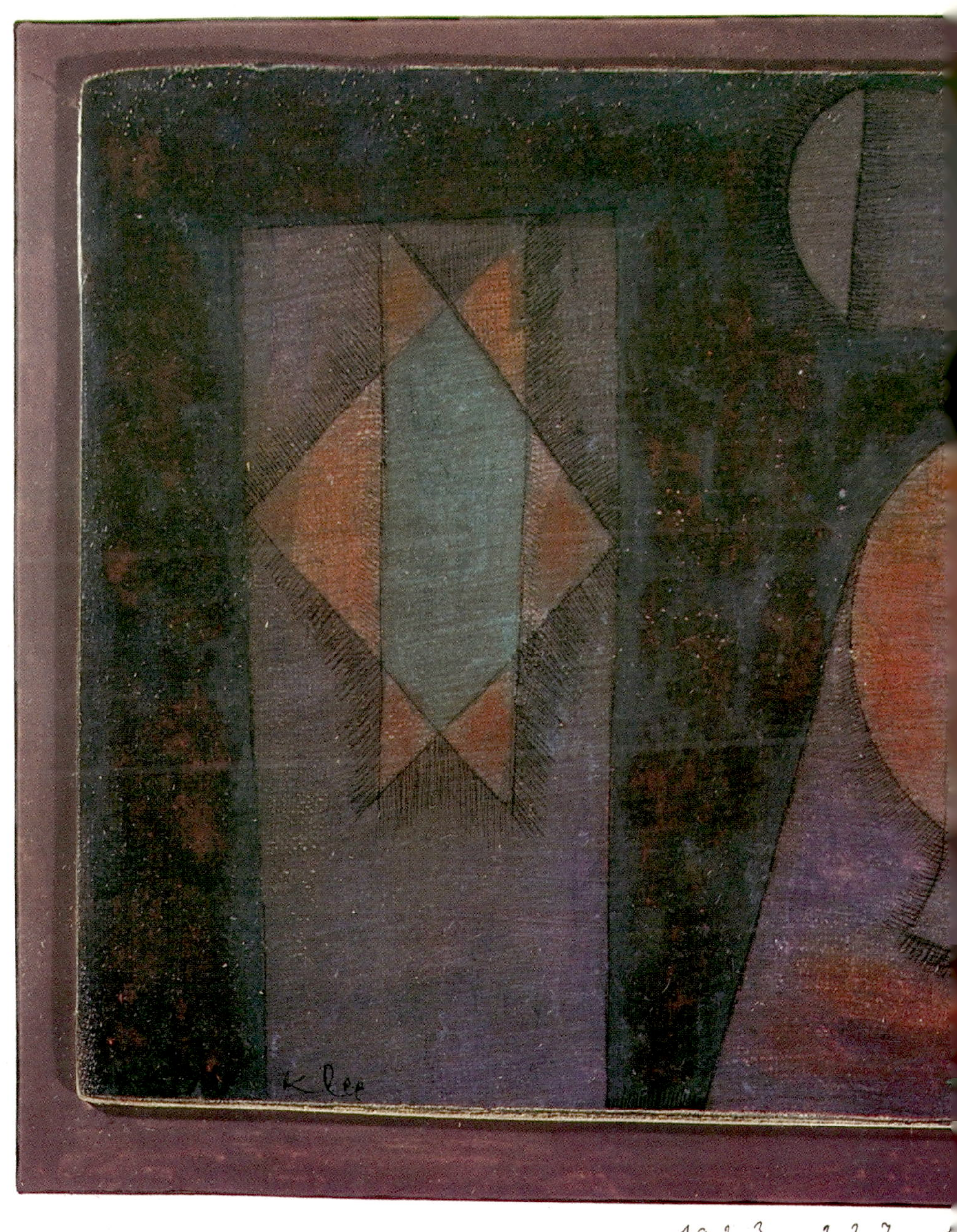
Klee
1923 237

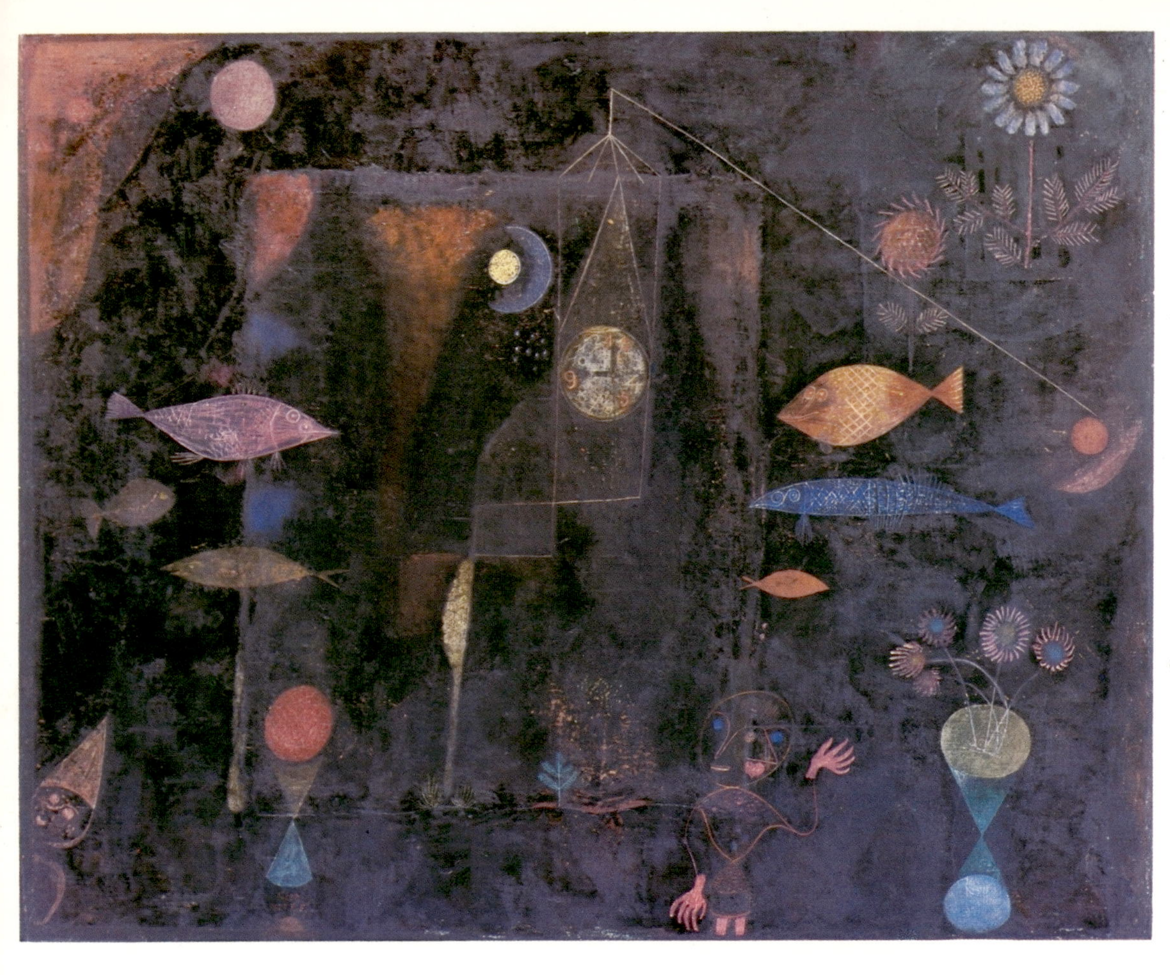

19 Klee *Fish Magic* 1925 Philadelphia Museum of Art

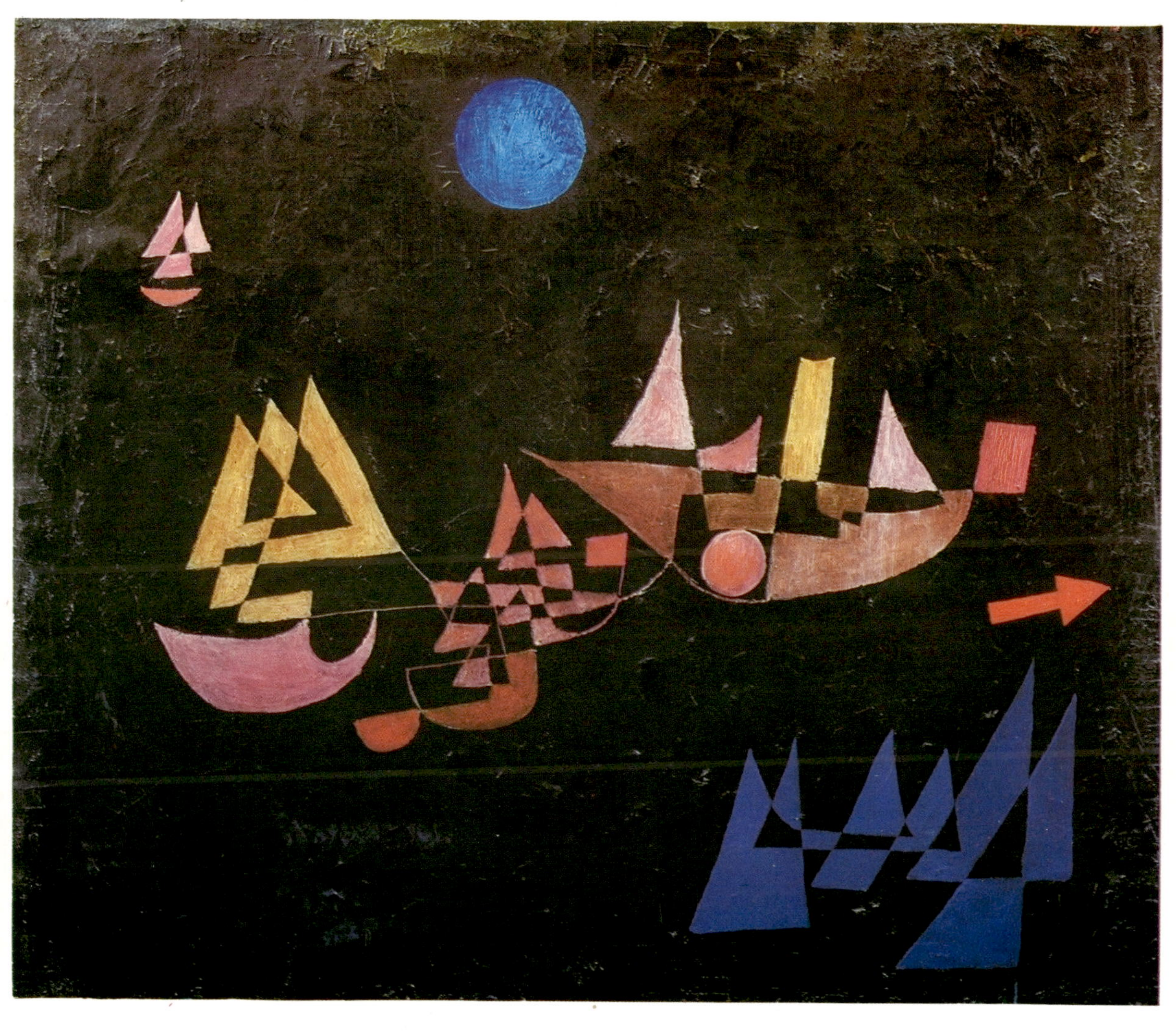

20 Klee *The Ships Depart* 1927 Private Collection New York

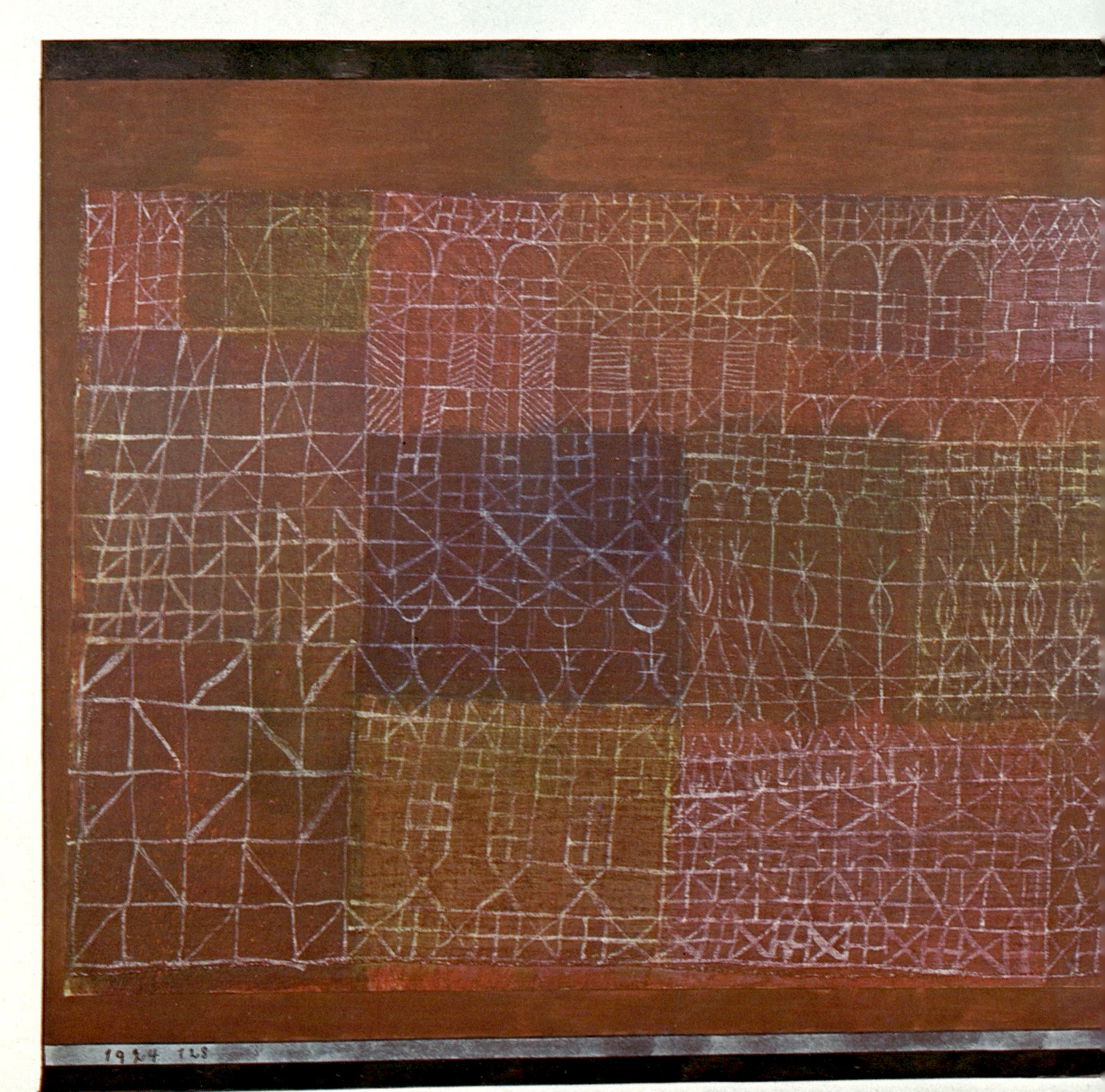

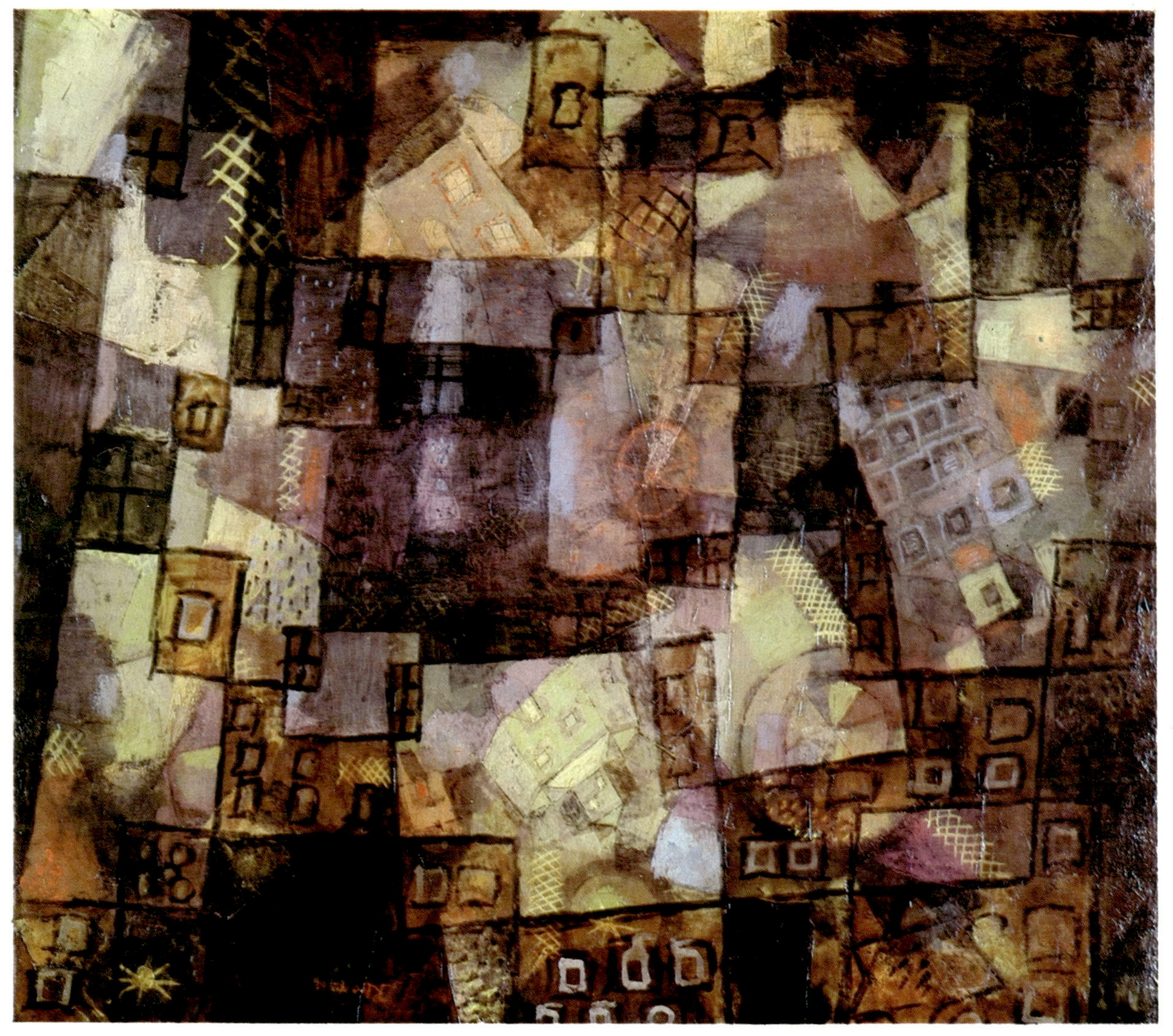

16 Klee *Villas and Huts* 1923 Private Collection

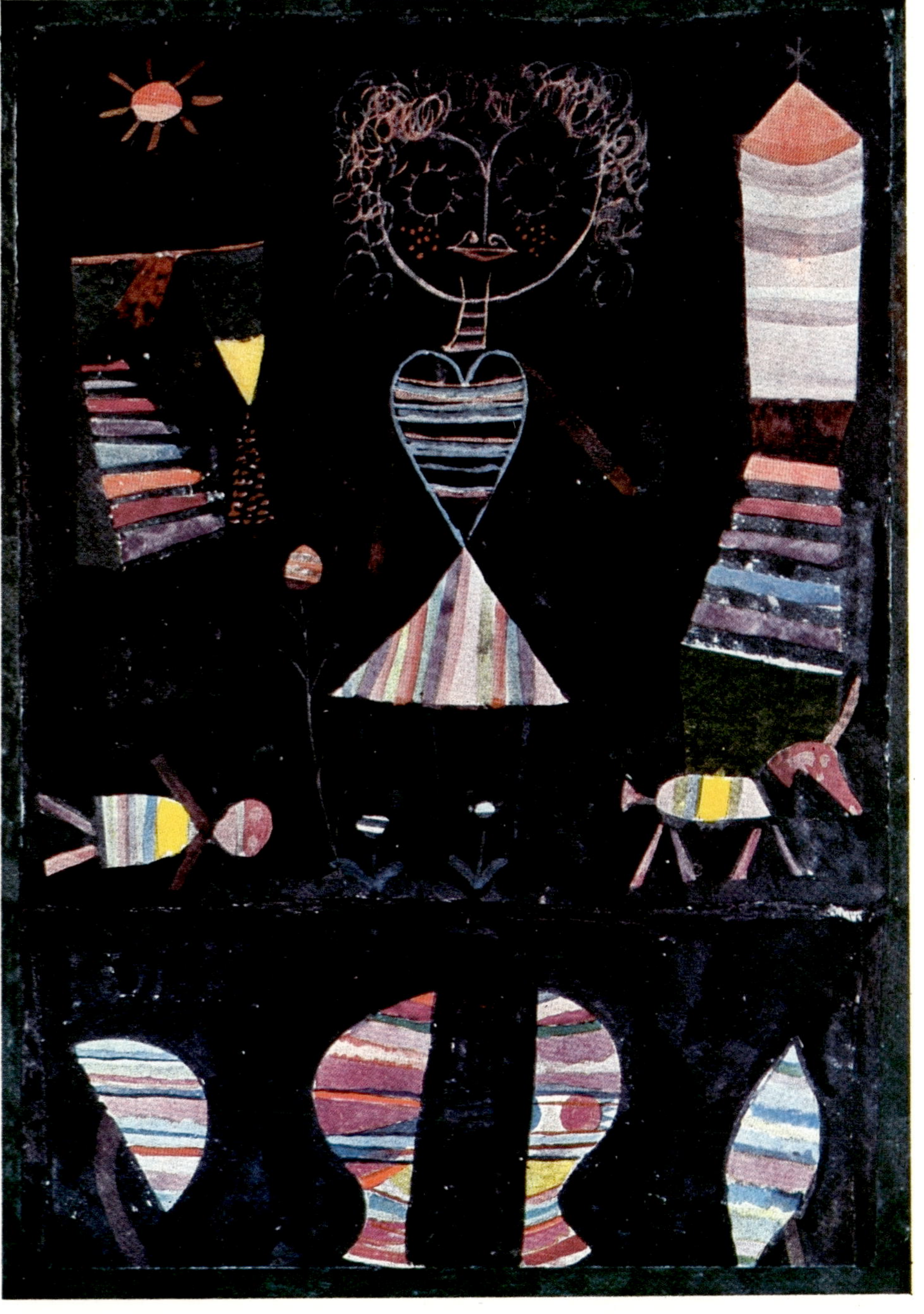

15 Klee *Puppet Show* 1923 Klee Foundation Bern

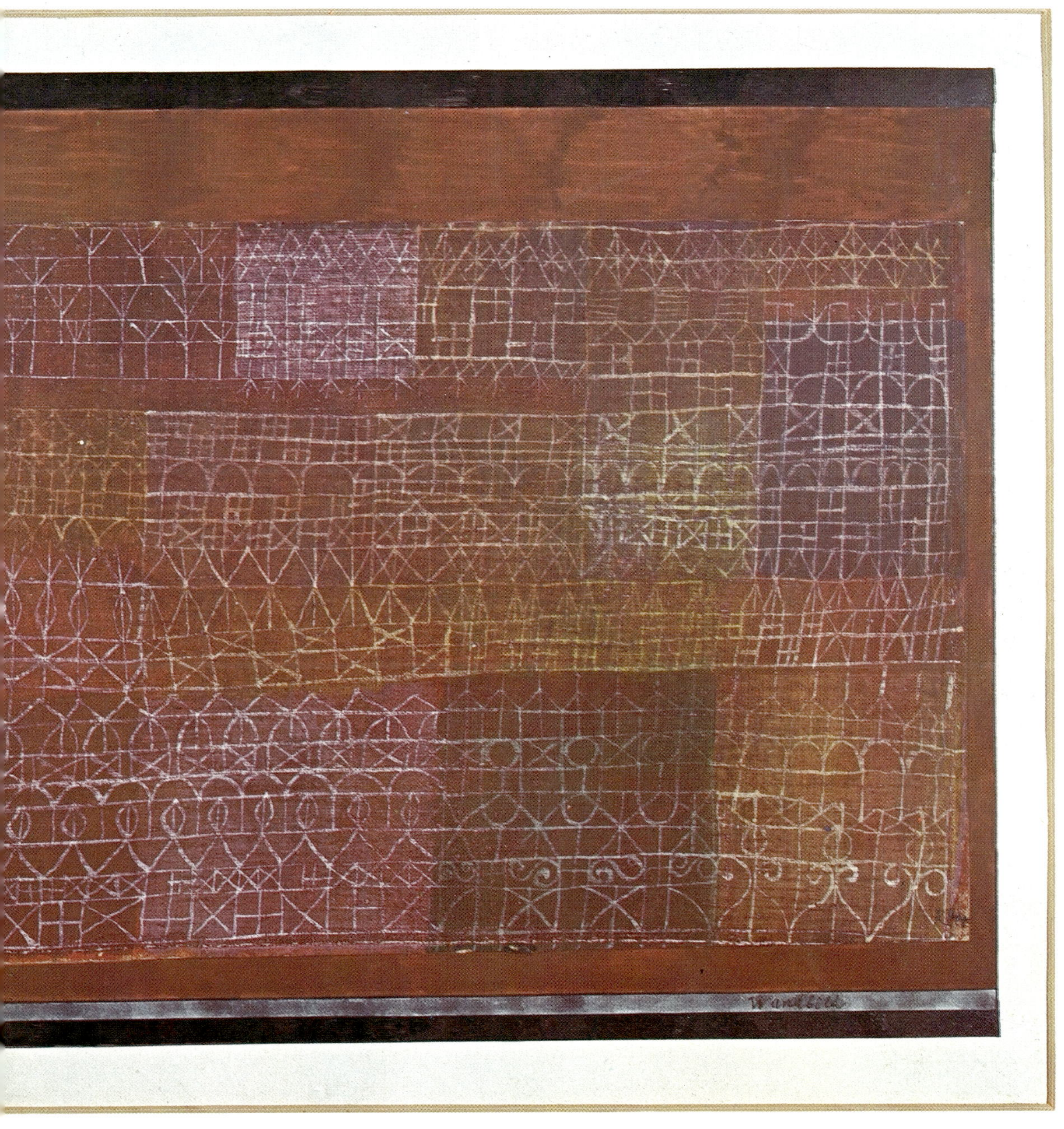

21 Klee *Mural* 1924 Klee Foundation Bern

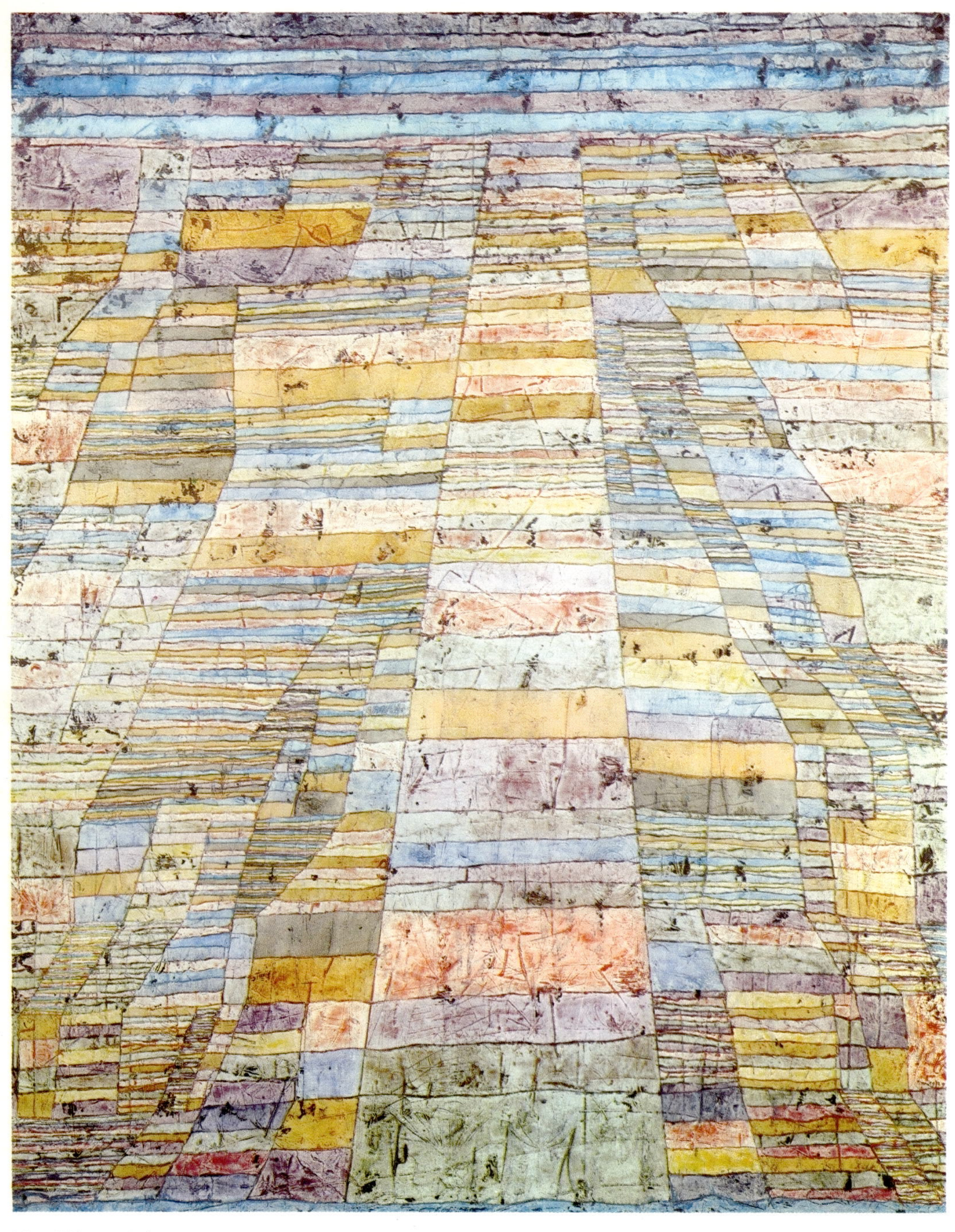

22 Klee *Highways and Byways* 1929 Private Collection Munich

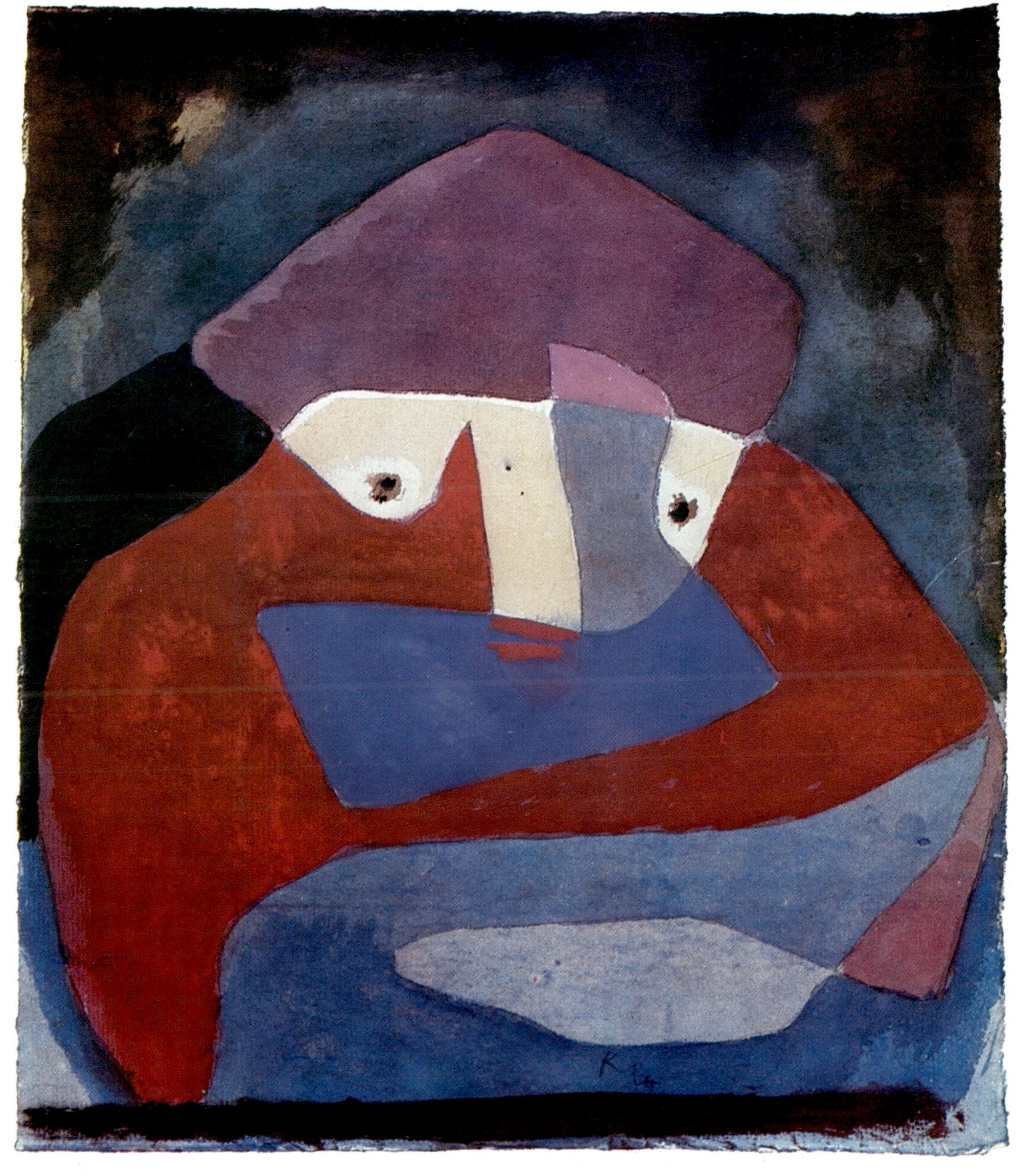

23 Klee *Female Dwarf* 1929 Galerie Beyeler Basel

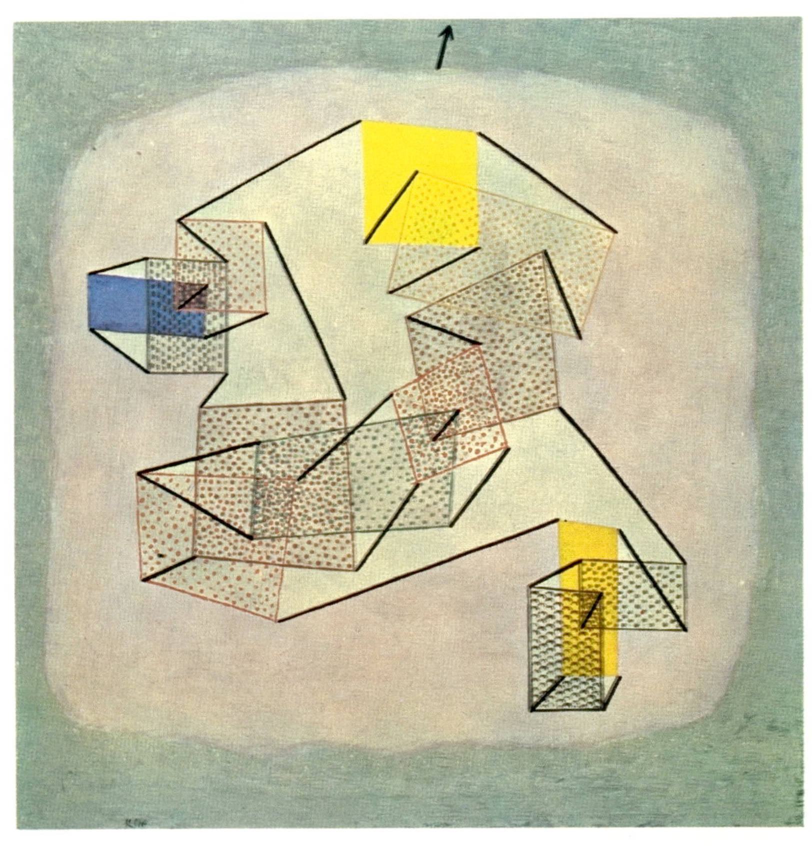

24 Klee *Hovering, before the Ascent* 1930 Klee Foundation Bern

25 Klee *Conqueror* 1930 Klee Foundation Bern→

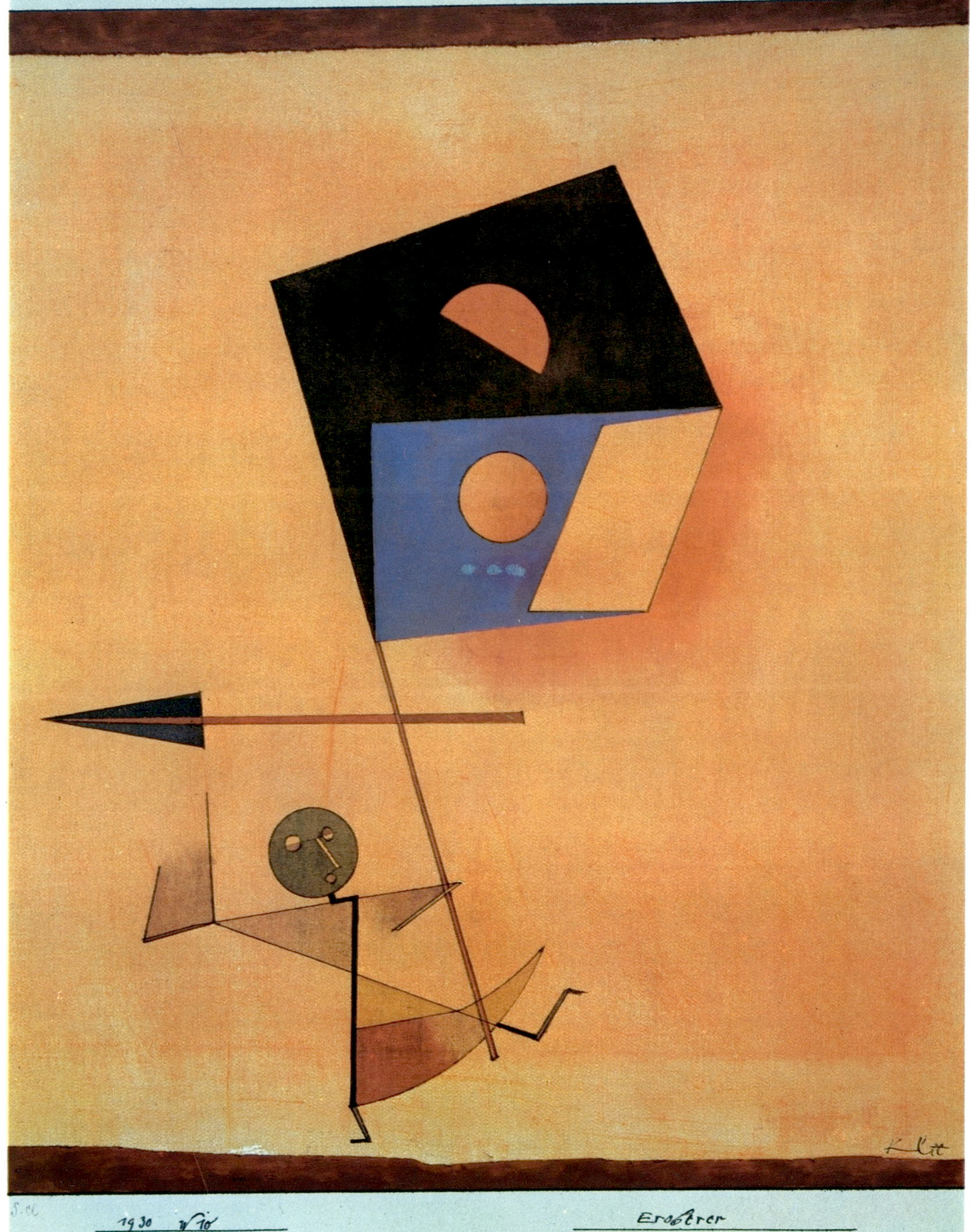

Klee
1930 W 10
Eroberer

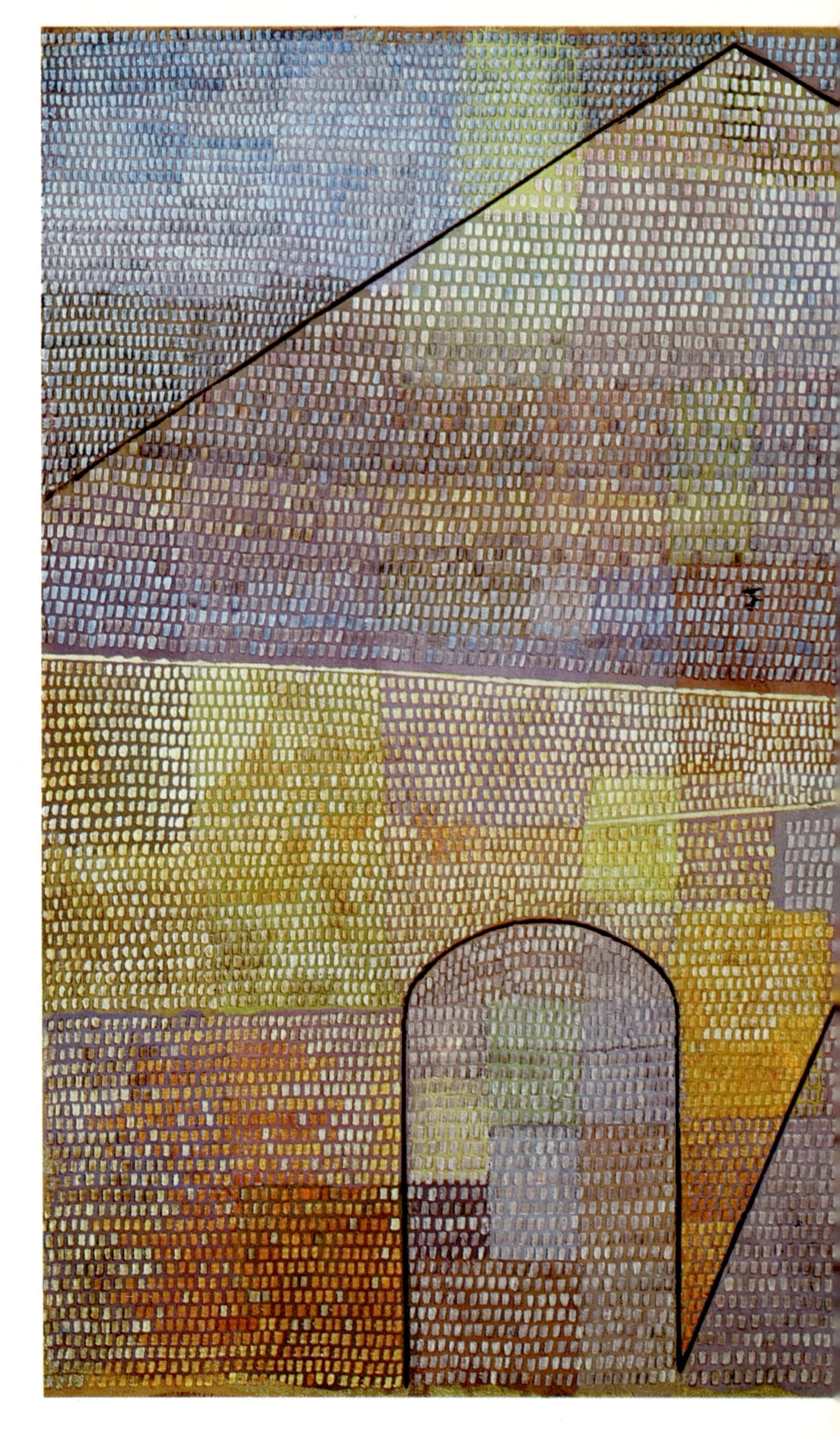

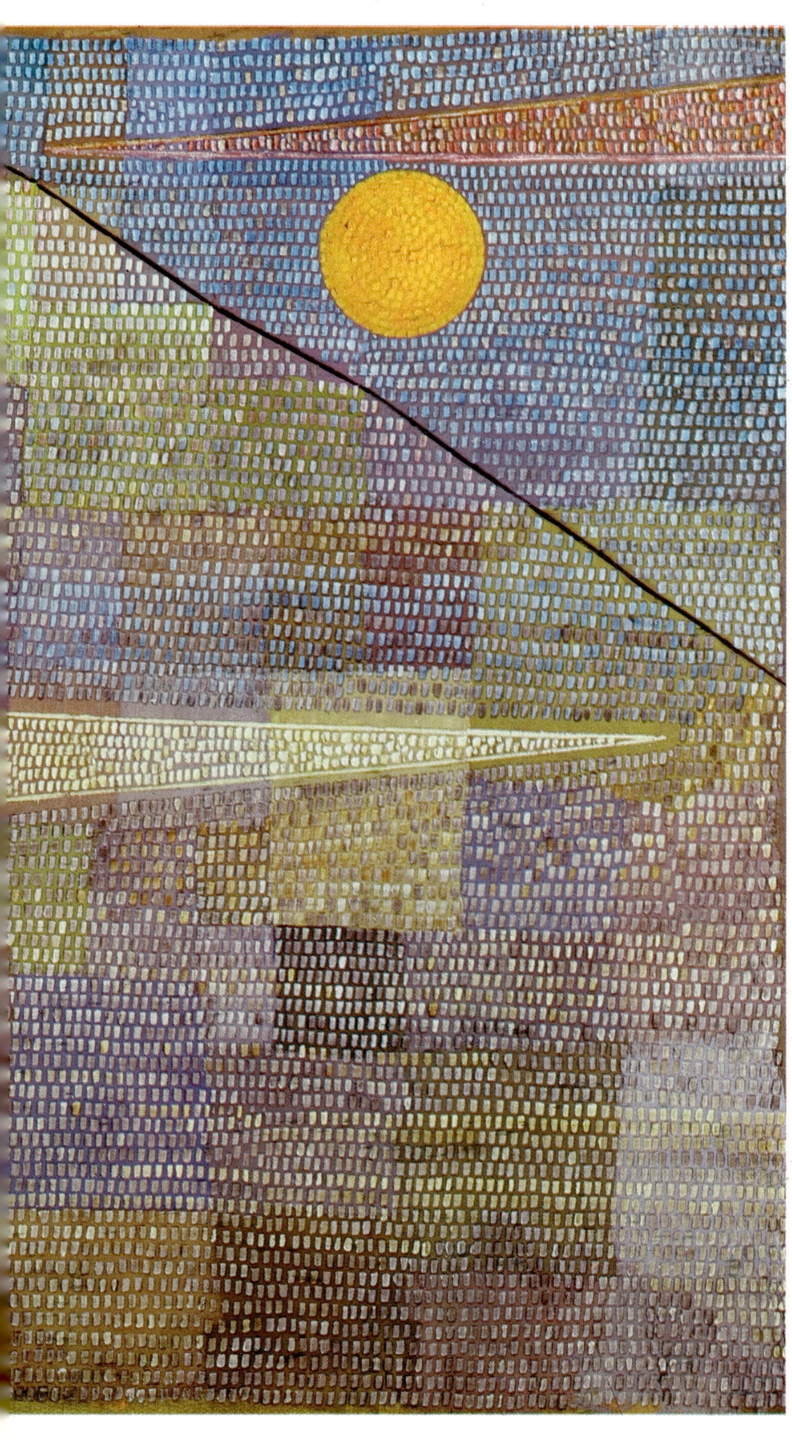

26 Klee *Ad Parnassum* 1932
Kunstmuseum Bern

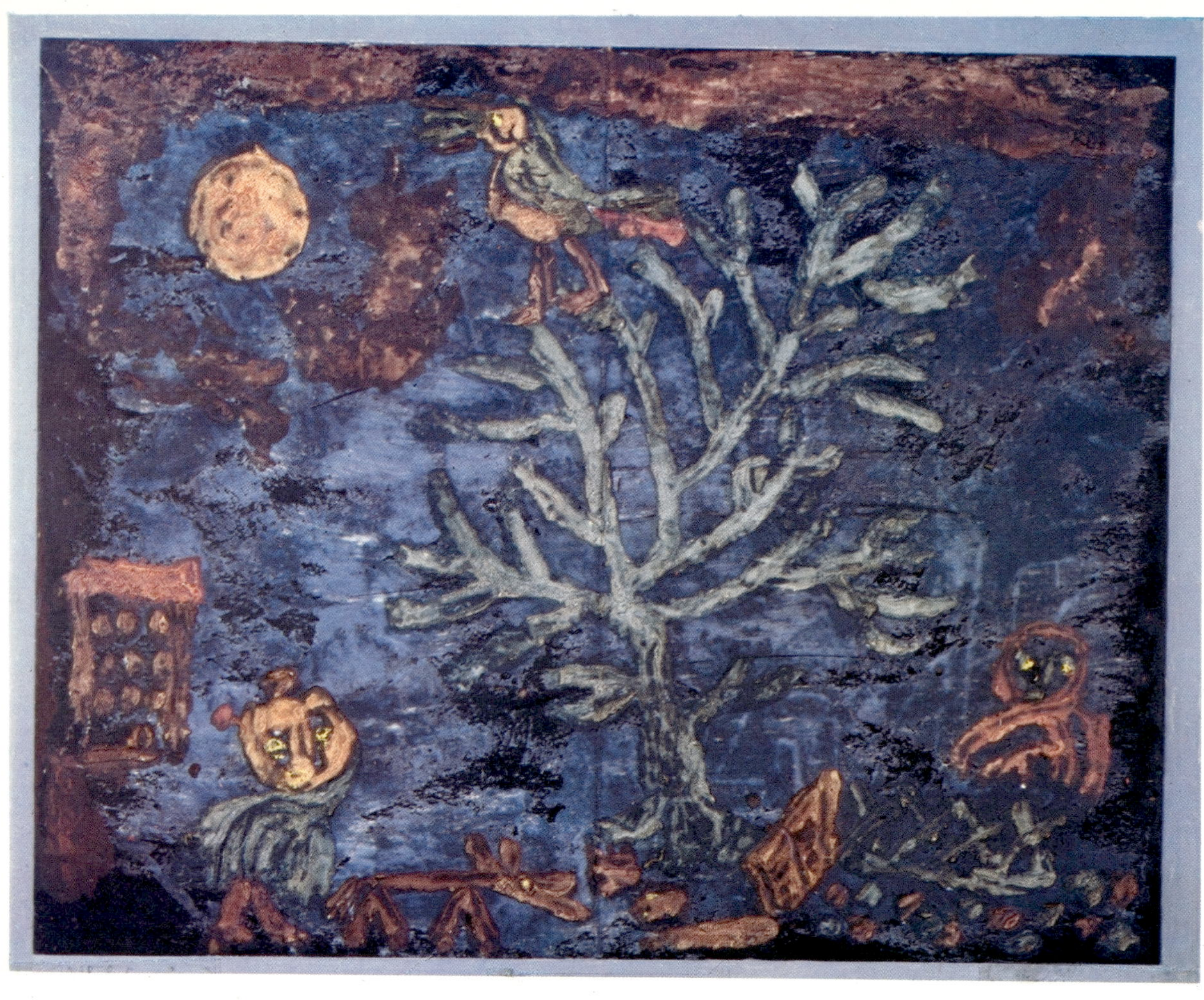

27 Klee *A Nordic Tale* 1930 Kunstmuseum Basel

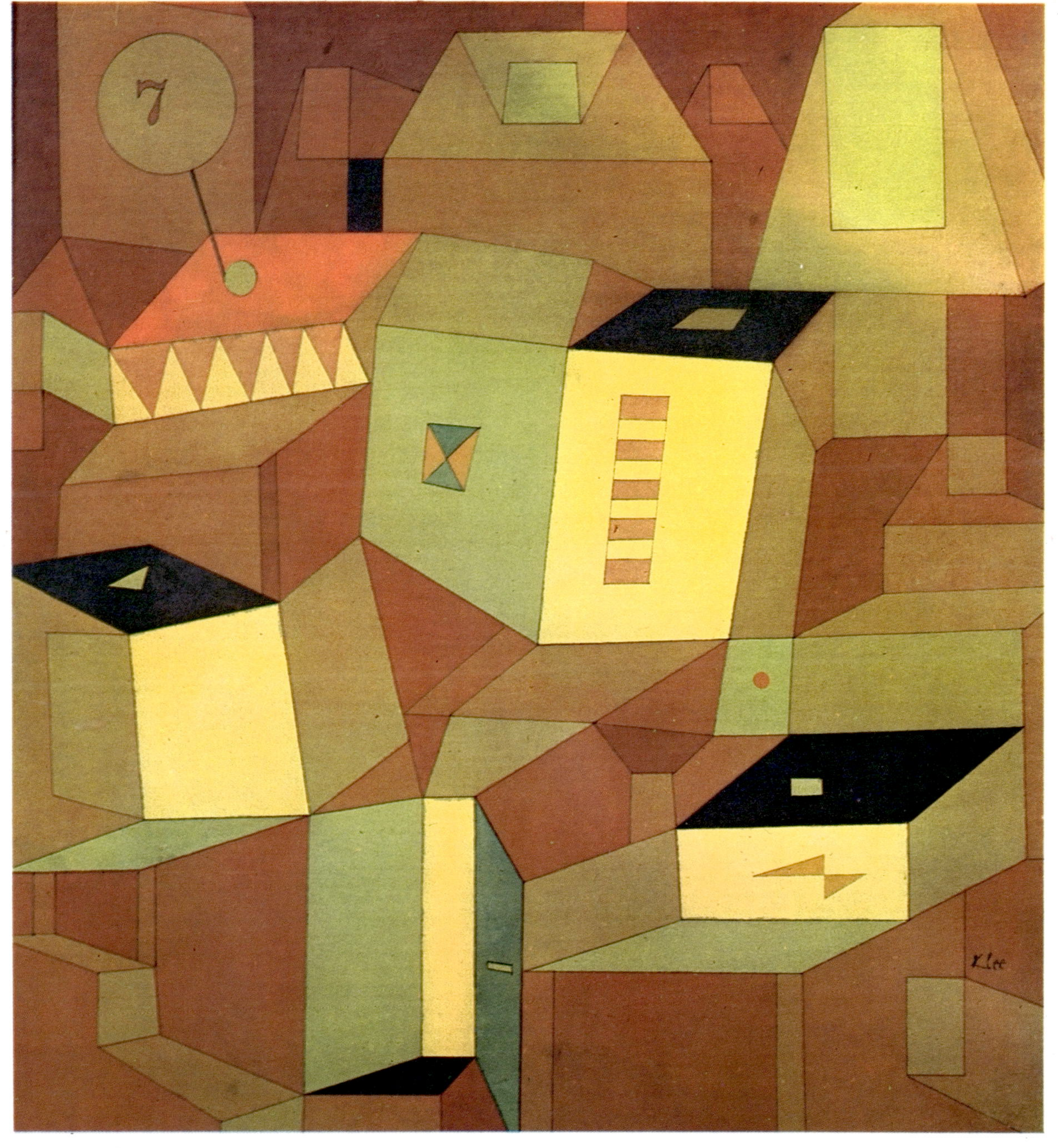

28 Klee *At Seven above the Roofs* 1930 Private Collection Paris

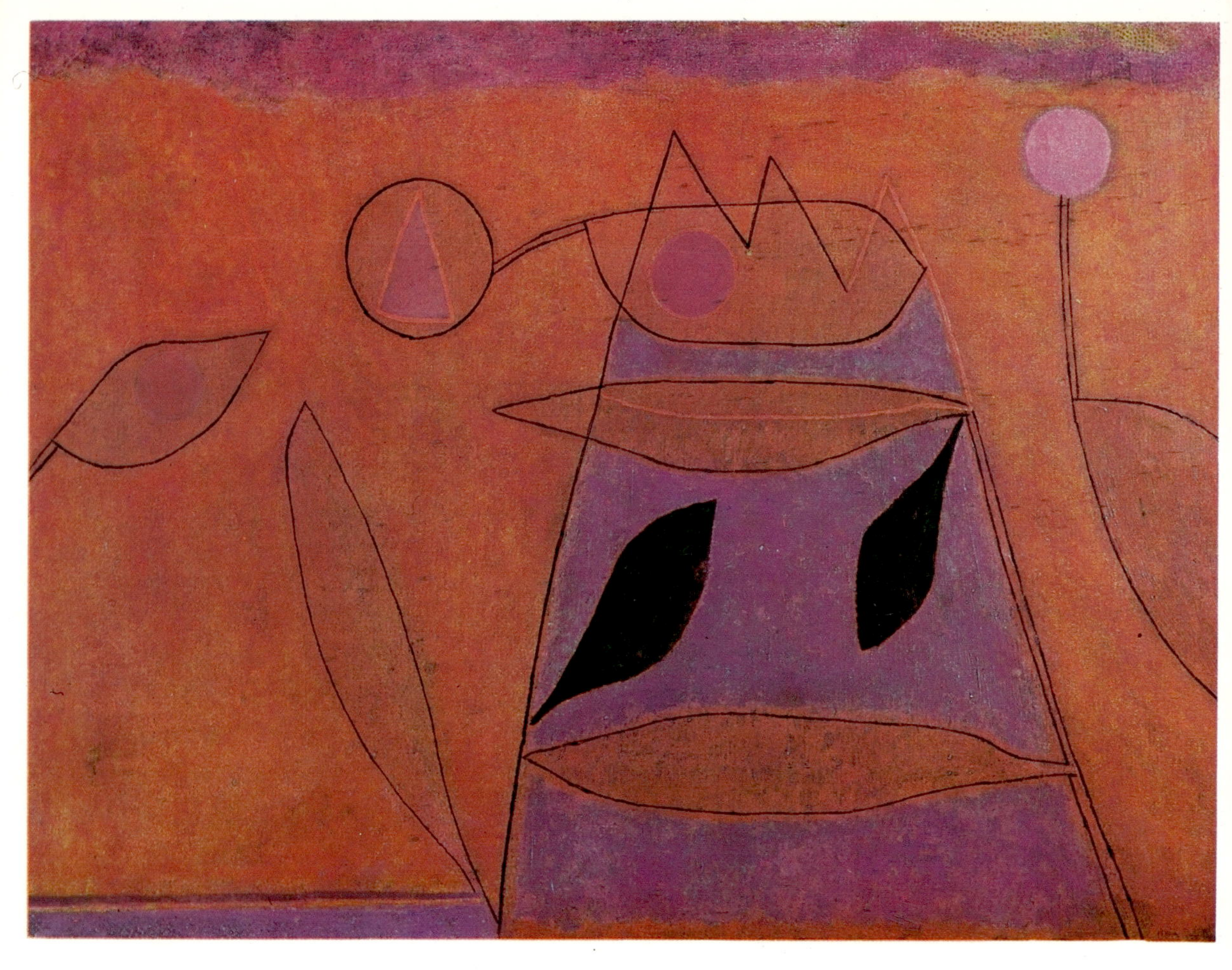

29 Klee *Something like a Plant* 1932 Galerie Beyeler Basel

30 Klee *Arab Song* 1932 Phillips Collection Washington→

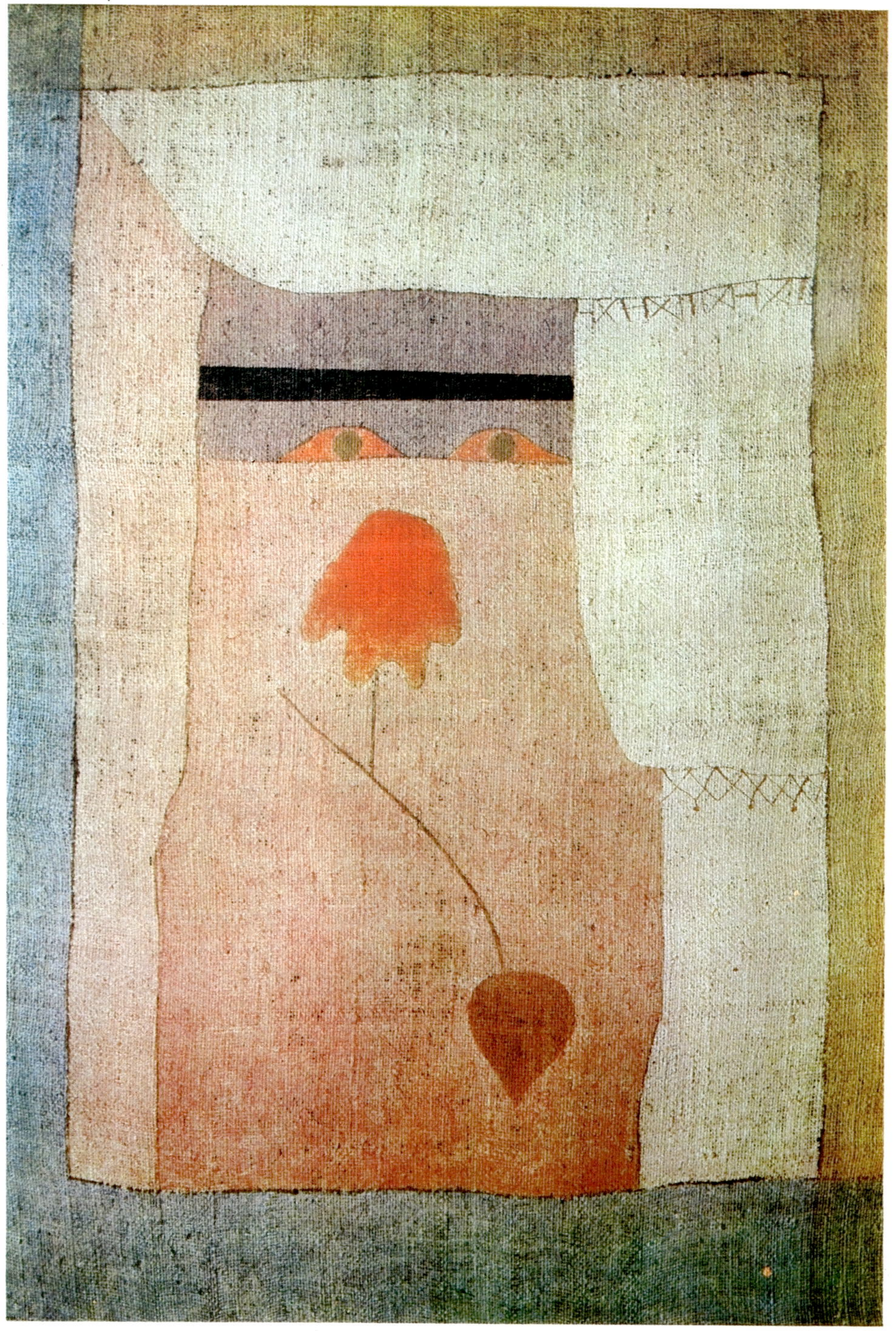

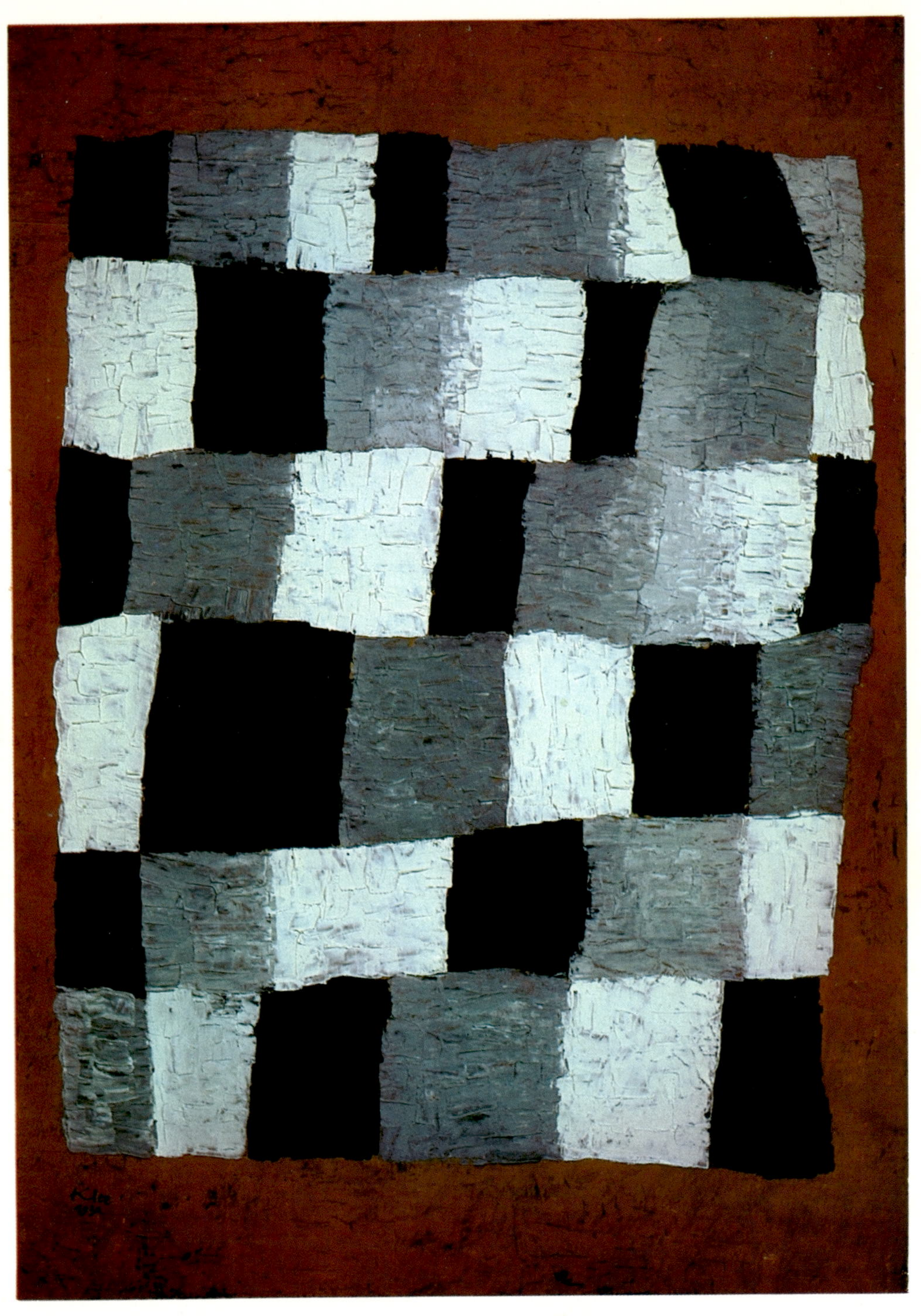

31
Klee *Rhythms*
1930 Private
Collection Bern

32
Klee *Negro Glanc*
1933 Klee Founc
tion Bern

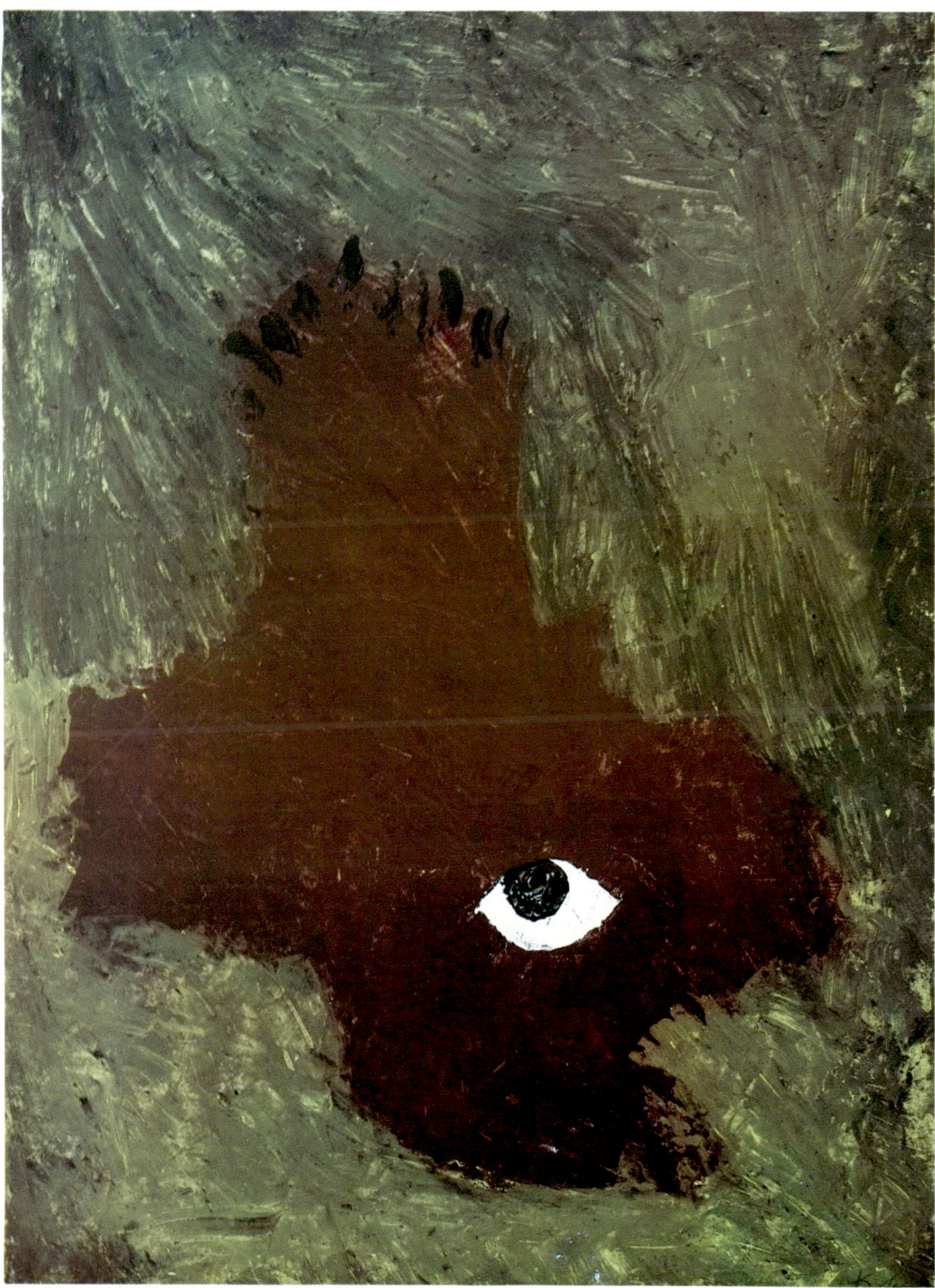

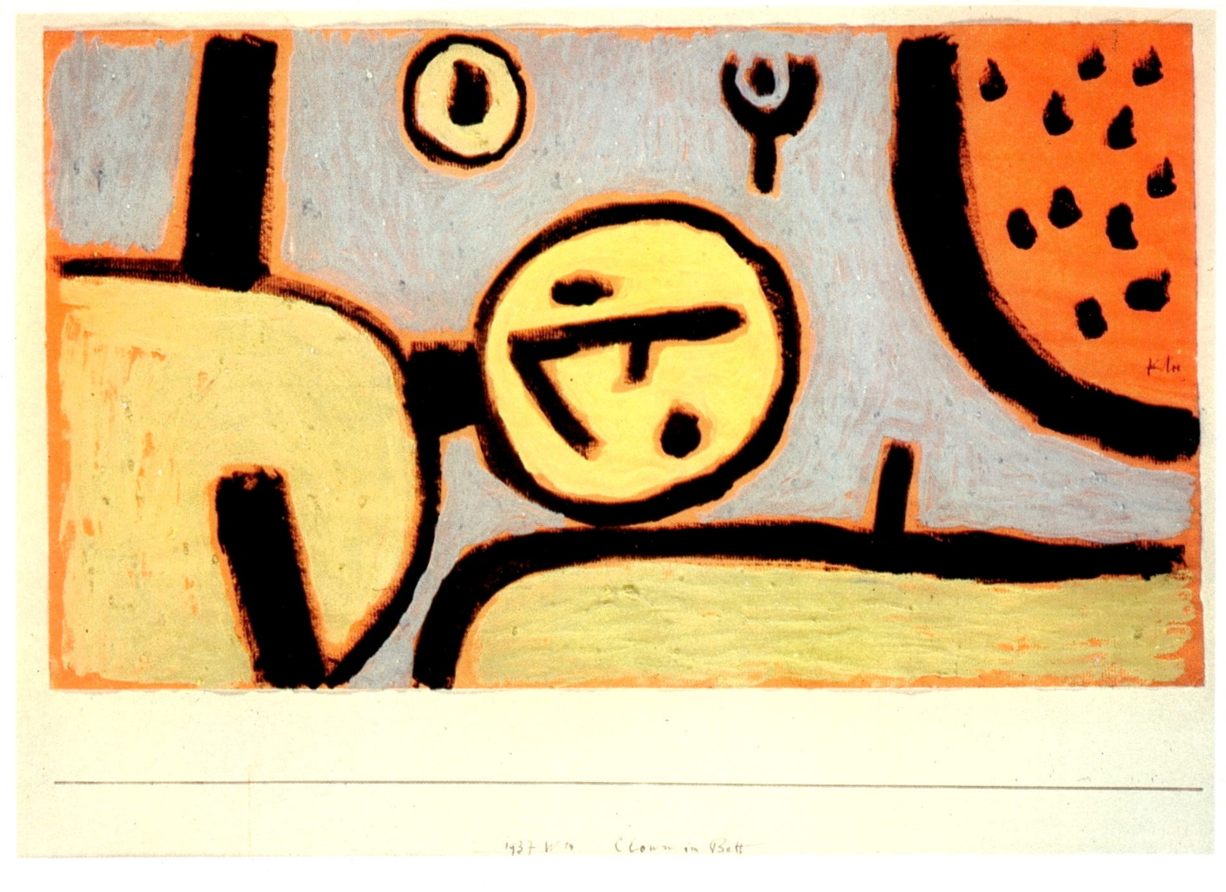

33 Klee *Clown in Bed* 1937 Klee Foundation Bern

34 Klee *Guarded Plant* 1937 Galerie Beyeler Basel→

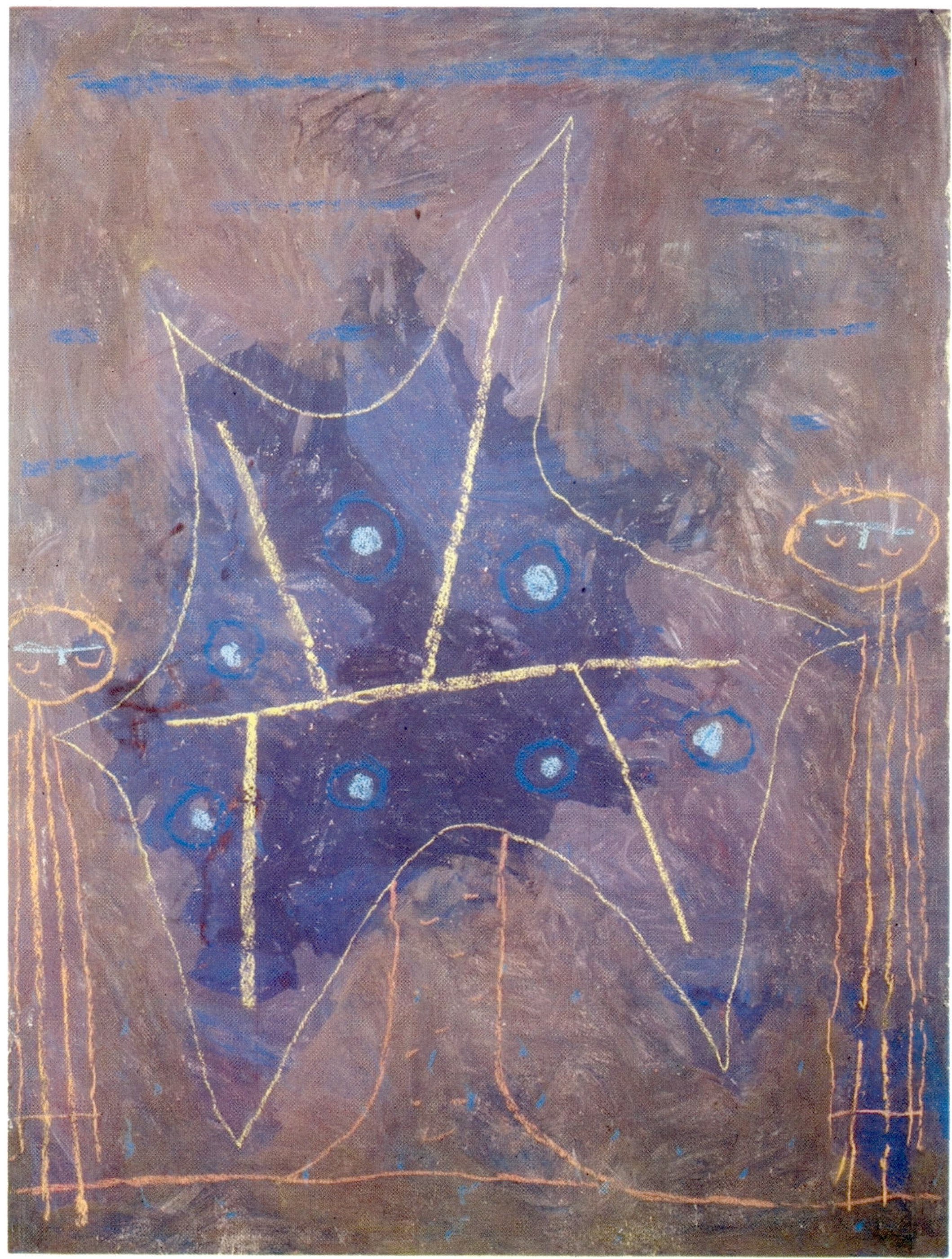

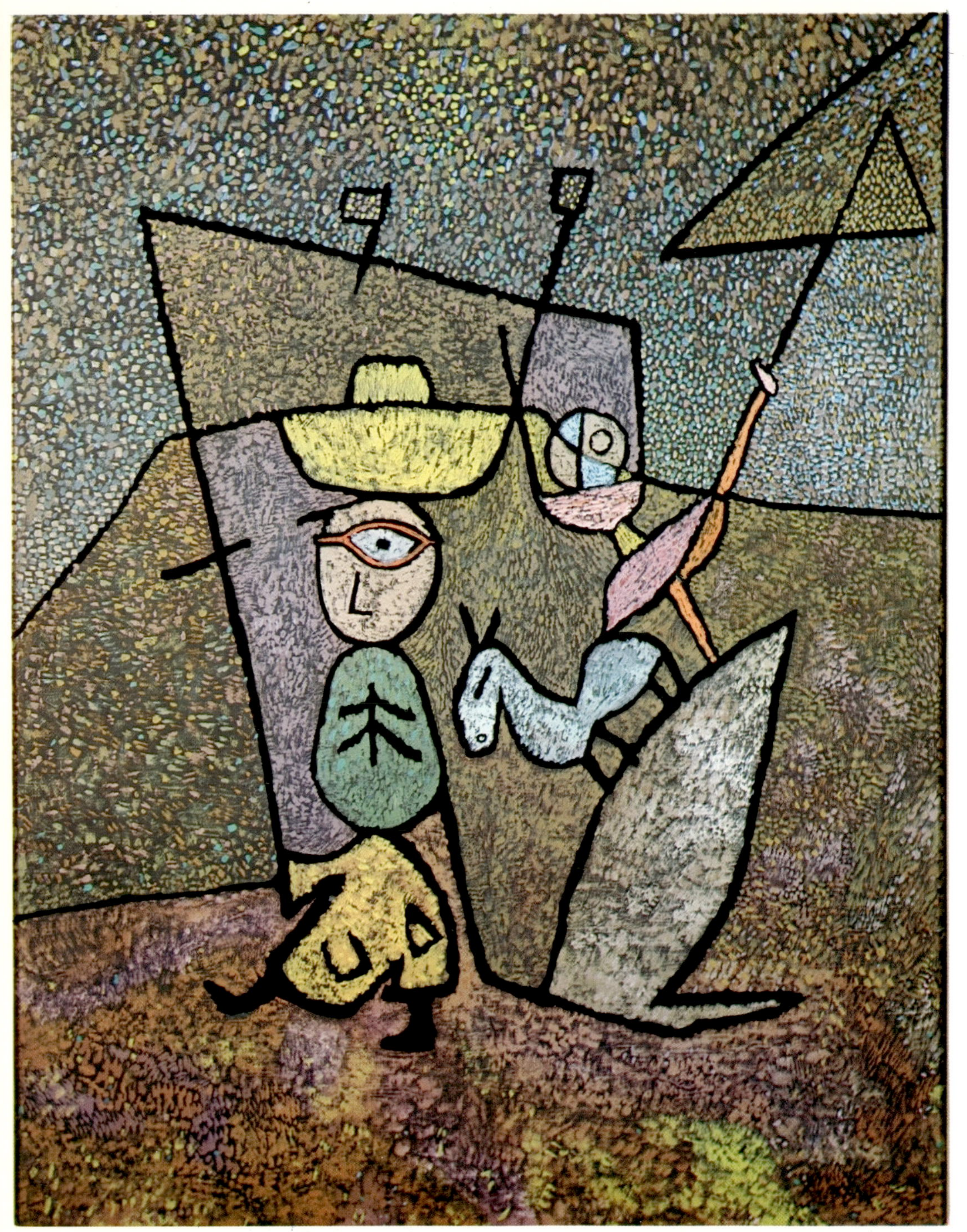

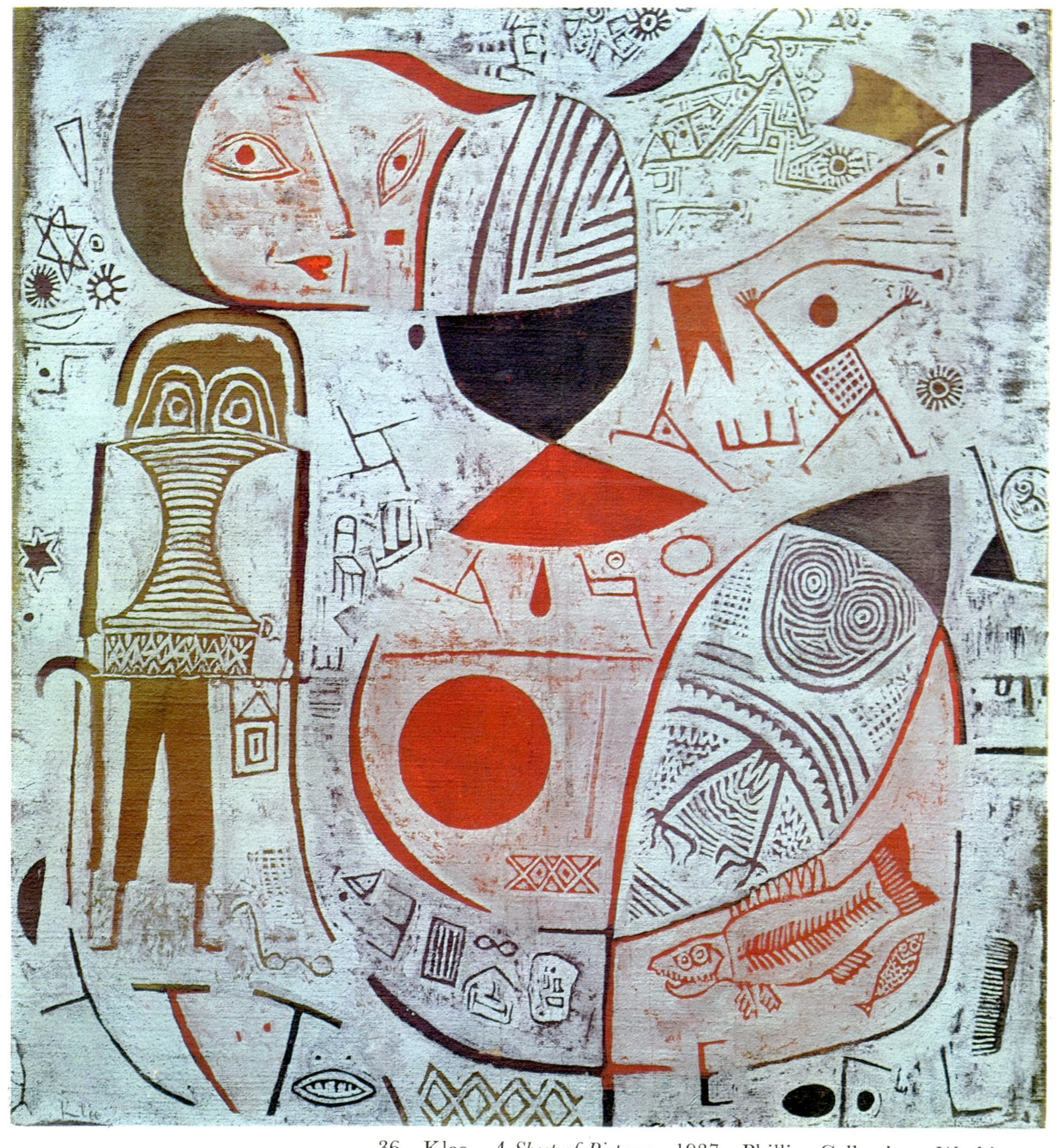

36 Klee *A Sheet of Pictures* 1937 Phillips Collection Washington

←35 Klee *Traveling Circus* 1937 Baltimore Museum of Art

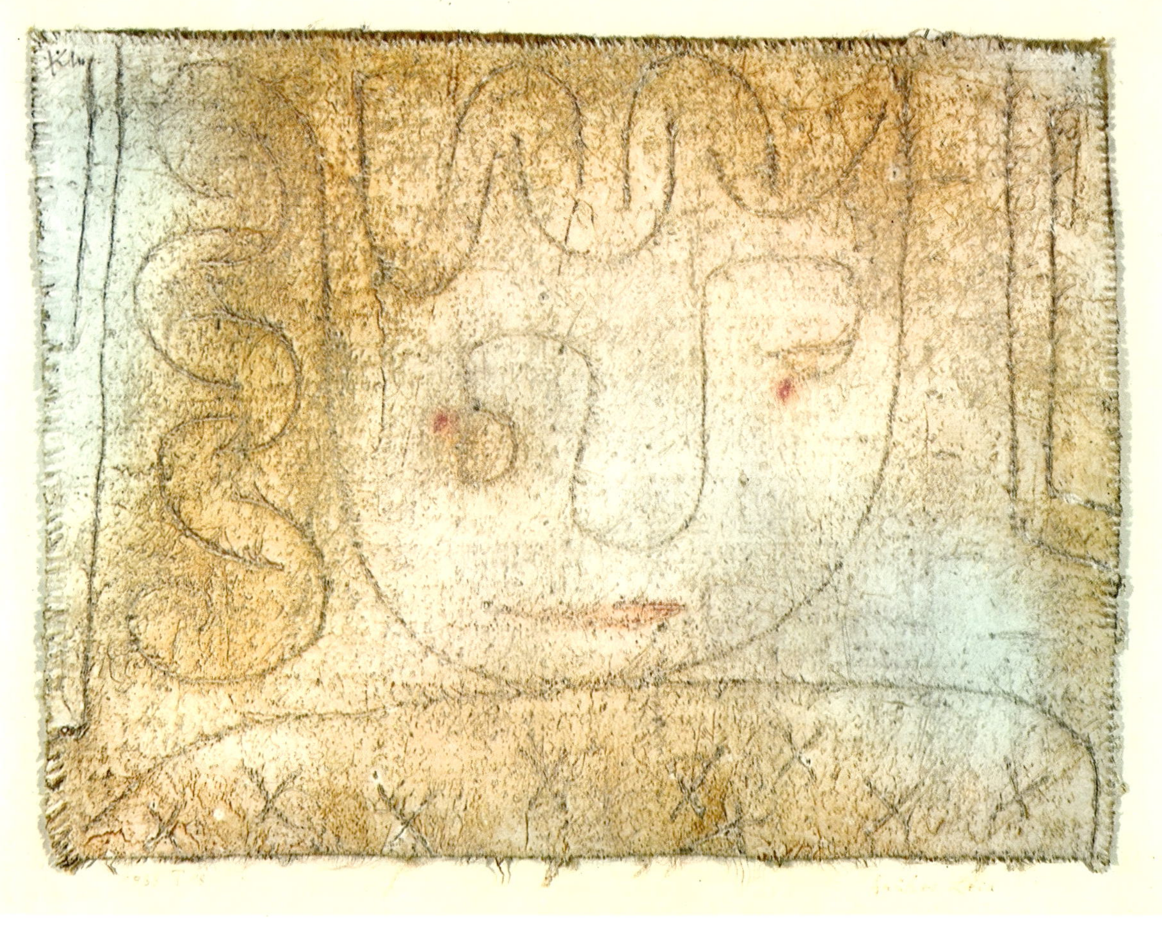

37 Klee *Early Sorrow* 1938 Klee Foundation Bern

38 Klee *Park near L(ucerne)* 1938 Klee Foundation Bern→

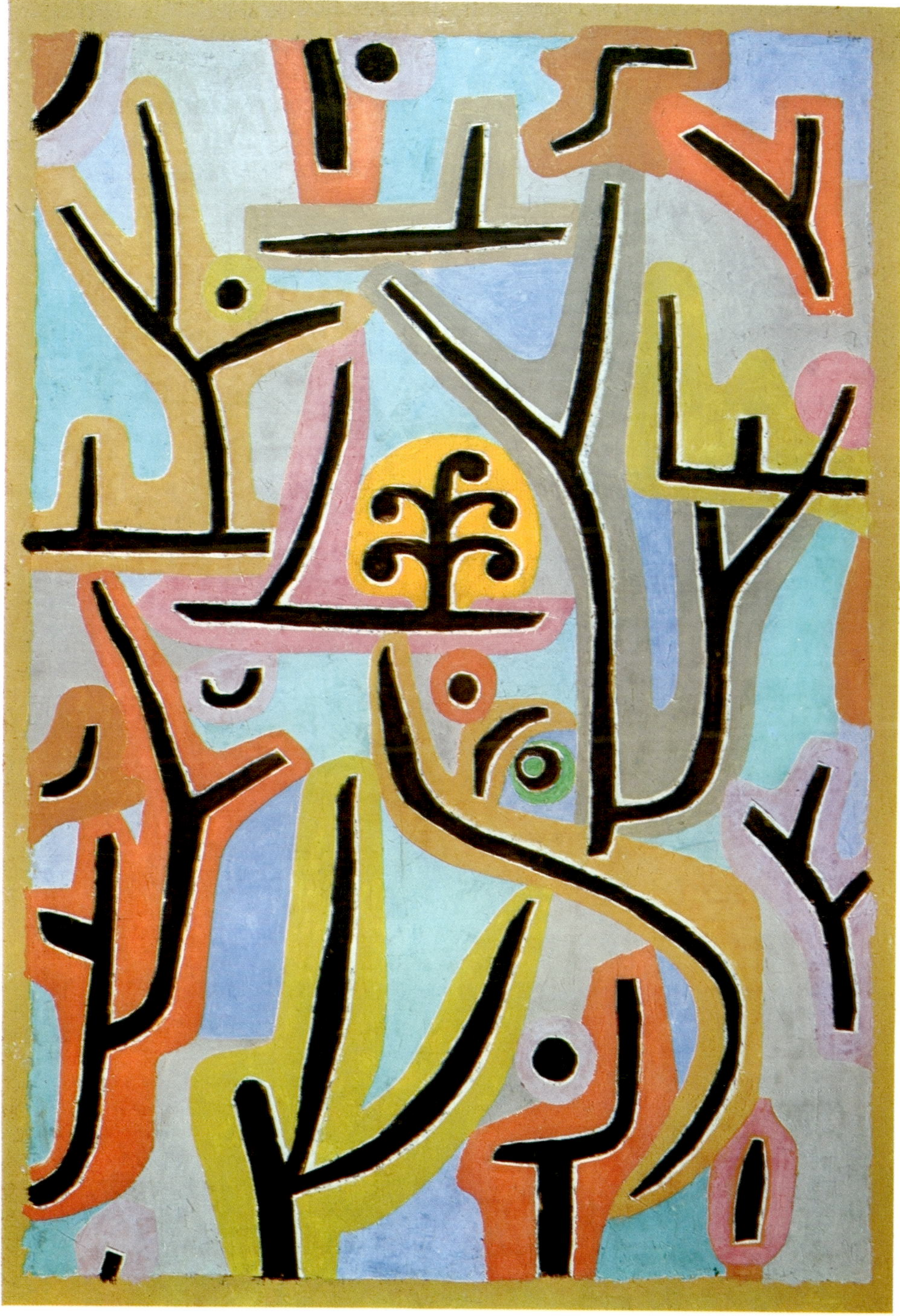

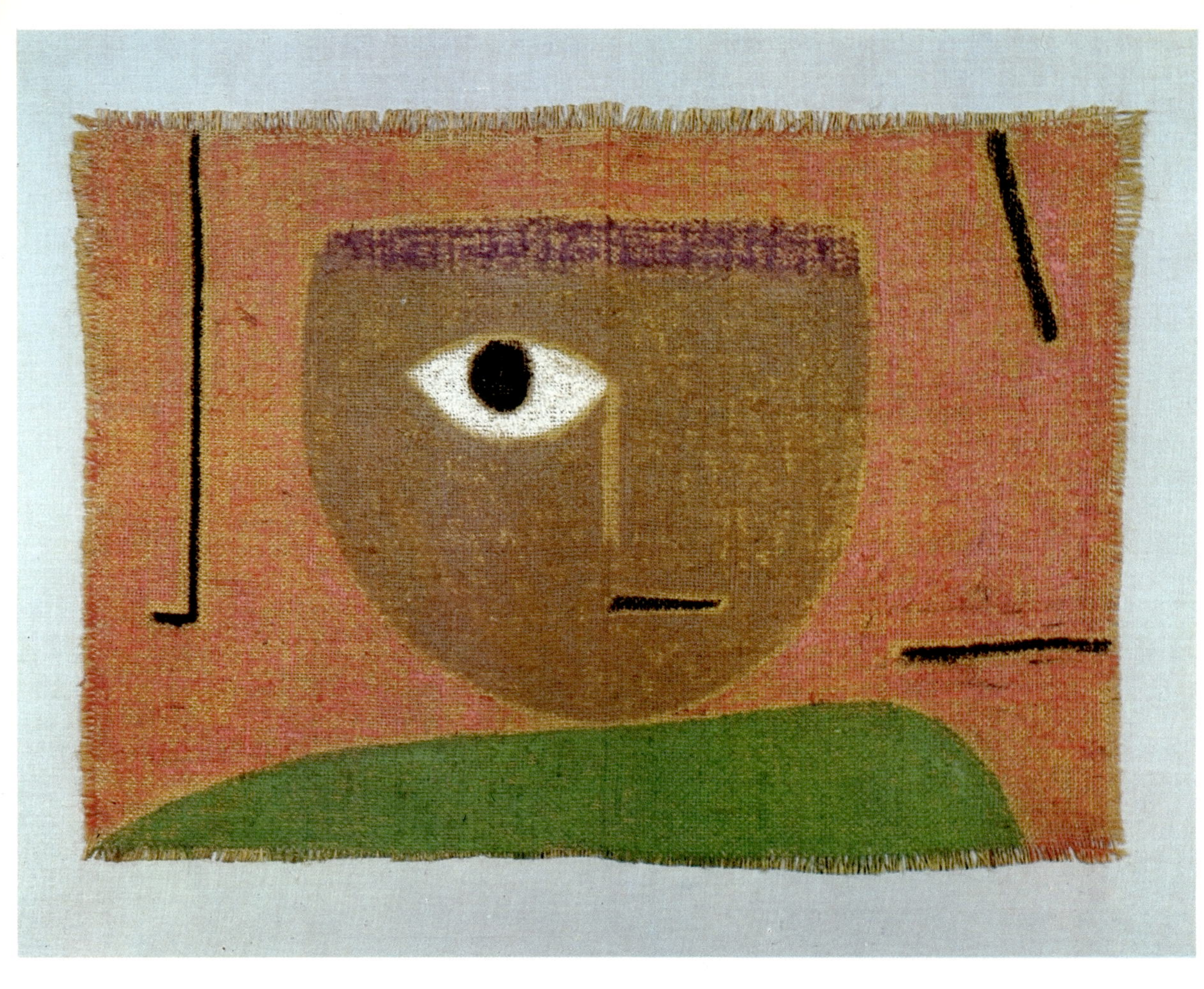

39 Klee *The Eye* 1938 Felix Klee Bern

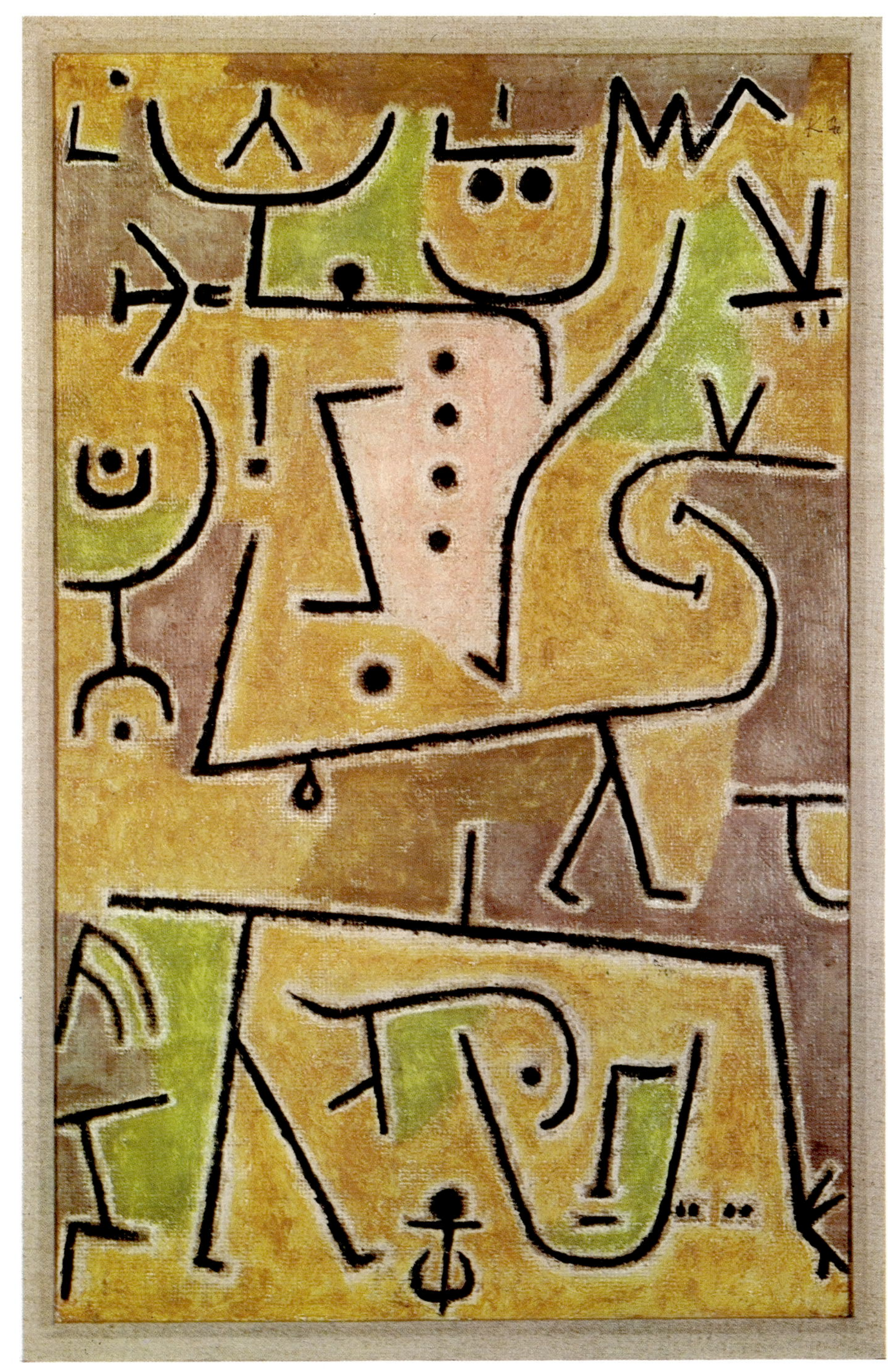

40
Klee *Red Waistcoat*
1938 Felix Klee Bern

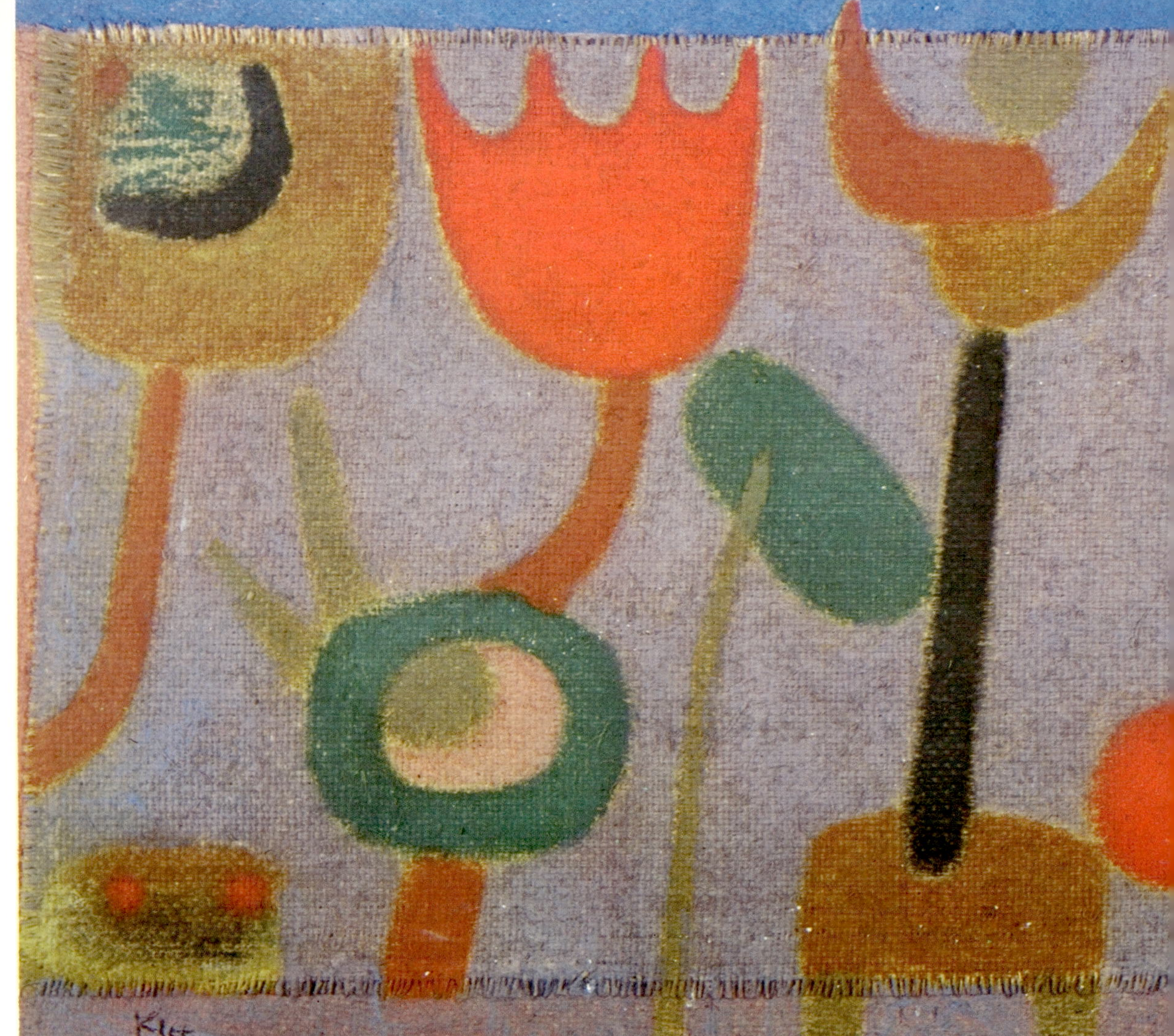
Klee

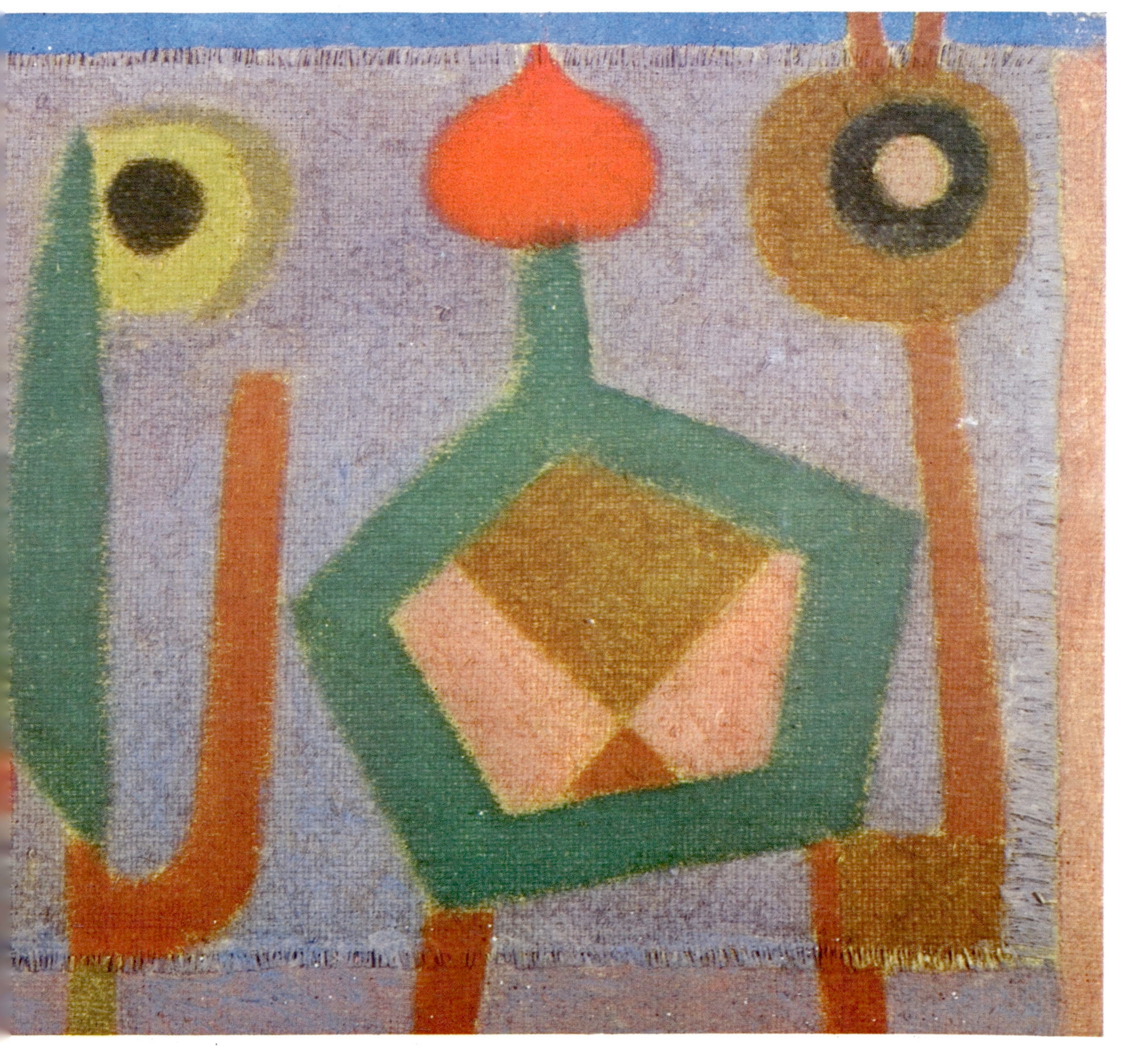

41 Klee *Twilight Blossoms* 1940 Klee Foundation Bern

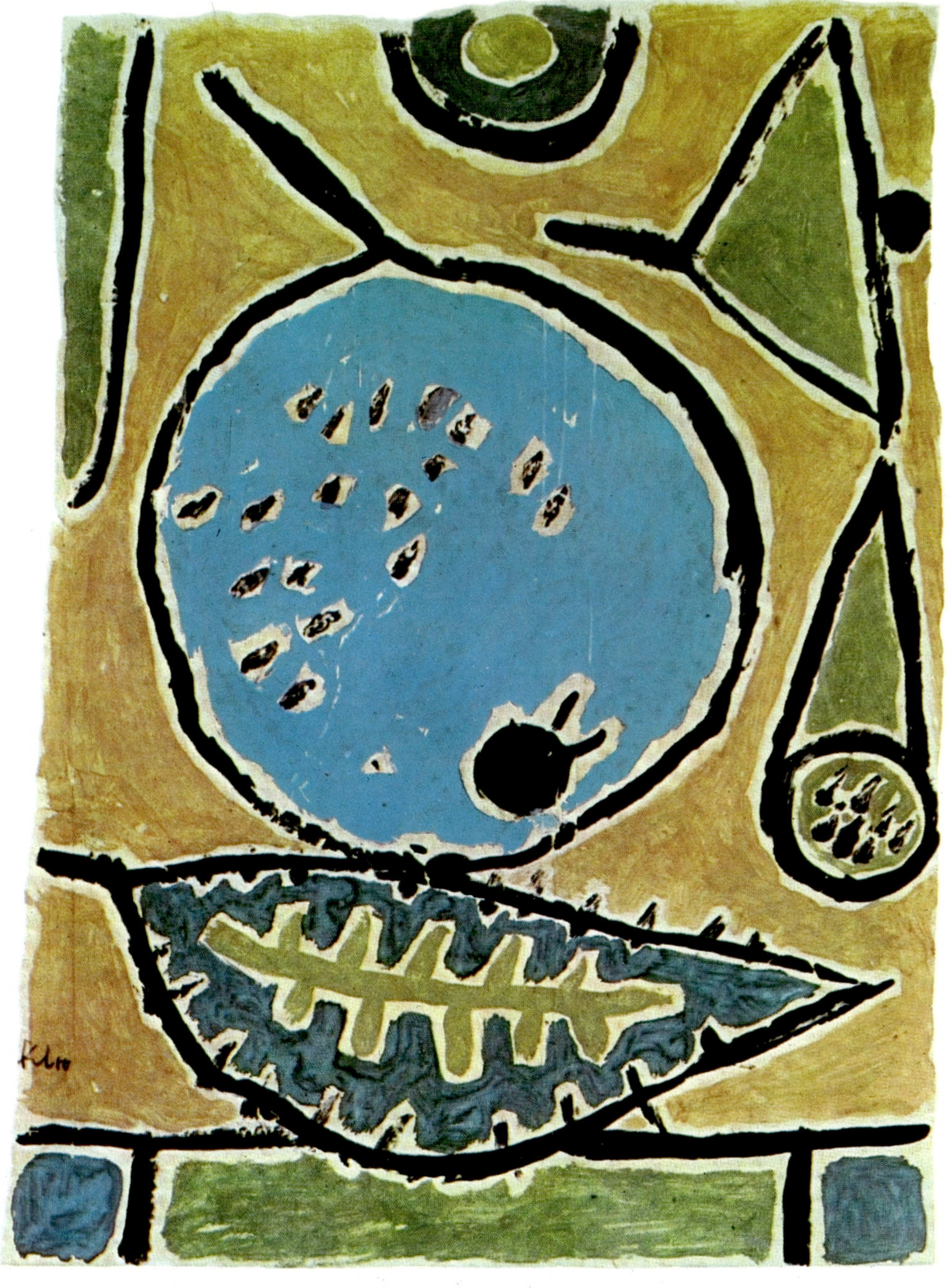

42 Klee *Coelin-Fruit* 1938 Klee Foundation Bern

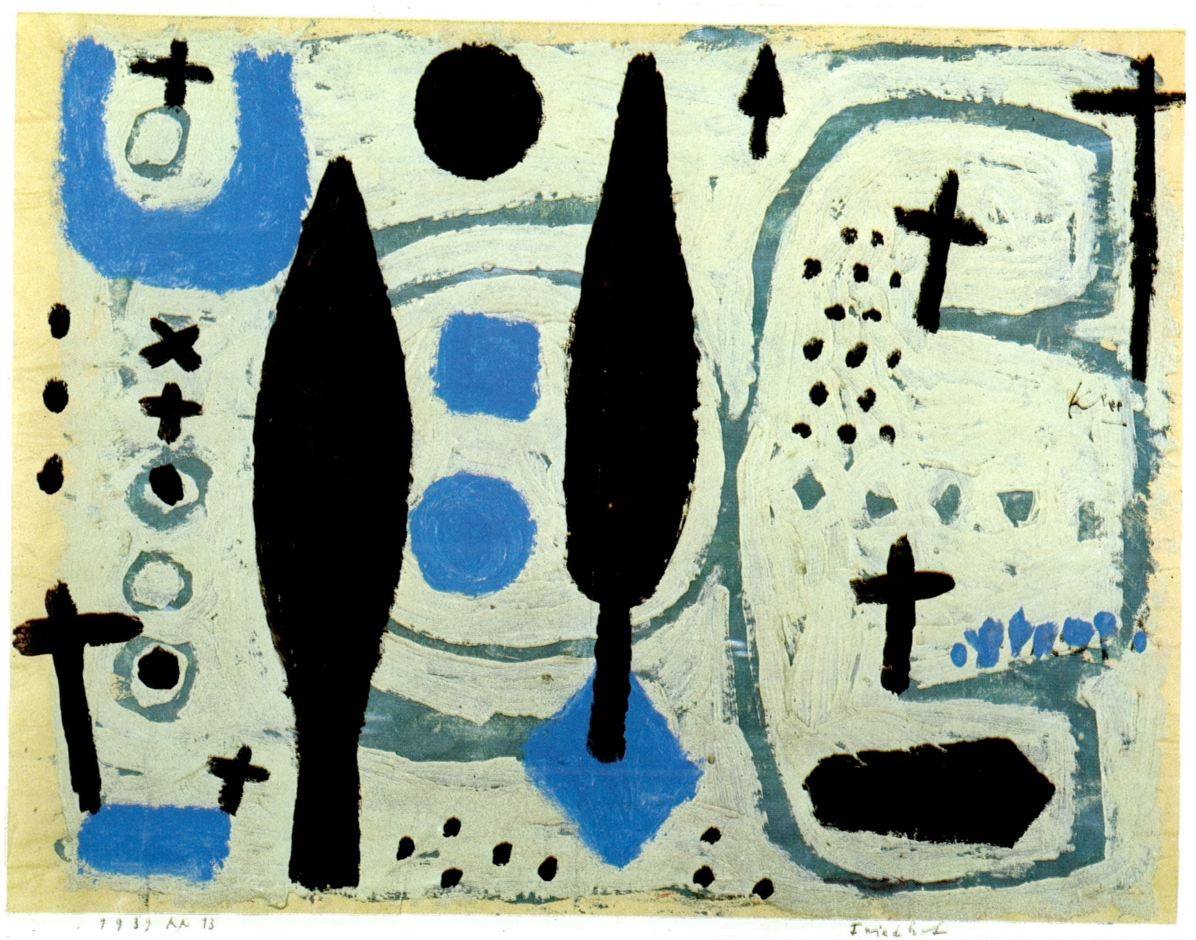

43 Klee *Graveyard* 1939 Klee Foundation Bern

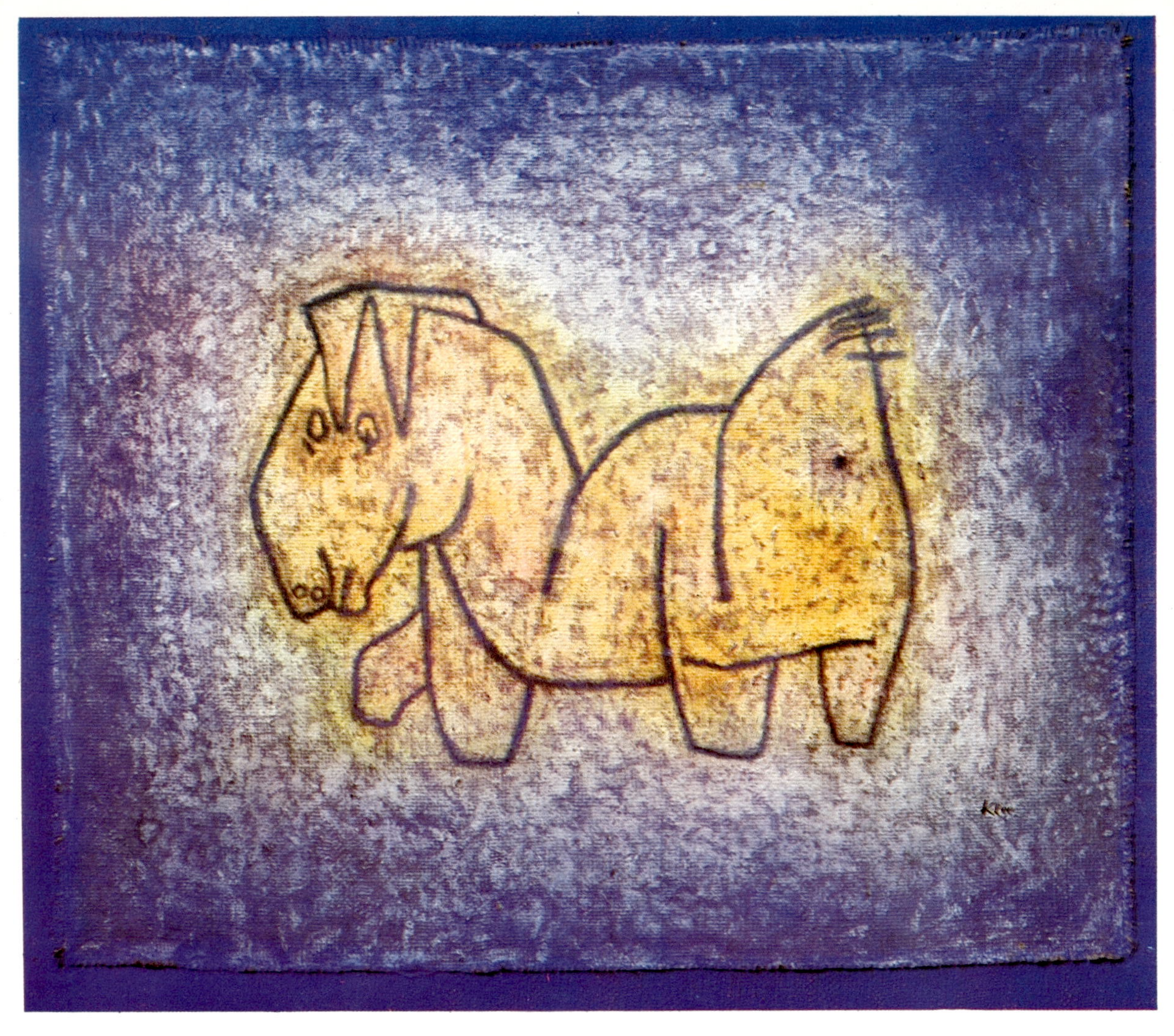

44 Klee *Bastard* 1939 Felix Klee Bern

45 Klee *A Face Yet on the Body* 1939 Felix Klee Bern→

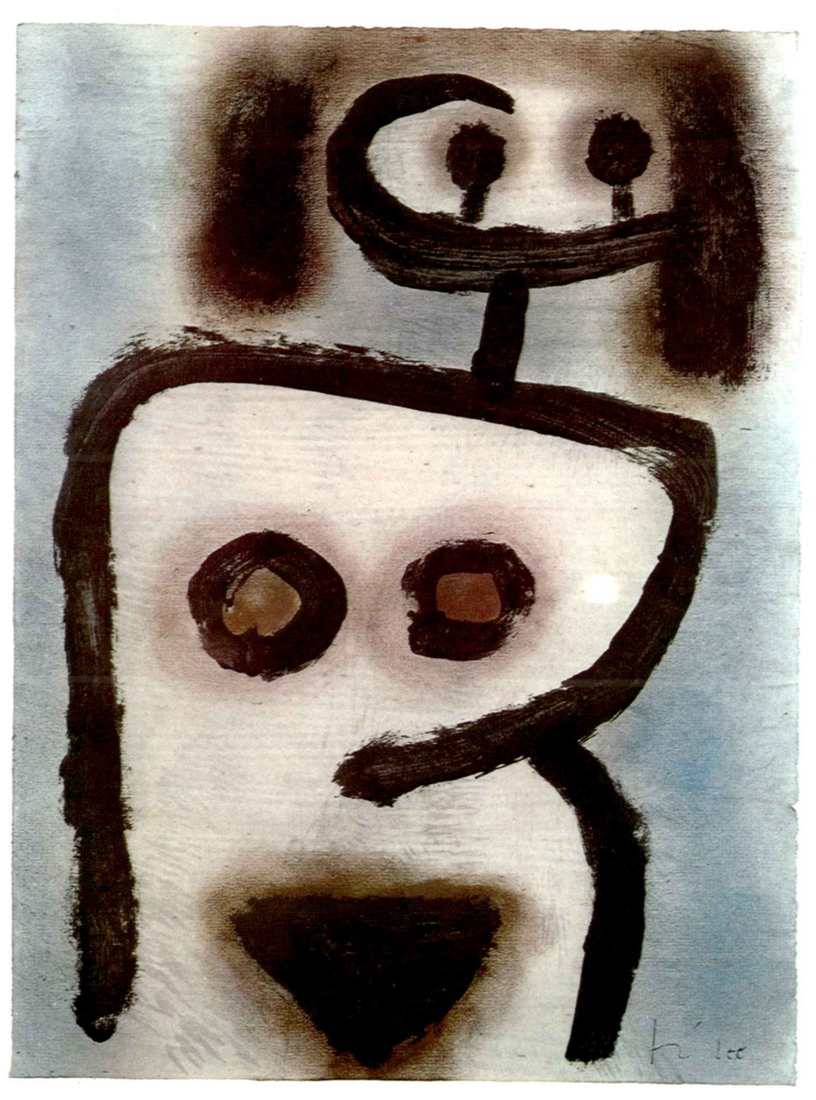

1939 H 19 ein Antlitz, auch des Leibes

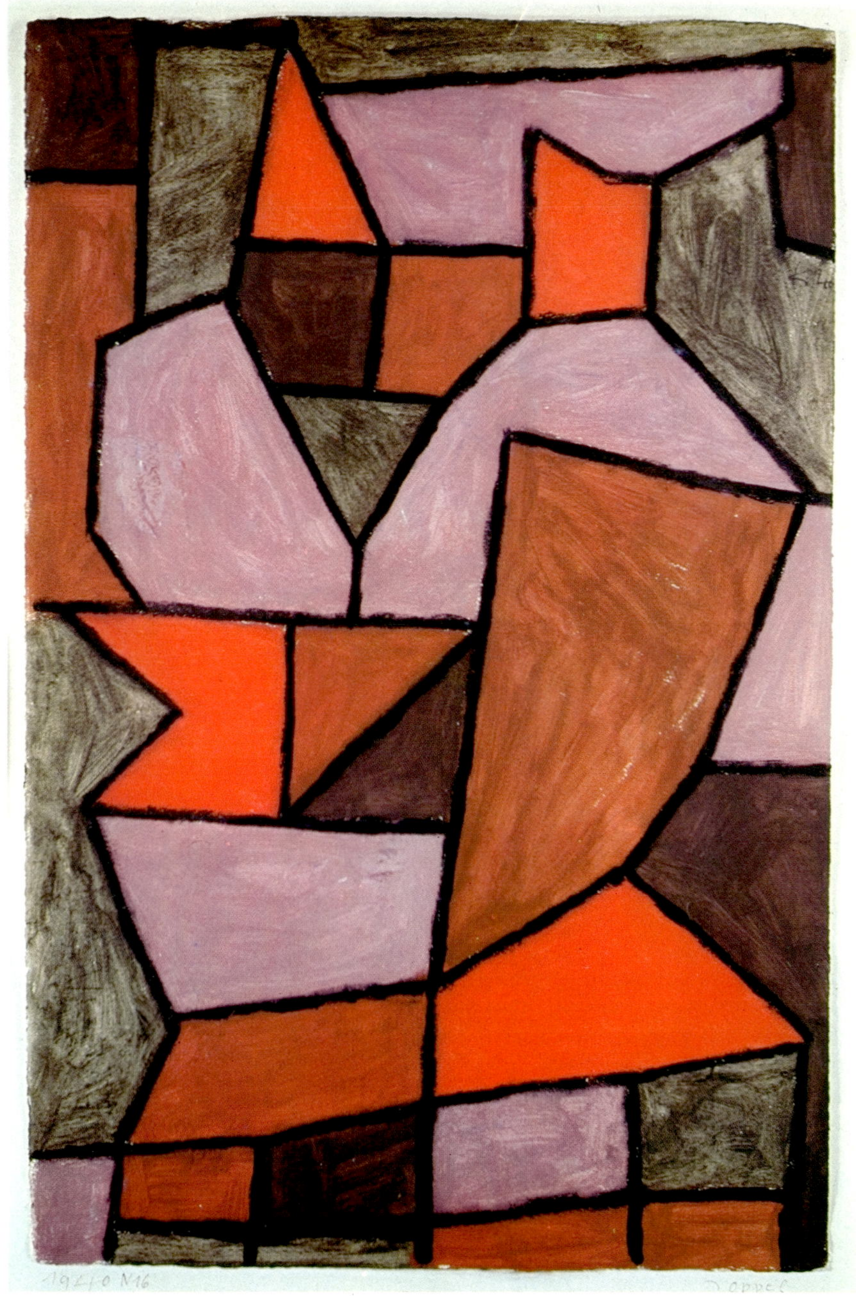

46 Klee *Double* 1940 Klee Foundation Bern

47 Klee *Still Life* 1940 Felix Klee Bern→

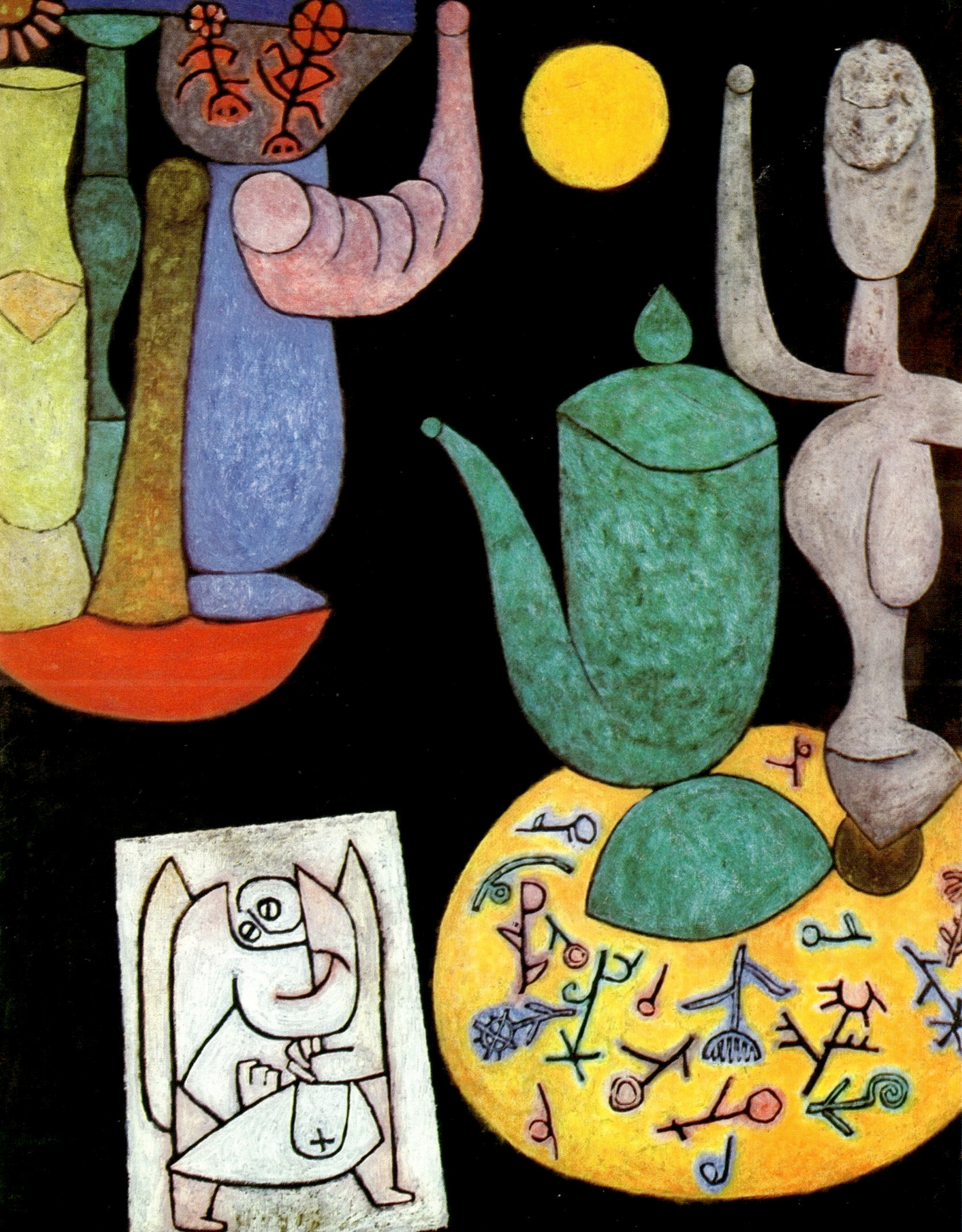

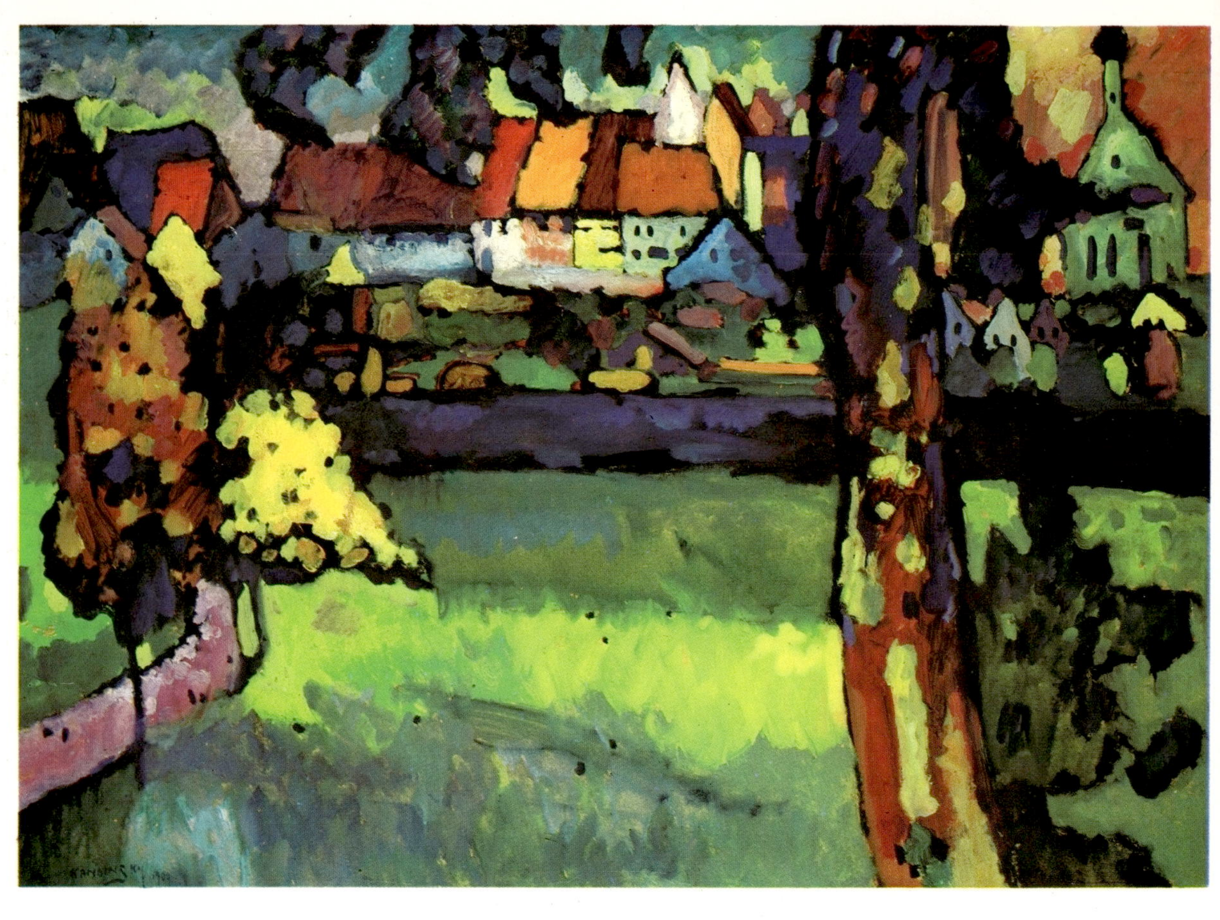

48 Kandinsky *Landscape with Tree* 1909 Museum of Düsseldorf

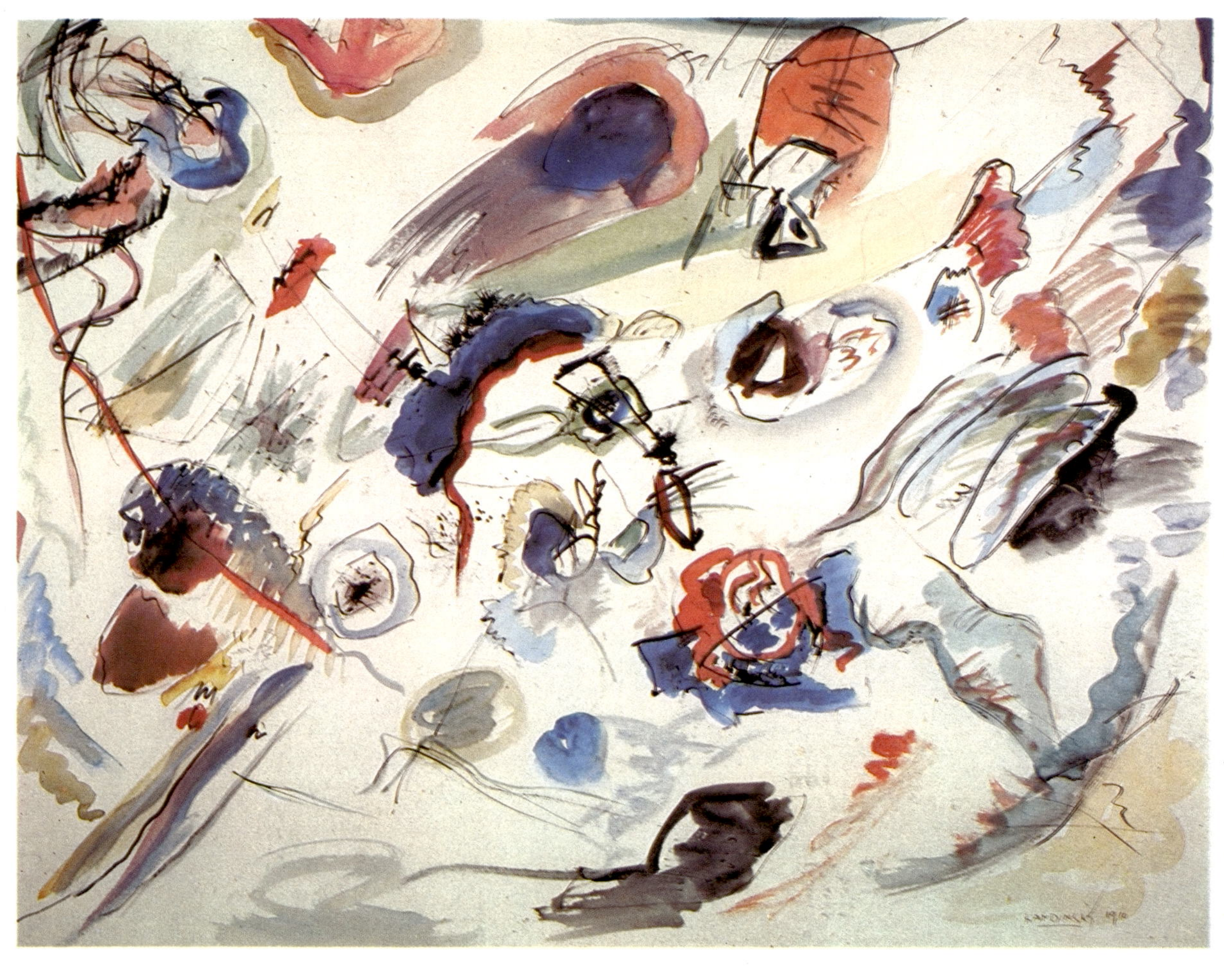

49 Kandinsky *First Abstract Water Color* 1910

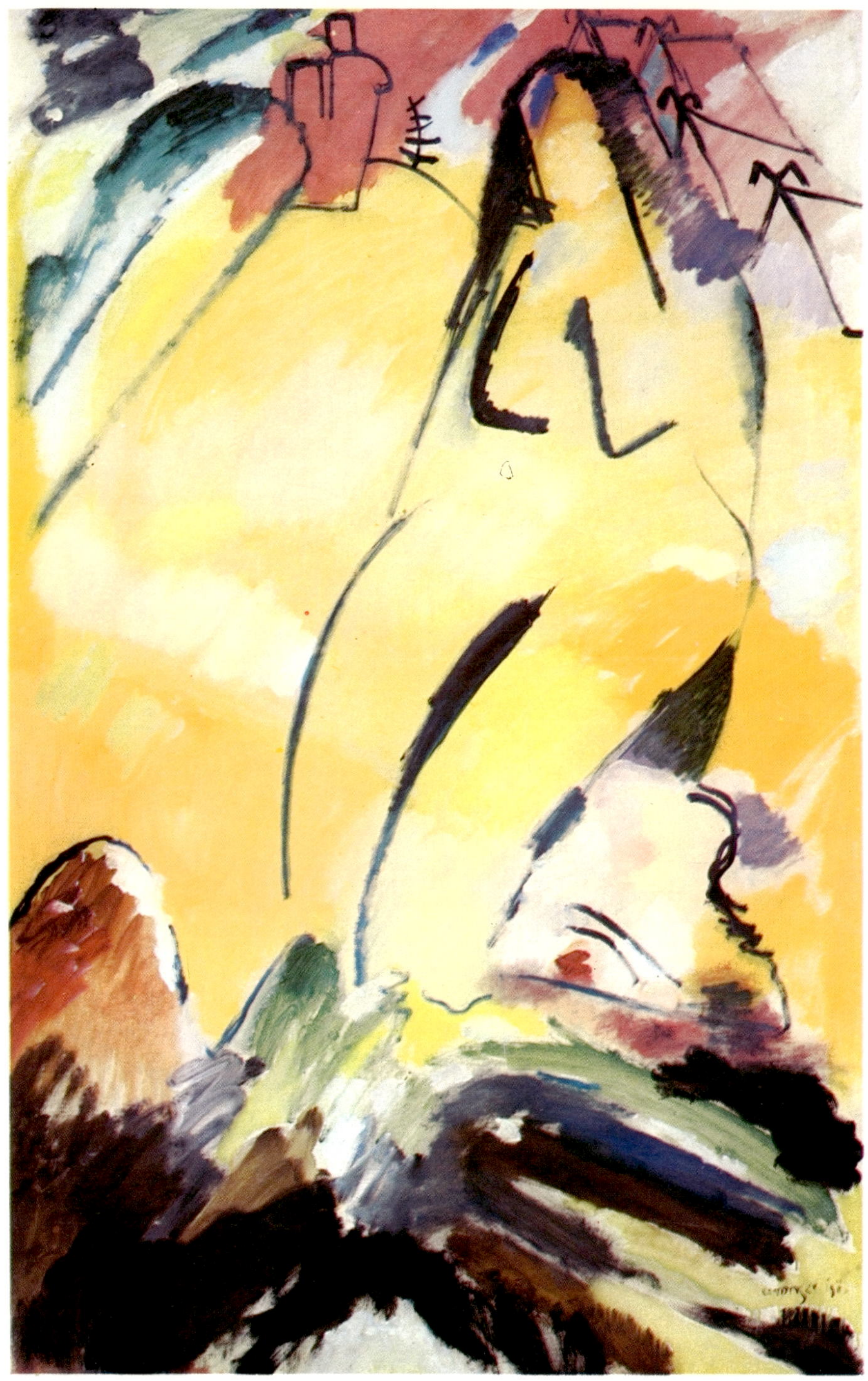

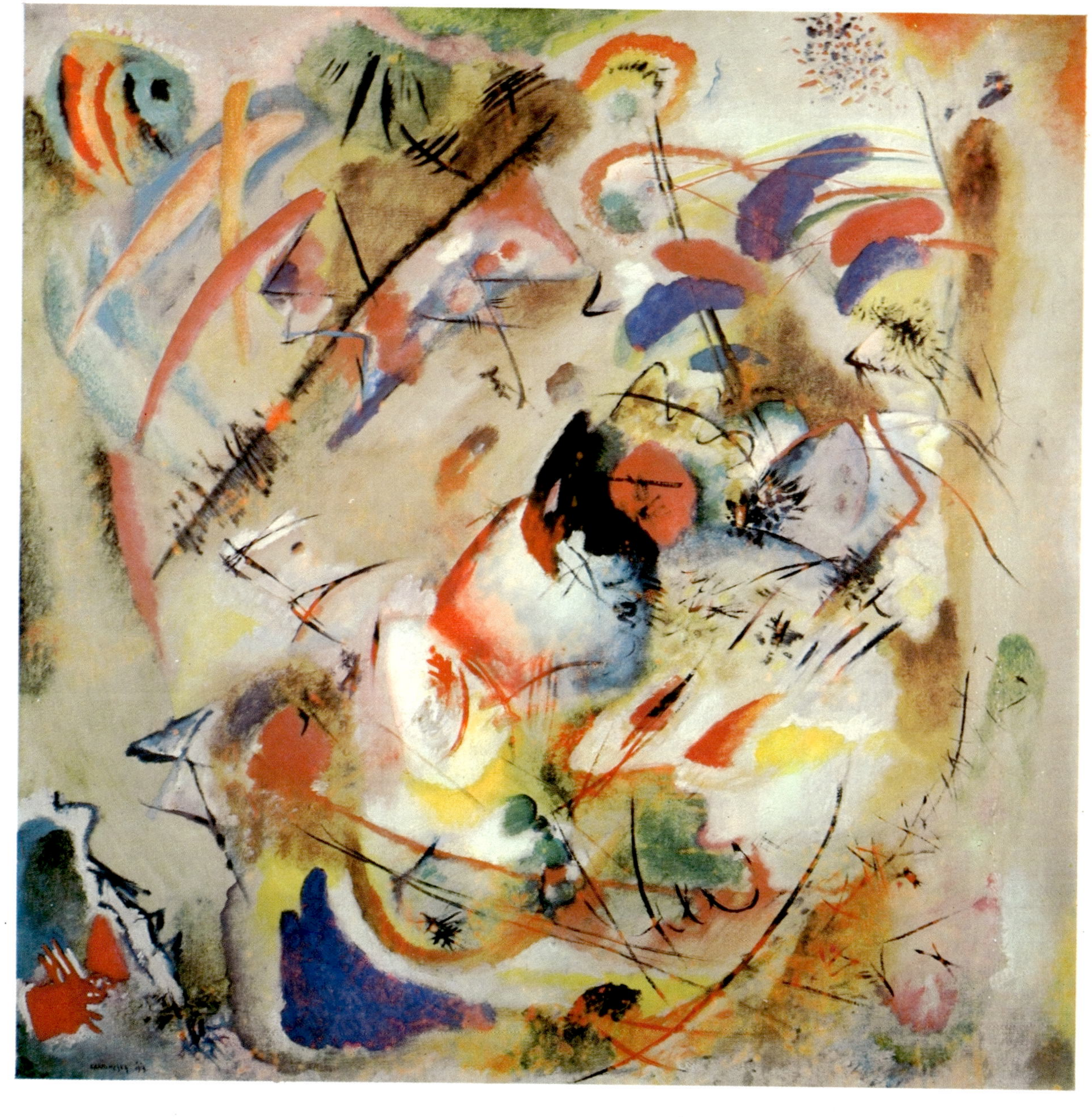

51 Kandinsky *Dreamy Improvisation* 1913 Private Collection New York

←50 Kandinsky *Nude* 1911 Galerie Beyeler Basel

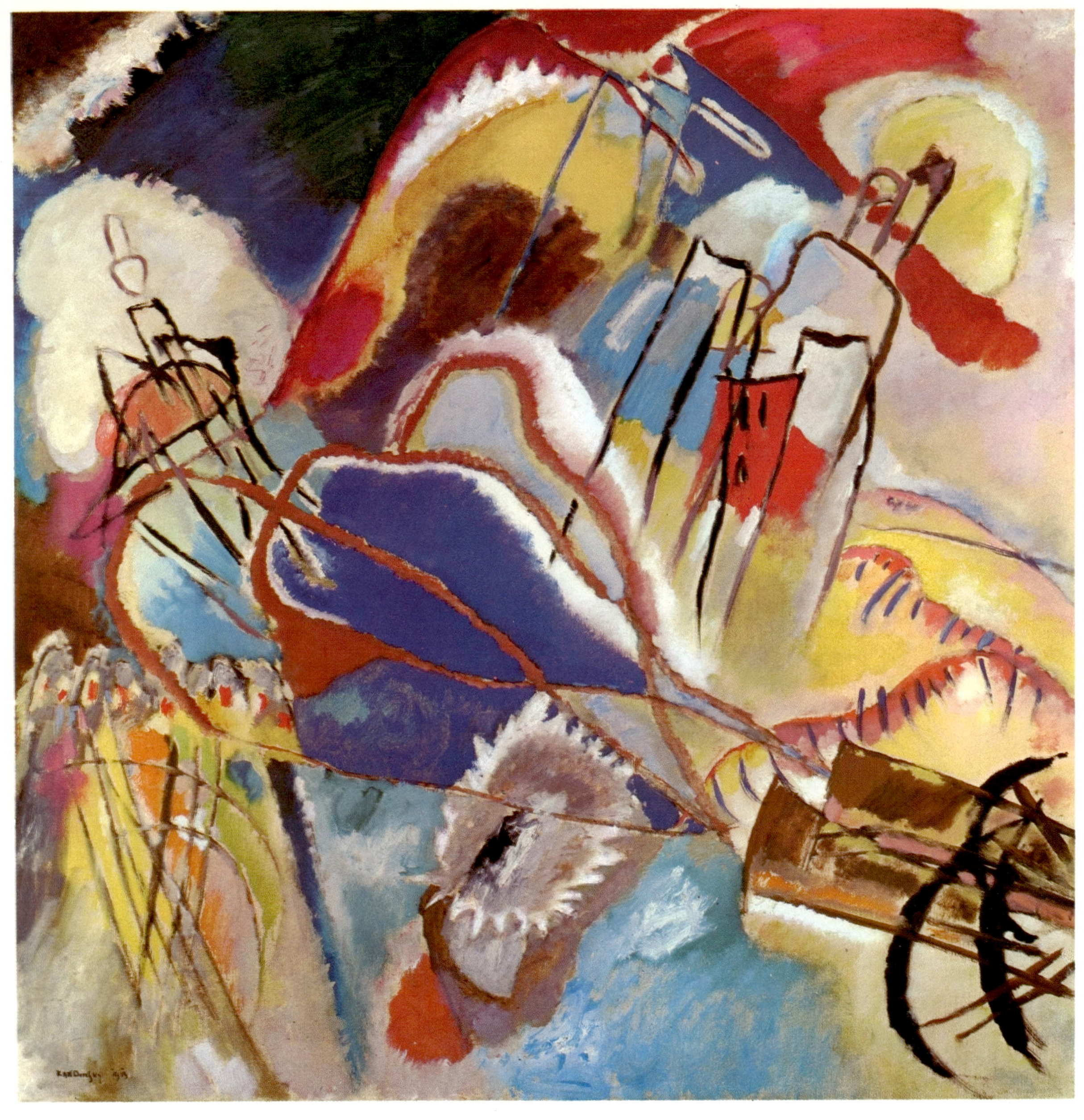

52 Kandinsky *Improvisation 30* 1913 Art Institute of Chicago

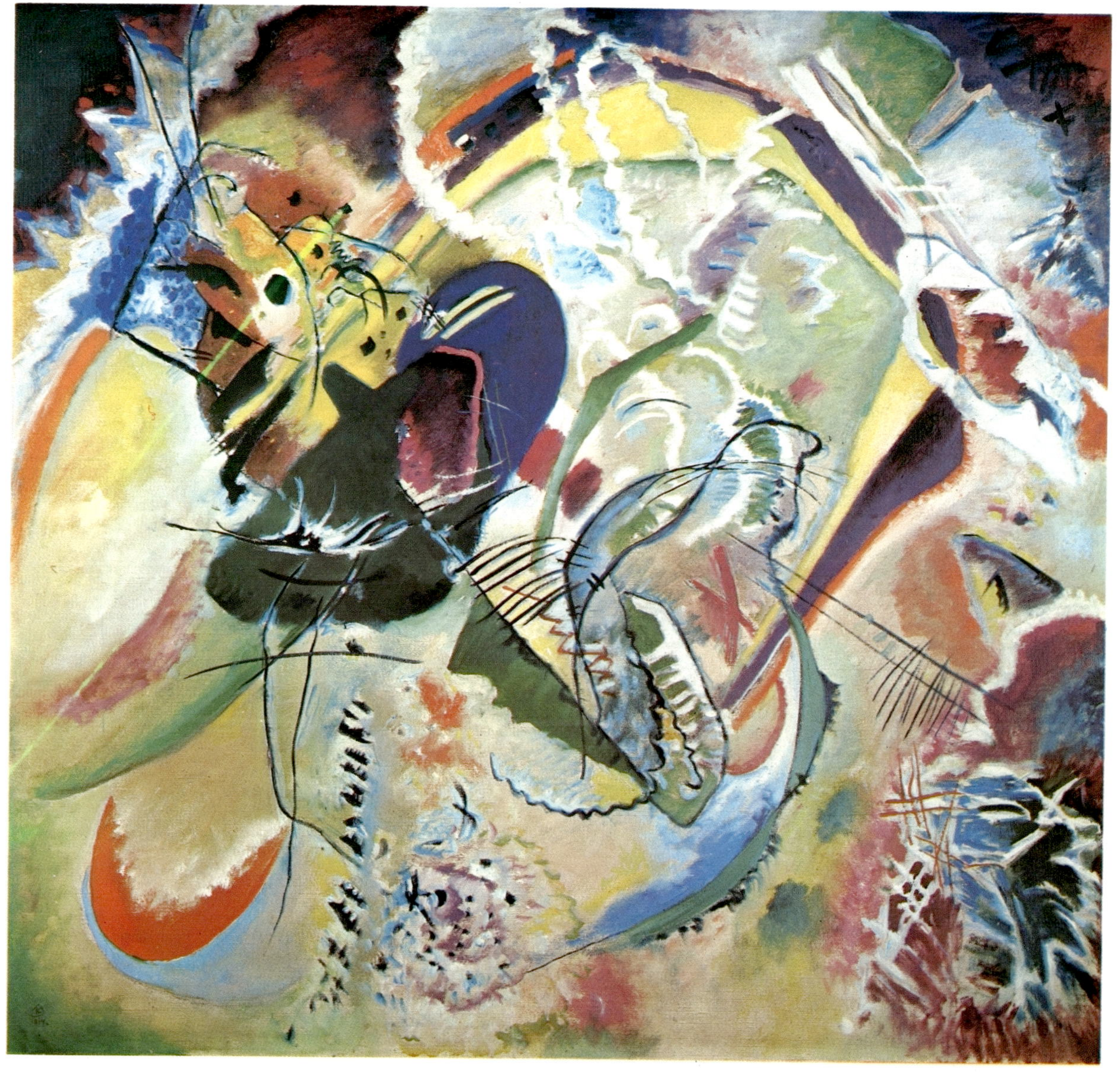

53 Kandinsky *Improvisation 35* 1914 Loaned to Kunstmuseum Basel

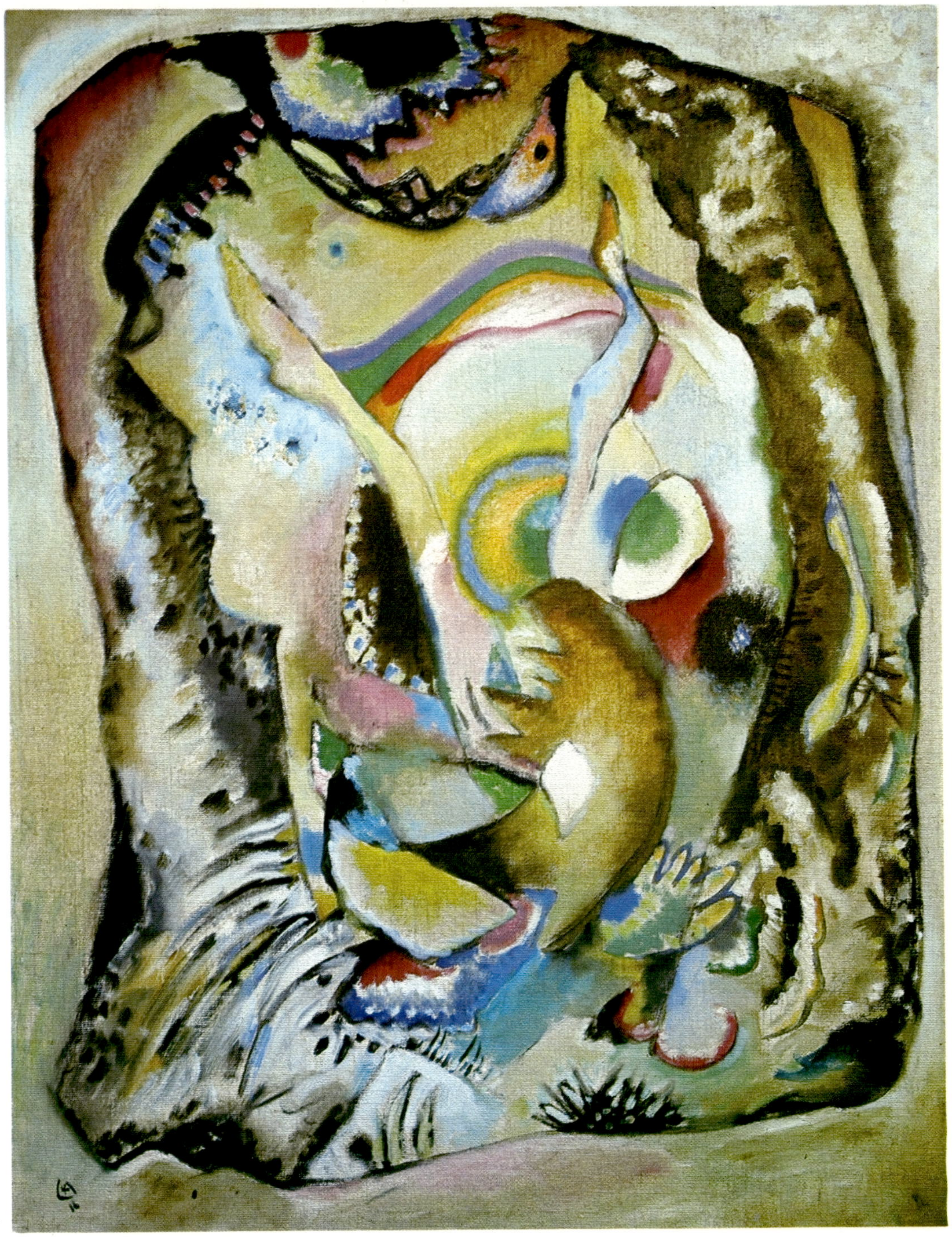

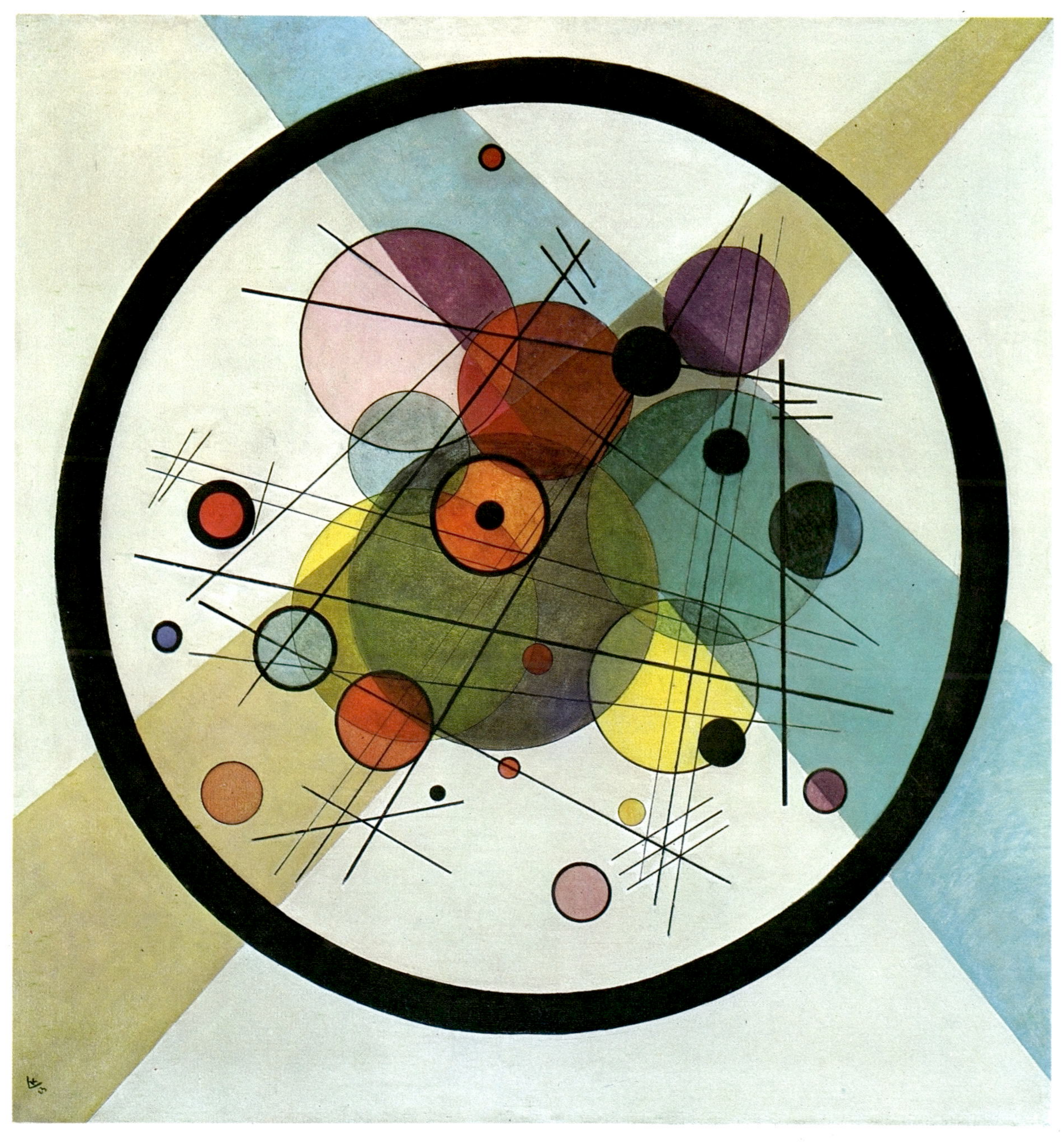

55 Kandinsky *Circle within the Circle* 1923 Philadelphia Museum of Art

–54 Kandinsky *Painting on Light Ground* 1916 Nina Kandinsky Paris

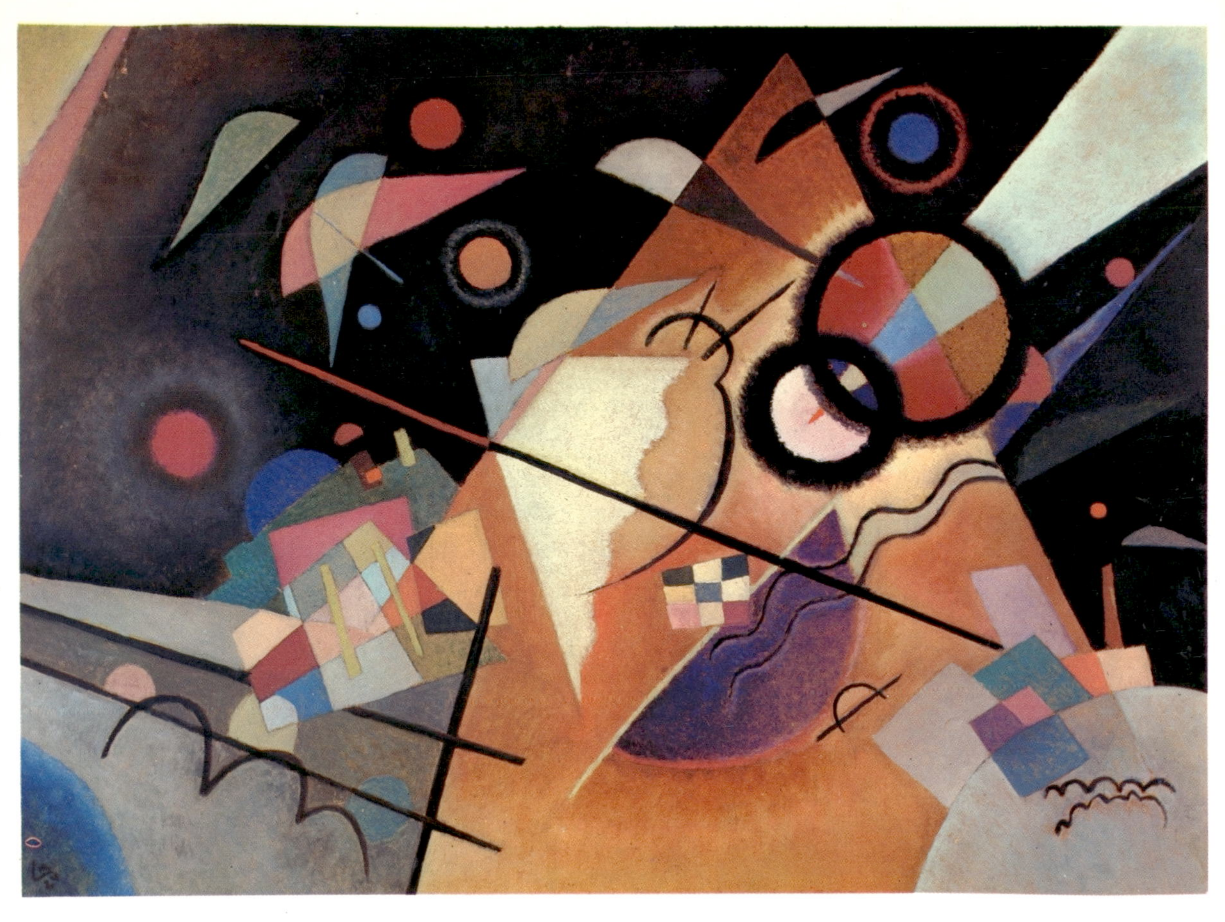

56 Kandinsky *Yellow Point* 1924 Private Collection

57 Kandinsky *Sharp-Calm Pink* 1924 Wallraf-Richartz-Museum Cologne→

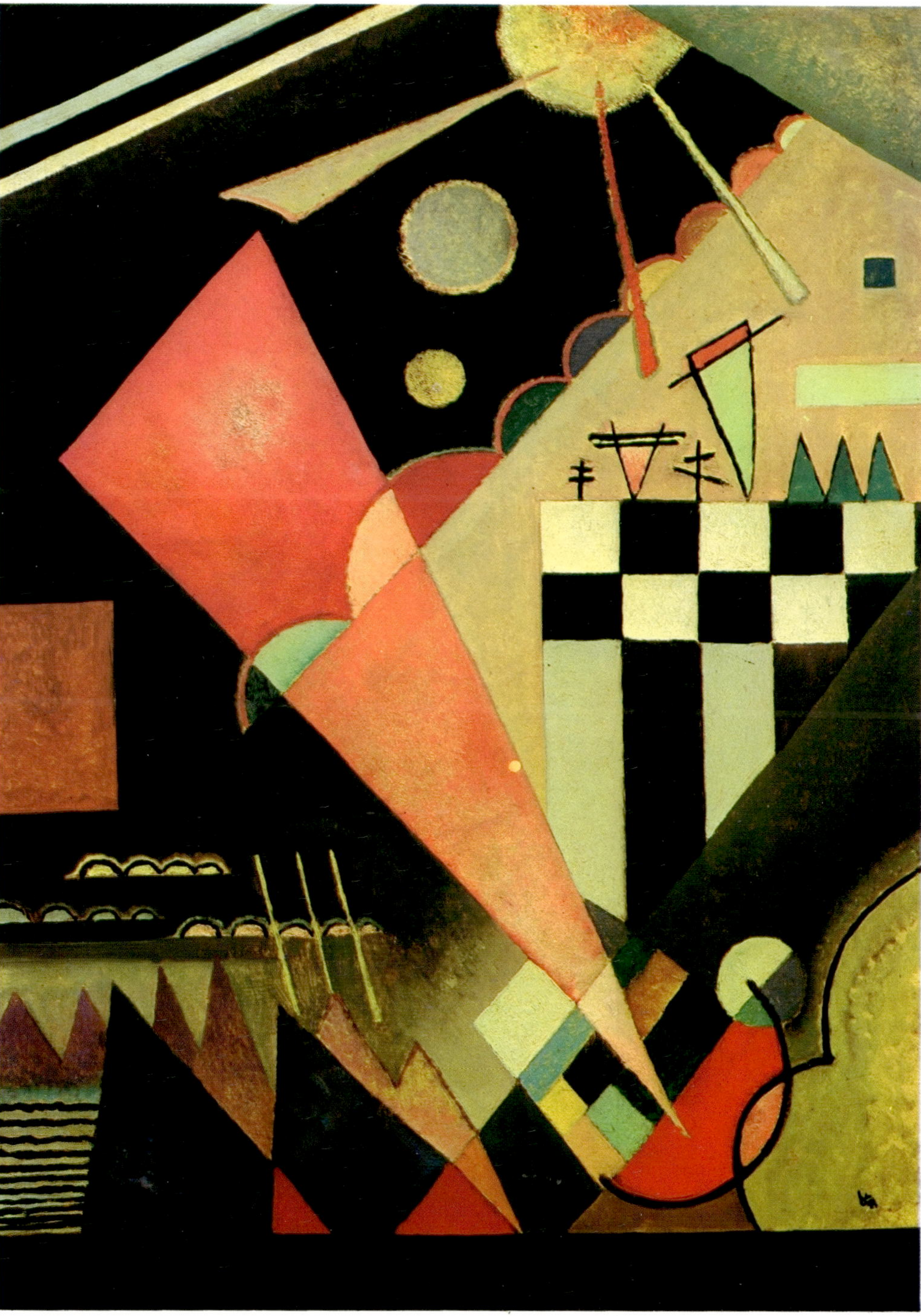

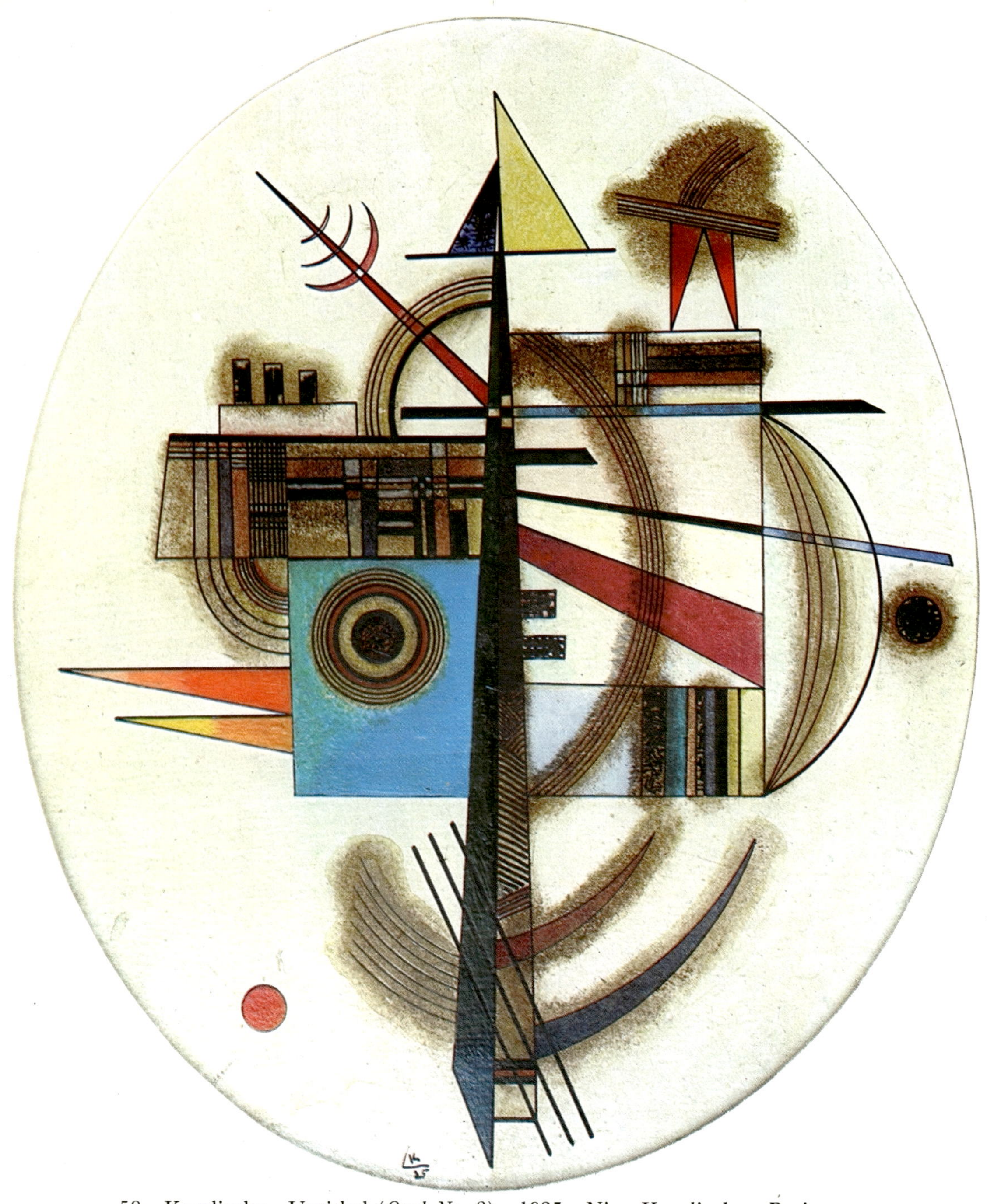

58 Kandinsky Untitled (*Oval No. 2*) 1925 Nina Kandinsky Paris

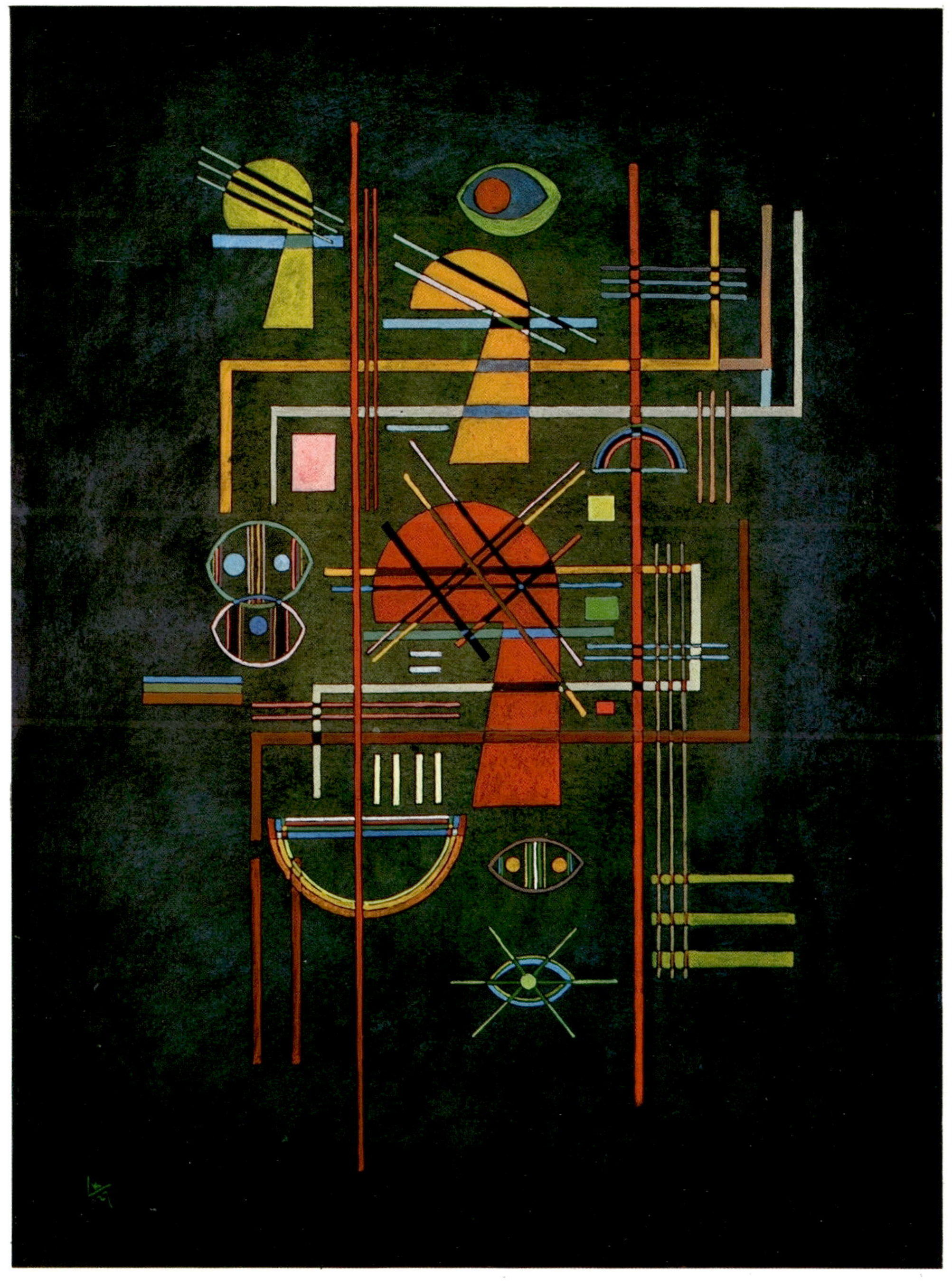

59 Kandinsky *Mild Hardness* 1927 Guggenheim Museum New York

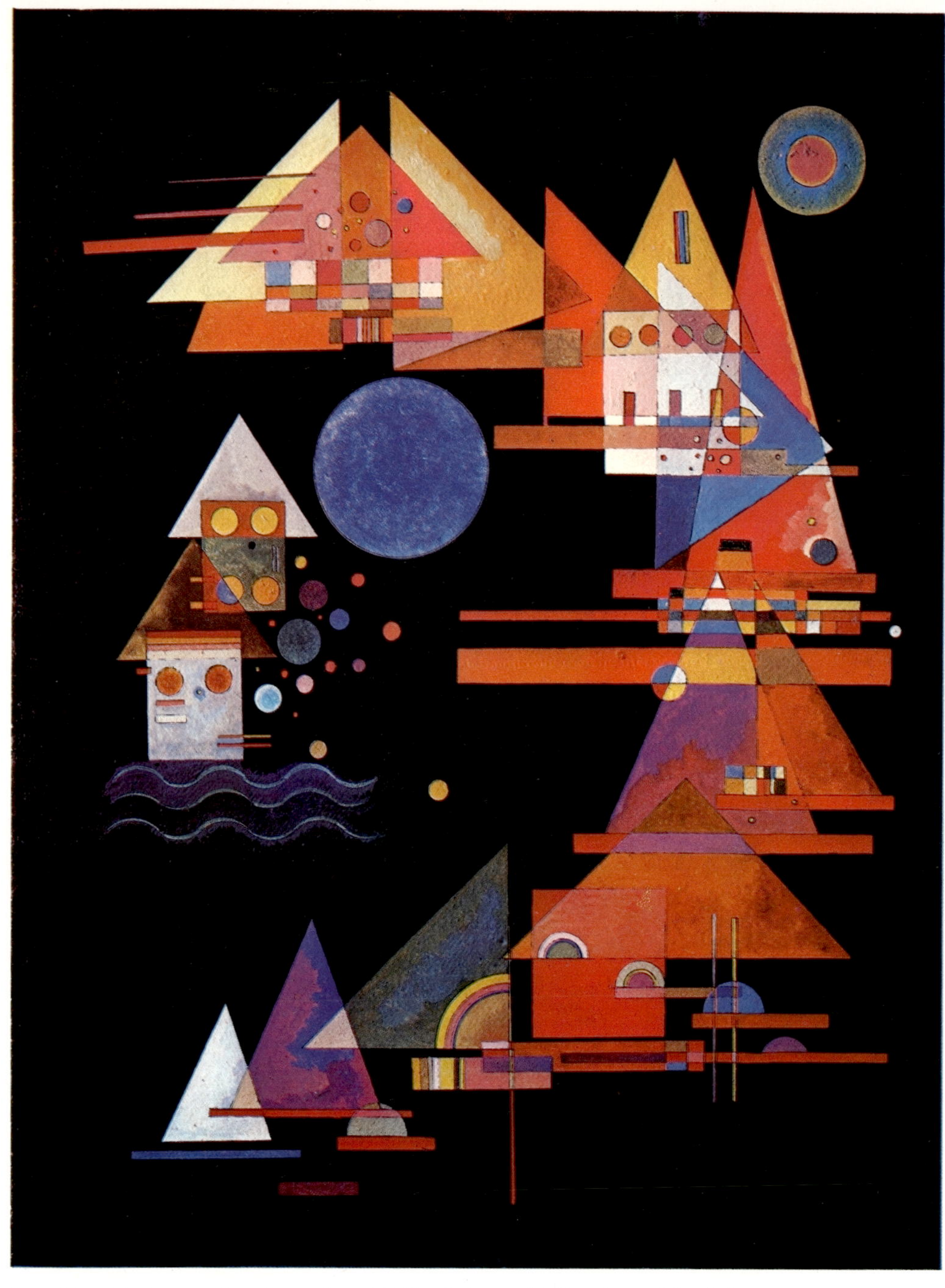

60 Kandinsky *Points in an Arc* 1927 Private Collection Munich

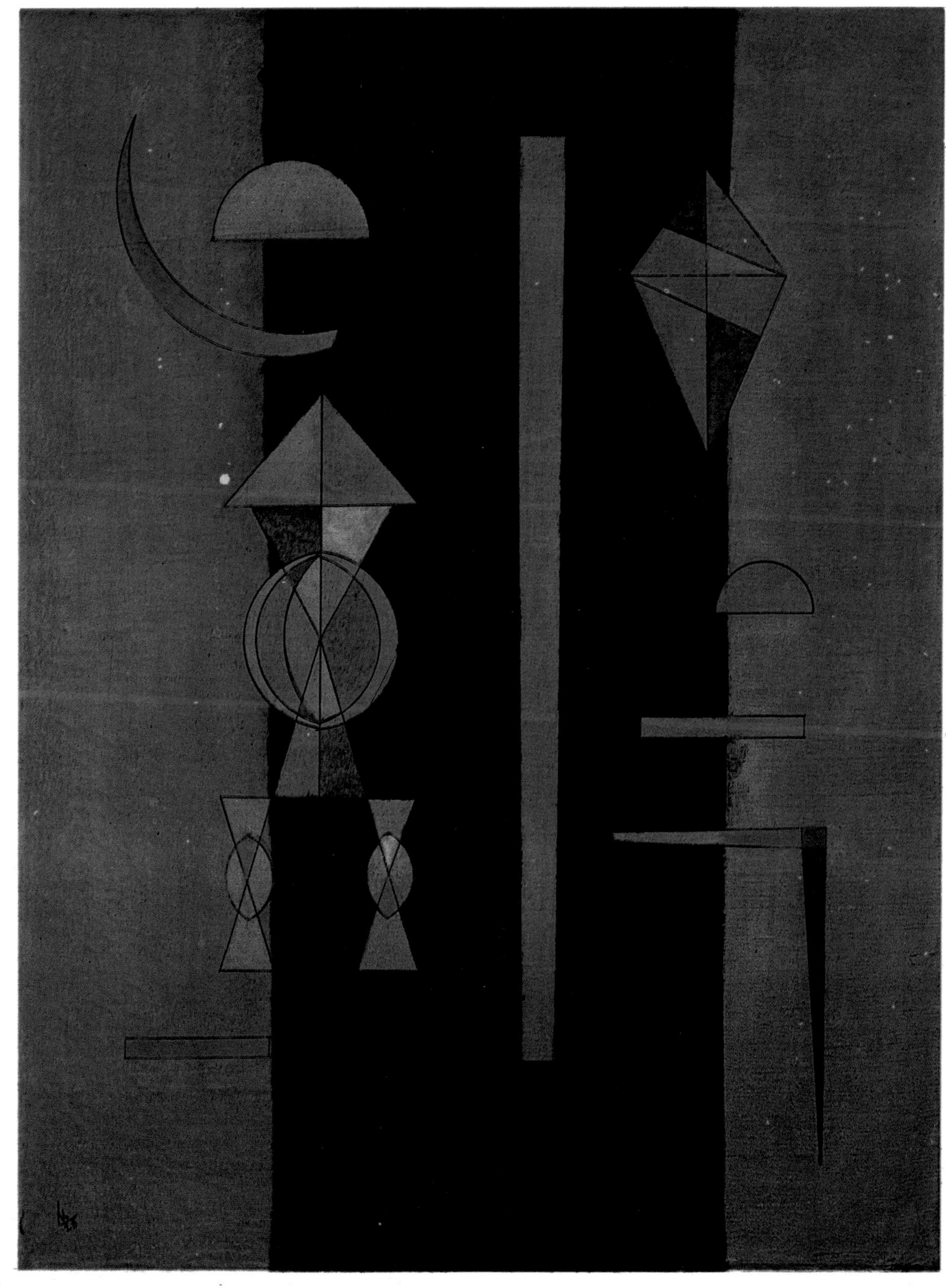

61 Kandinsky *Two Sides Red* 1928 Guggenheim Museum New York

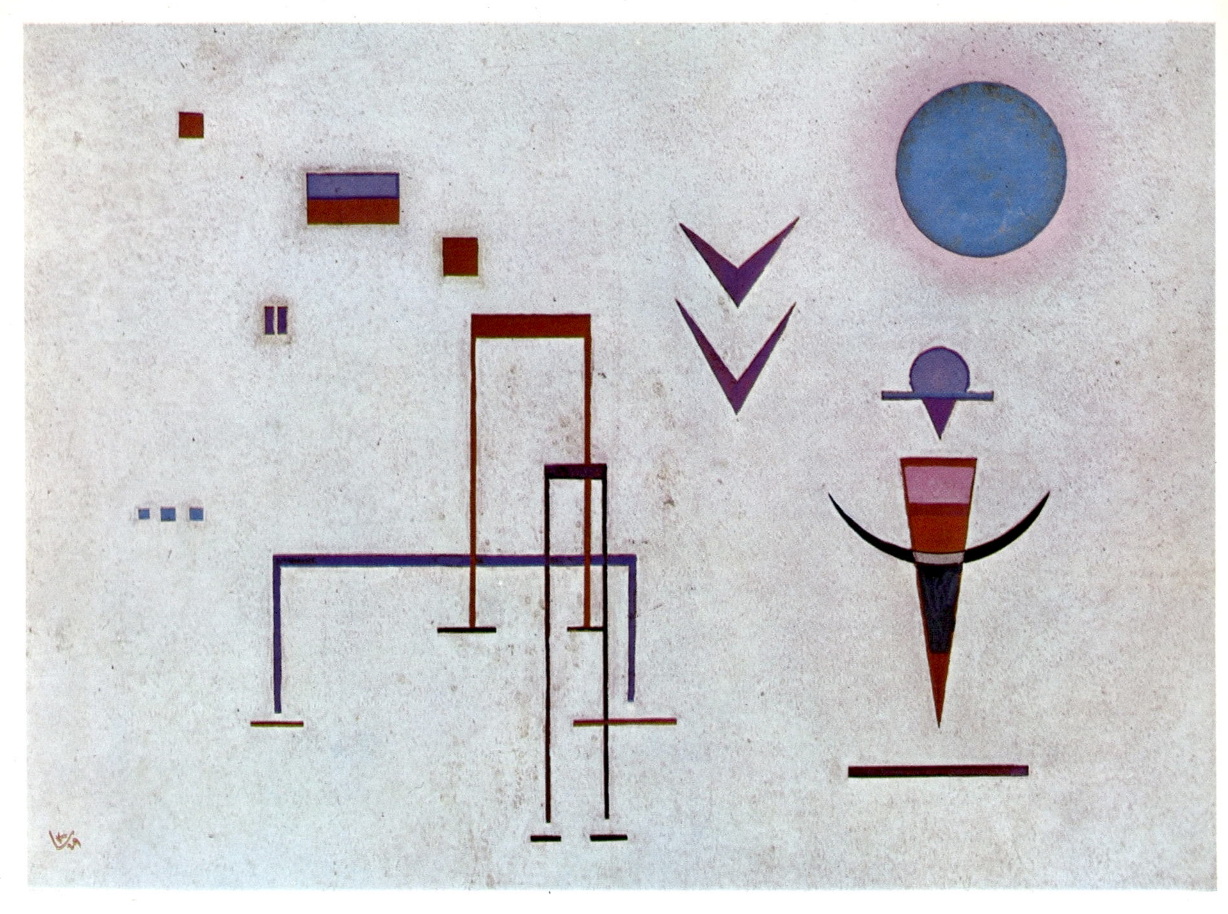

62 Kandinsky *Jocular Sound* 1929 Busch-Reisinger Museum Harvard

63 Kandinsky *Thirteen Rectangles* 1930 Nina Kandinsky Paris→

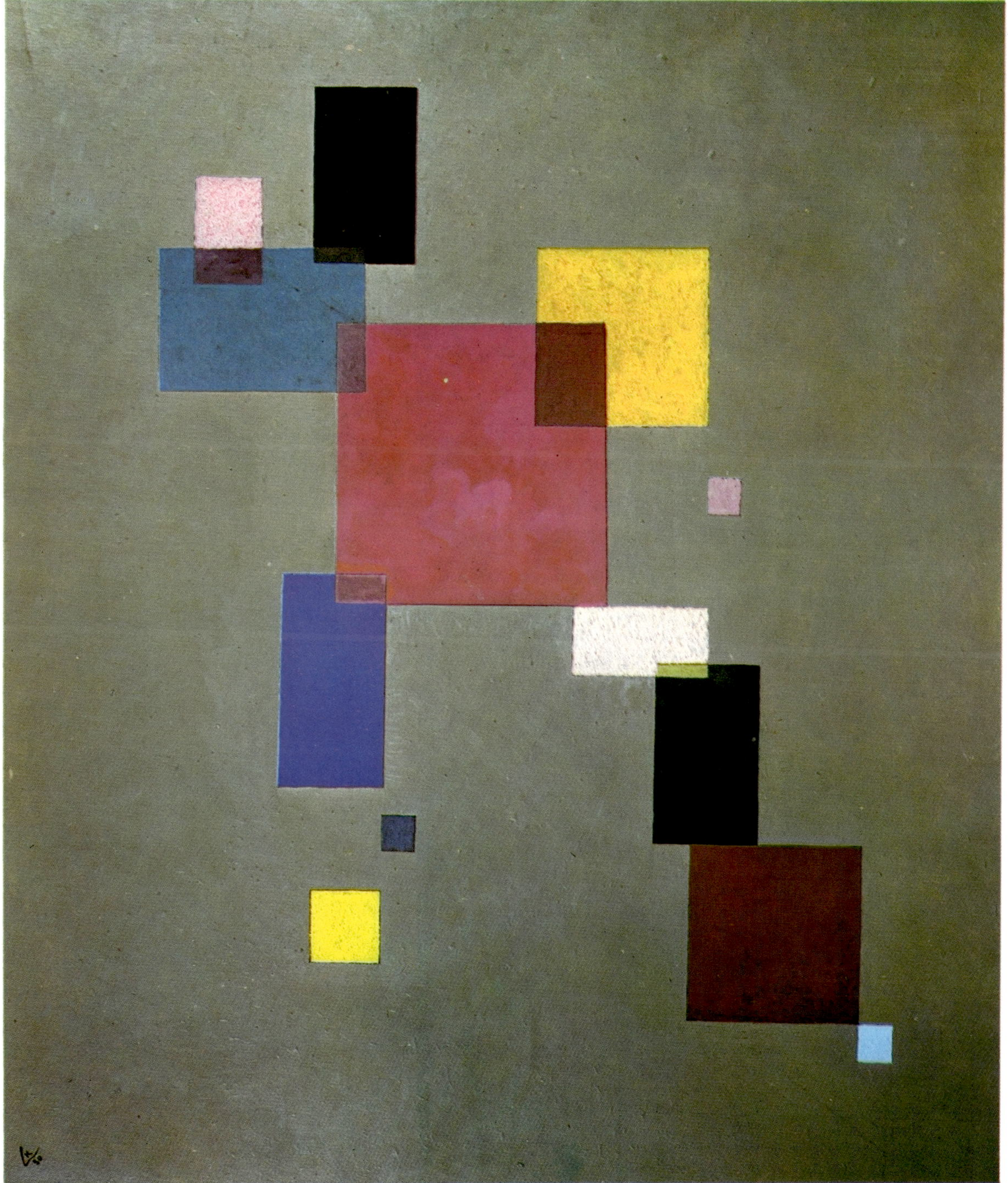

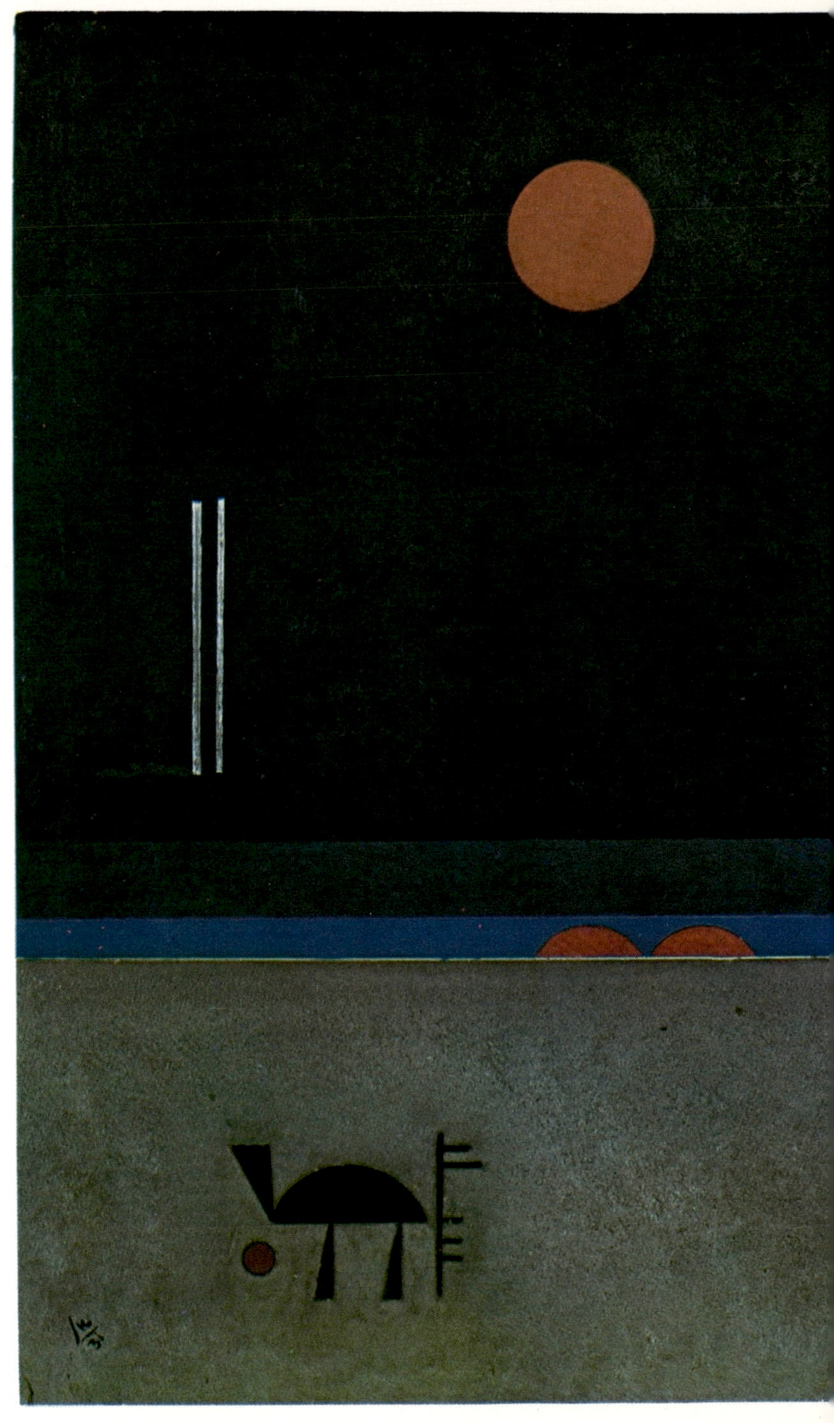

64
Kandinsky *Brownish*
1931 San Francisco
Museum of Art

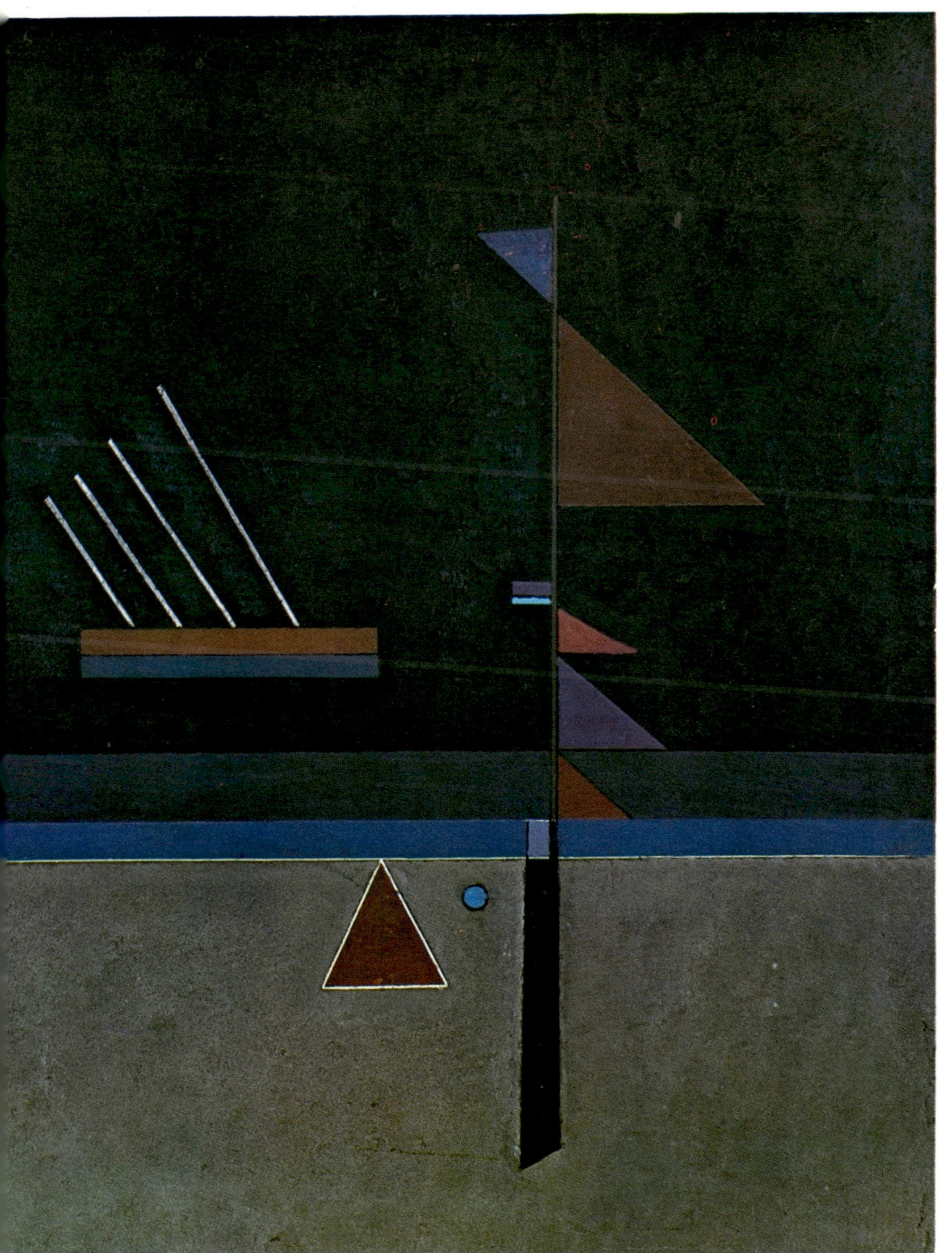

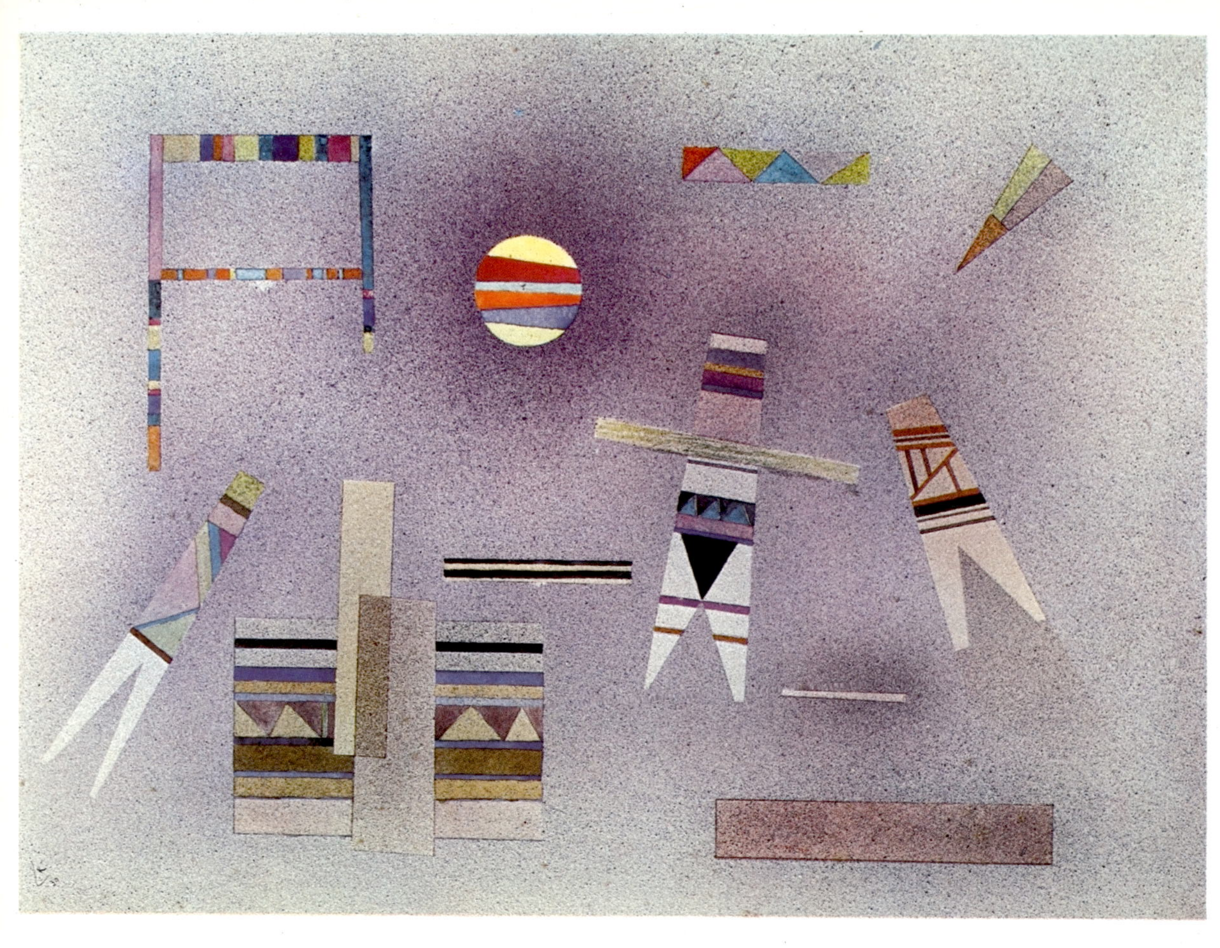

65 Kandinsky *Composition* National Museum of Art Mannheim

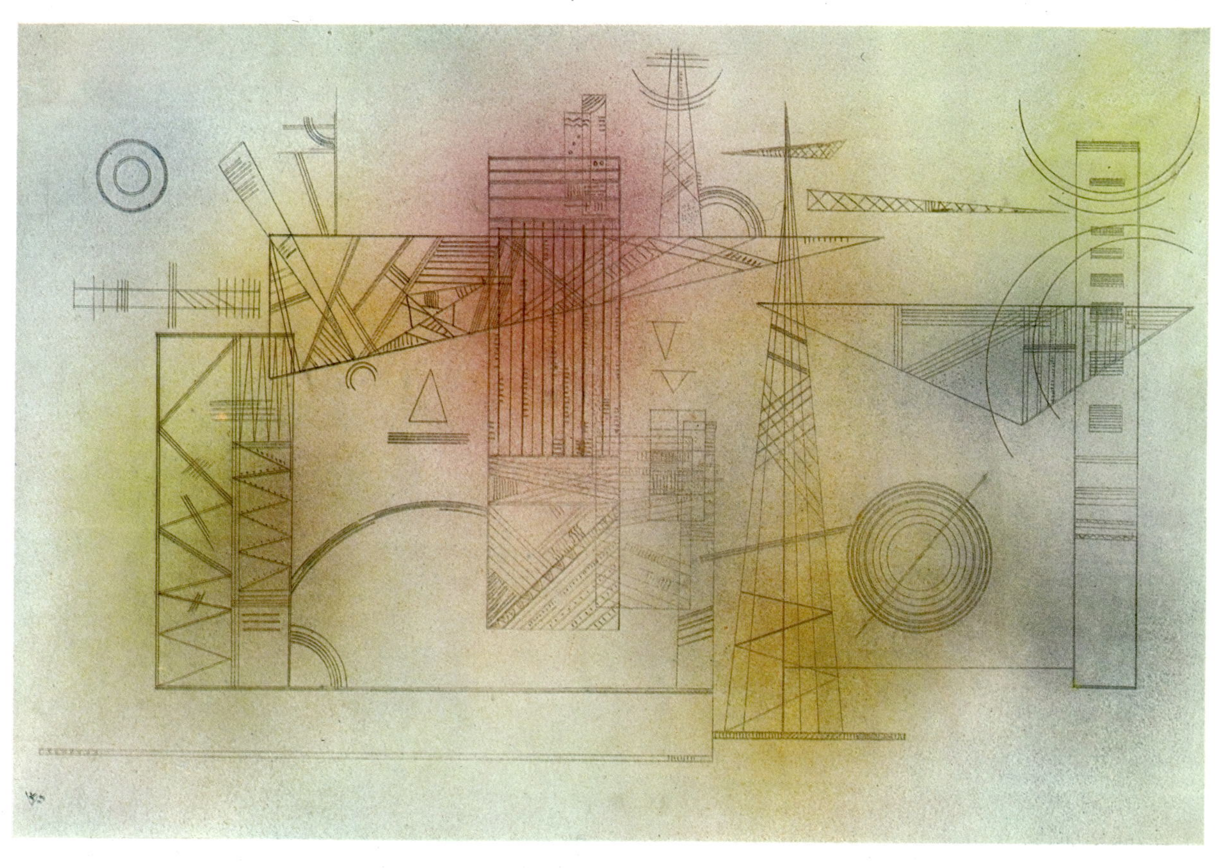

66 Kandinsky *Gradated Drawing* Galerie Beyeler Basel

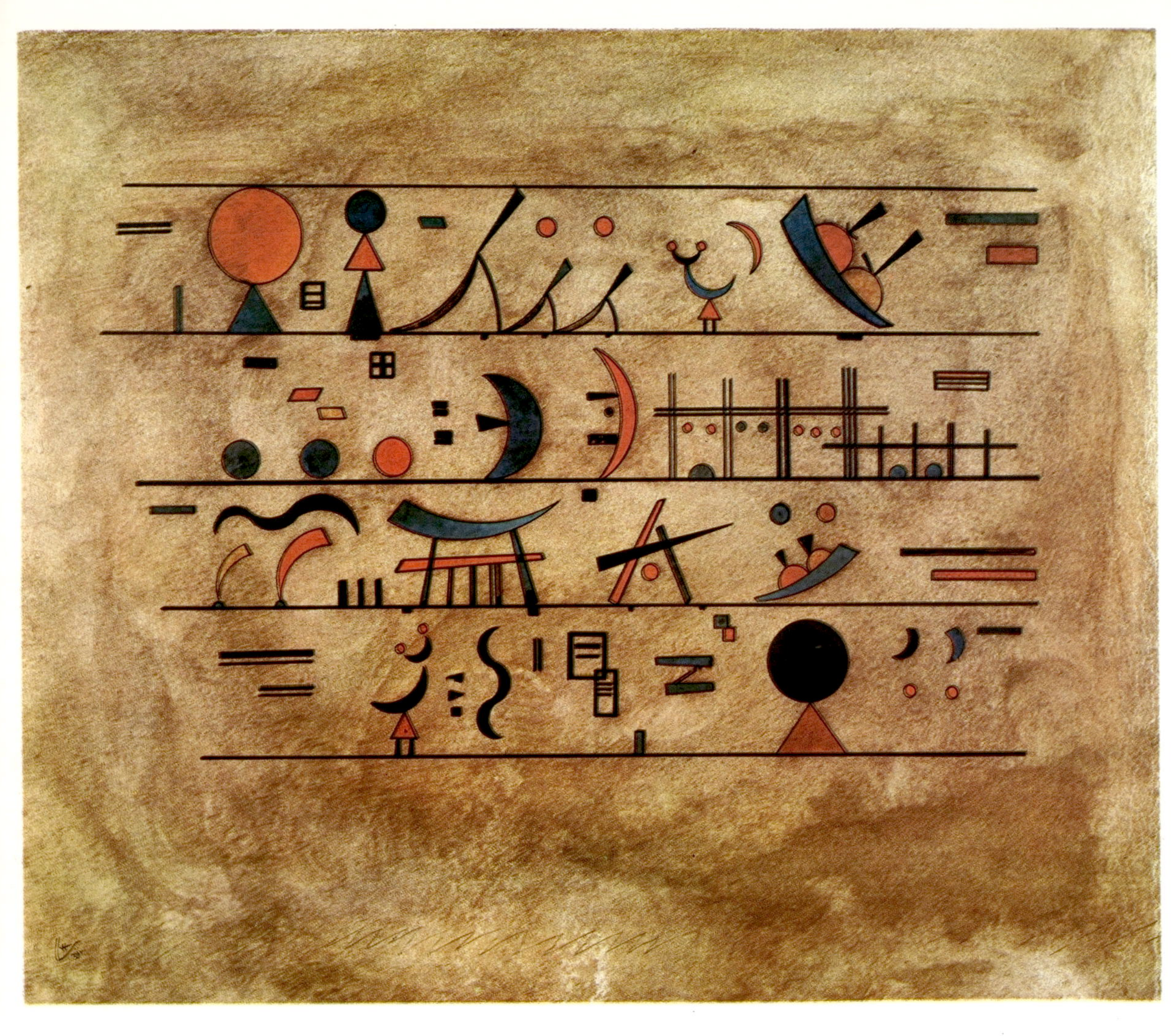

67 Kandinsky *Line of Marks* 1931 Kunstmuseum Basel

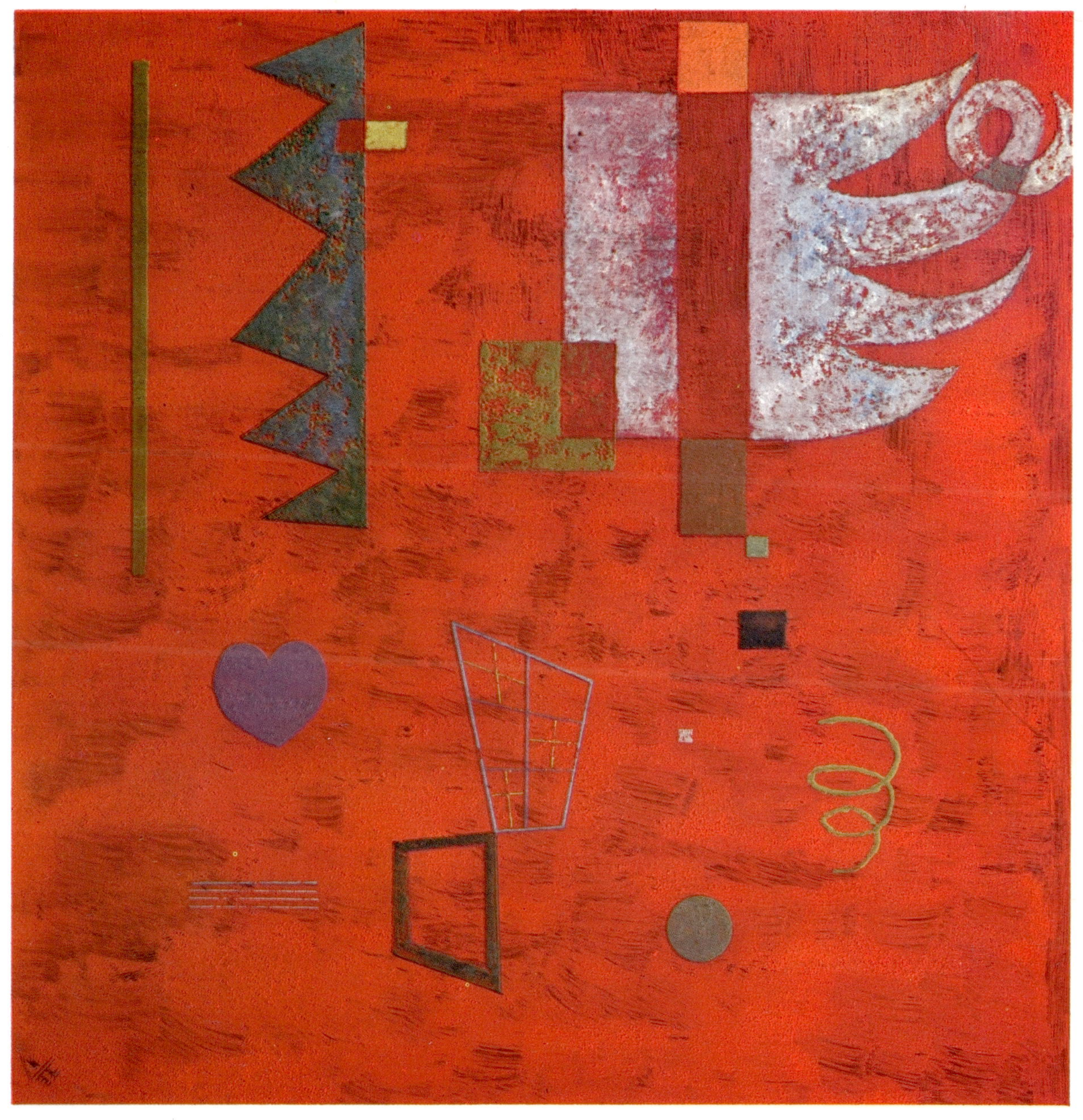

68 Kandinsky *Cool Distance* 1932 Nina Kandinsky Paris

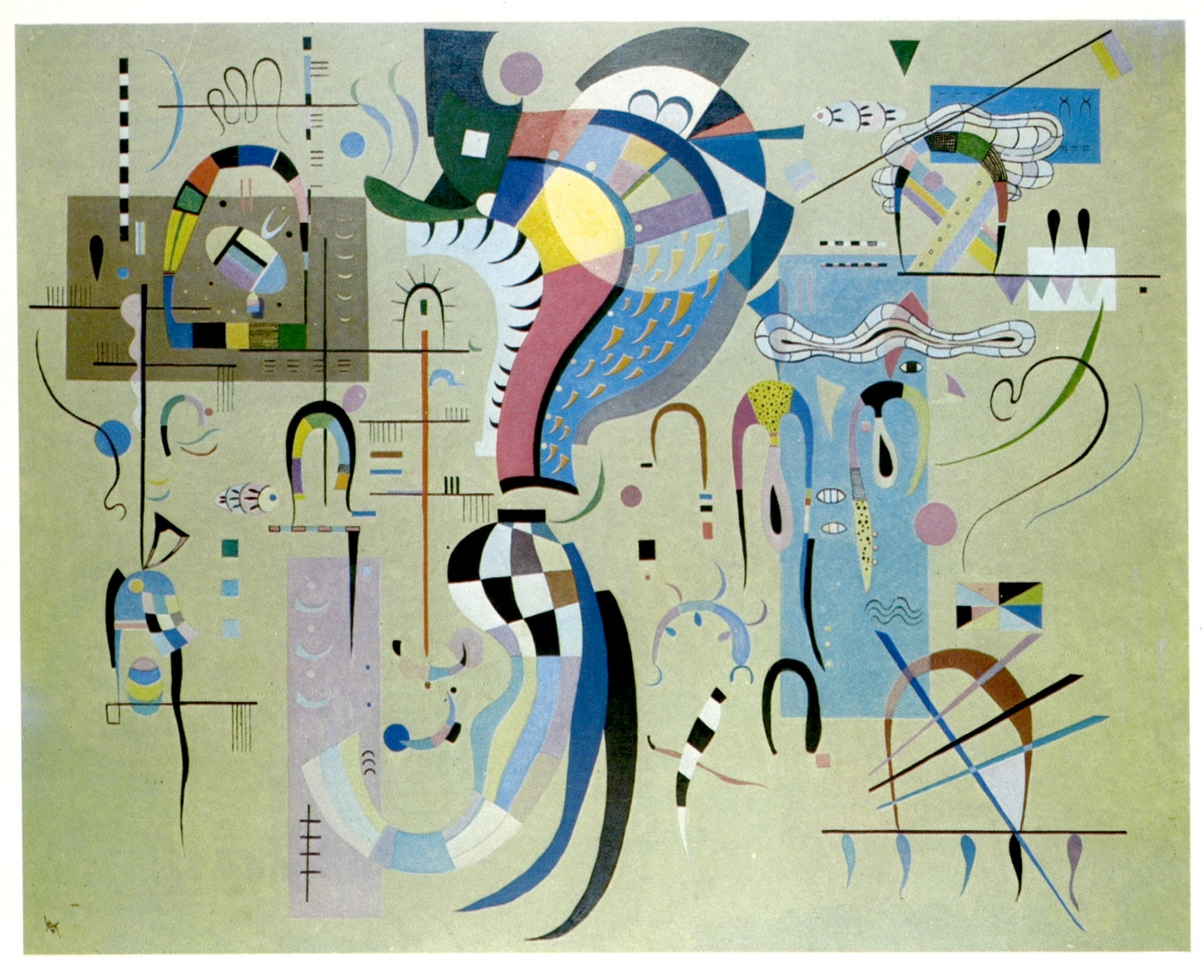

69 Kandinsky *Center with Accompaniment* 1937 Collection Aimé Maeght Paris

70 Kandinsky *Many-colored Ensemble* 1938 Baltimore Museum of Art→

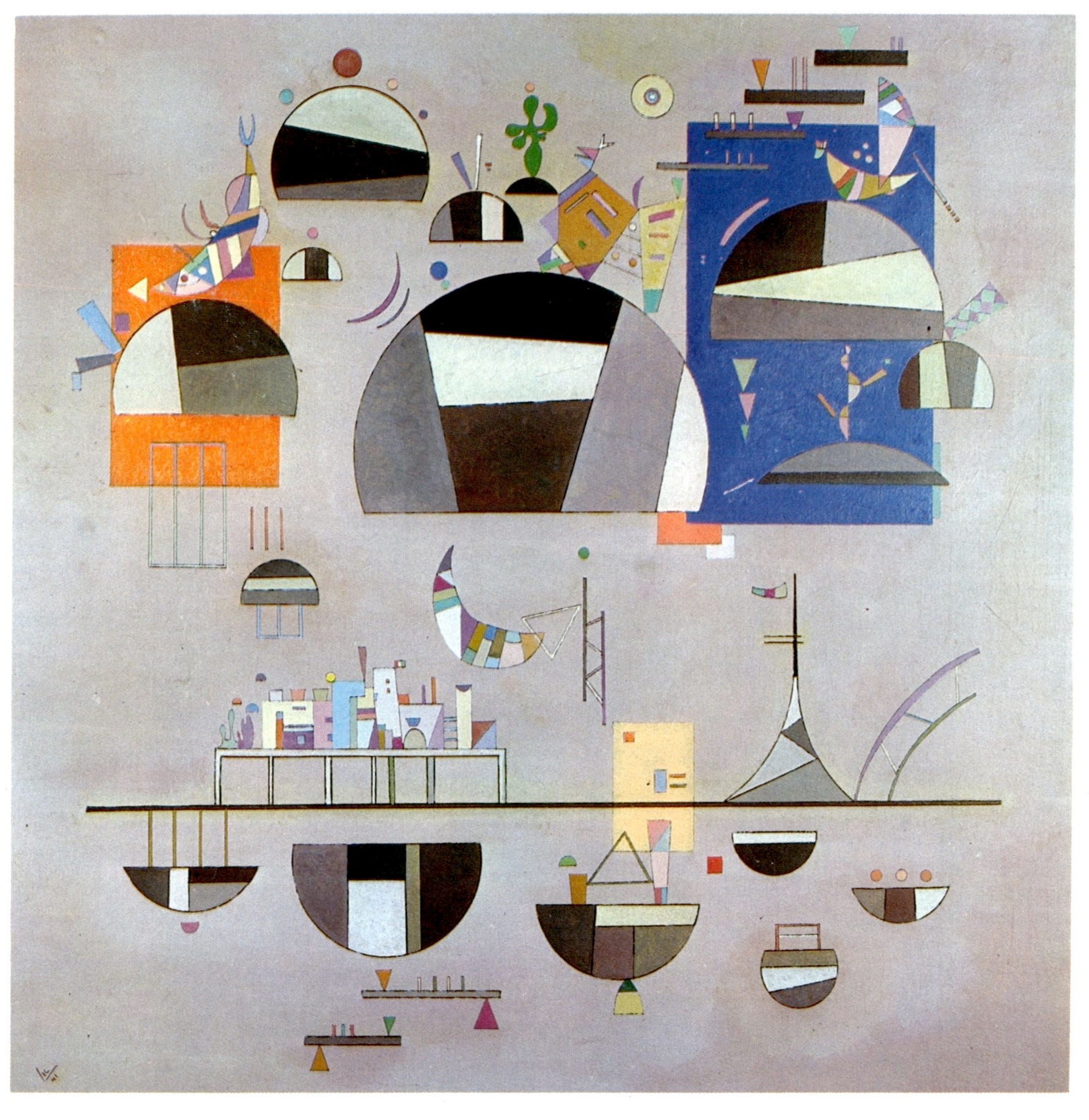

73 Kandinsky *Moderate Variation* 1941 Collection Aimé Maeght Paris

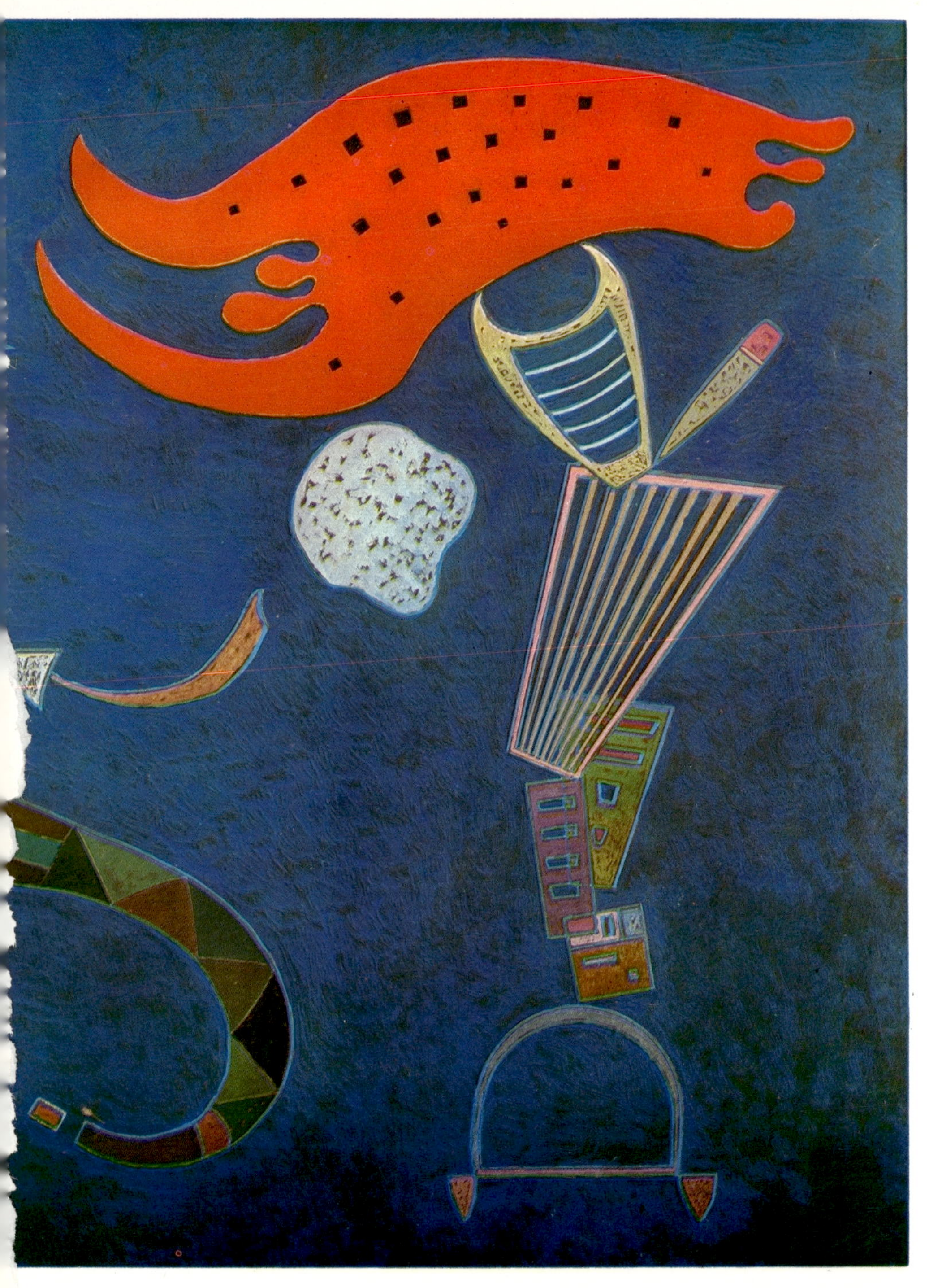

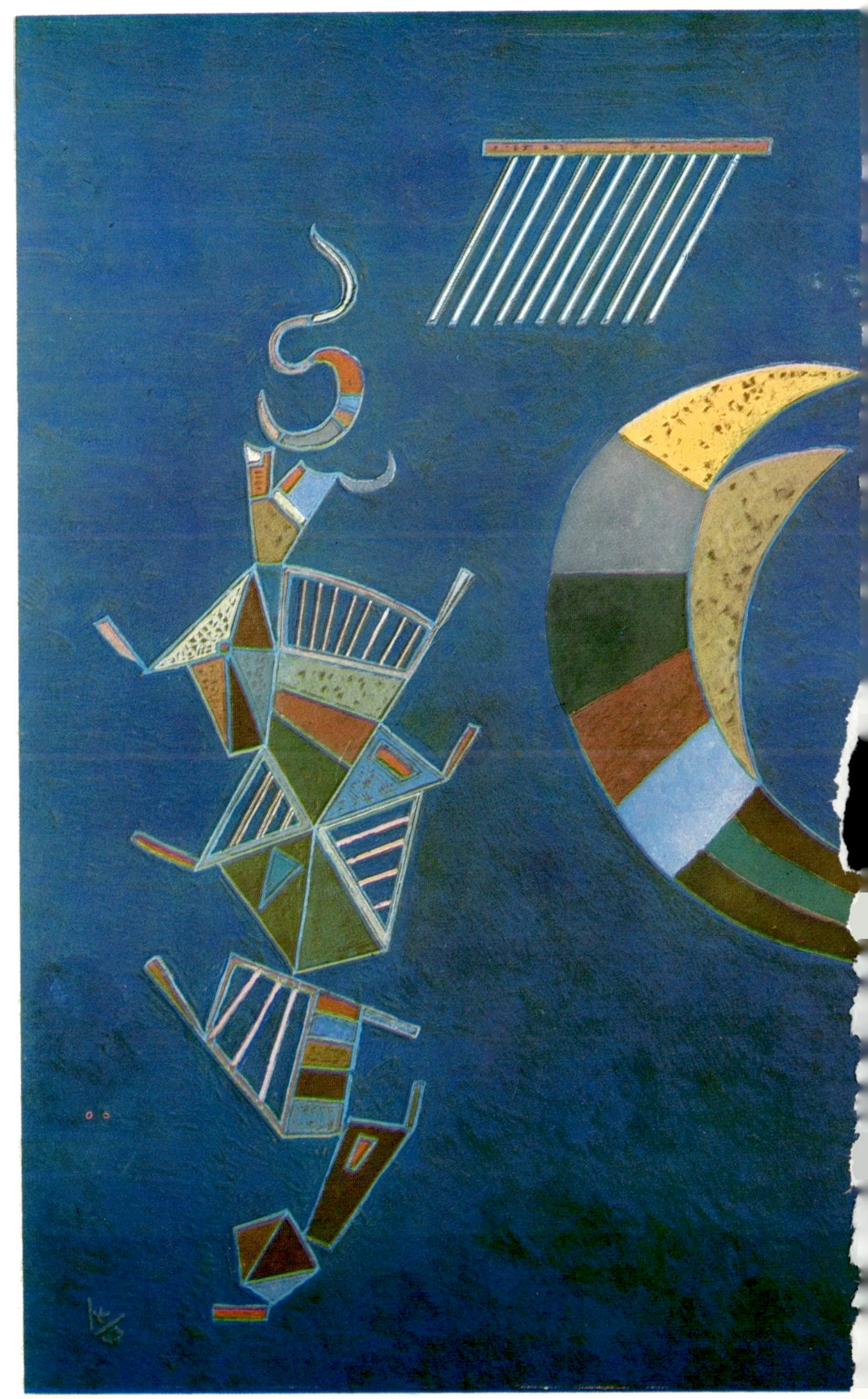

←71
Kandinsky *Circuit*
1939 Nina Kandinsky
Paris

72
Kandinsky *The Arrow*
1943 Kunstmuseum
Basel

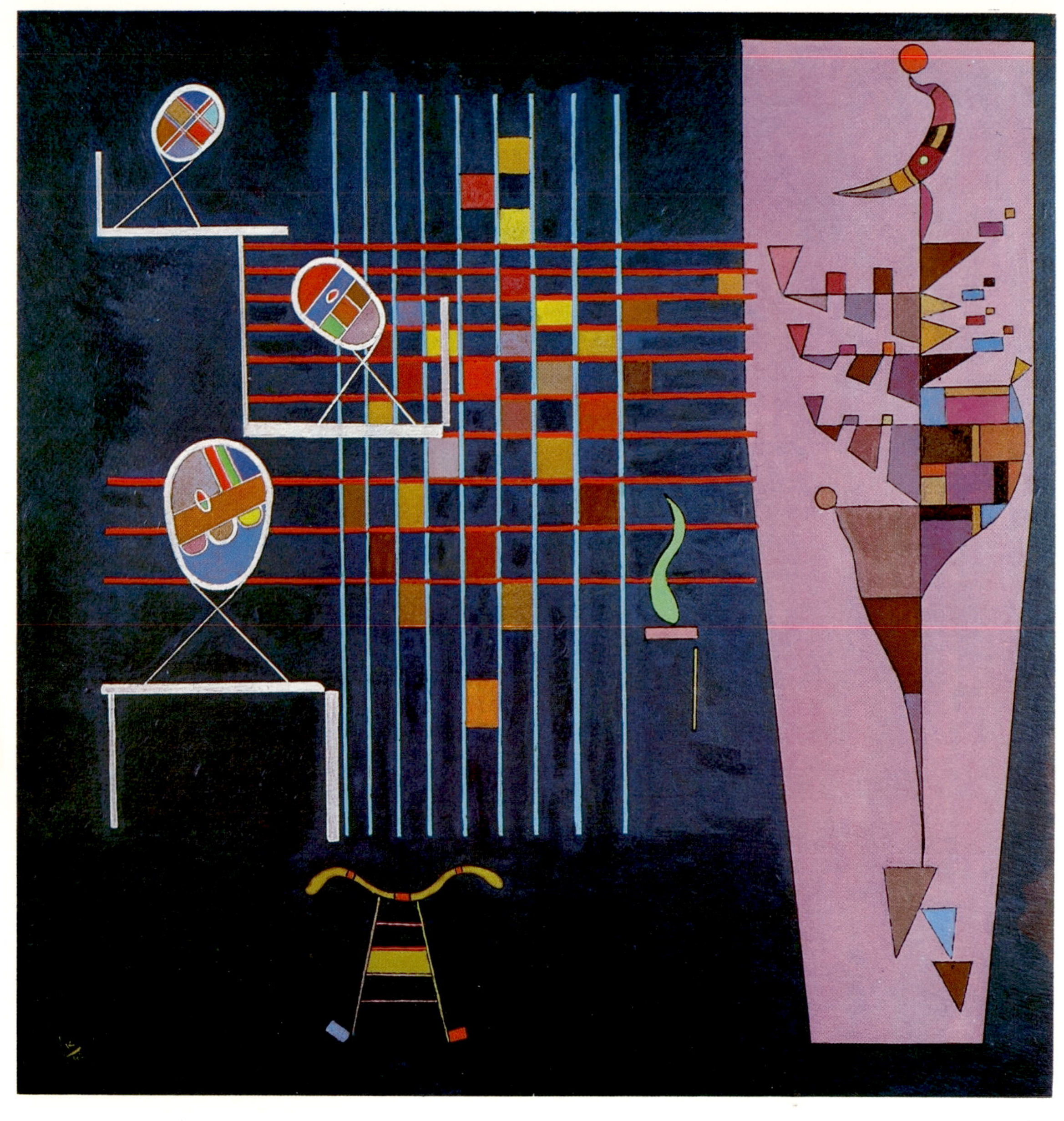

74 Kandinsky *Three Ovals* 1942 Collection Aimé Maeght Paris

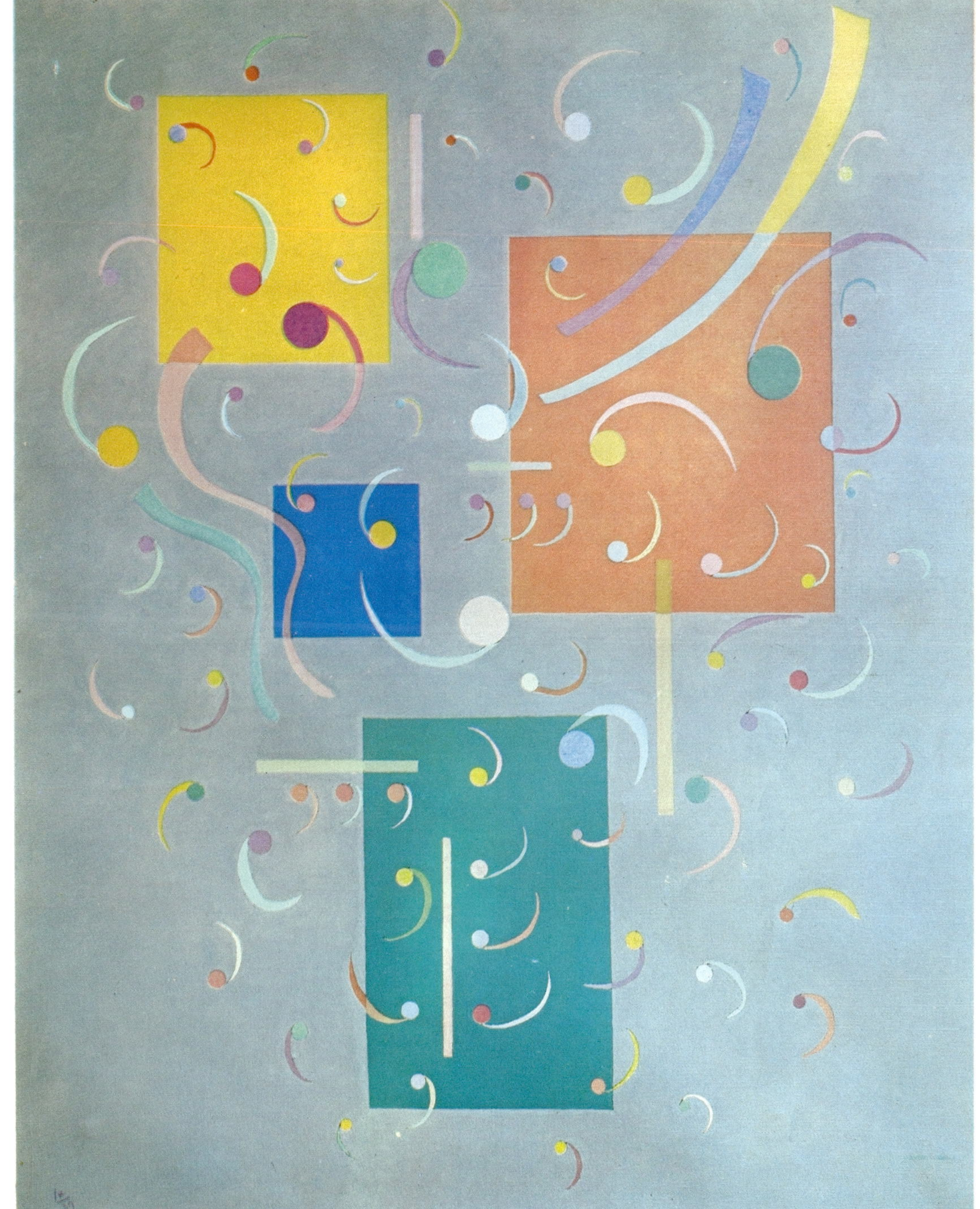

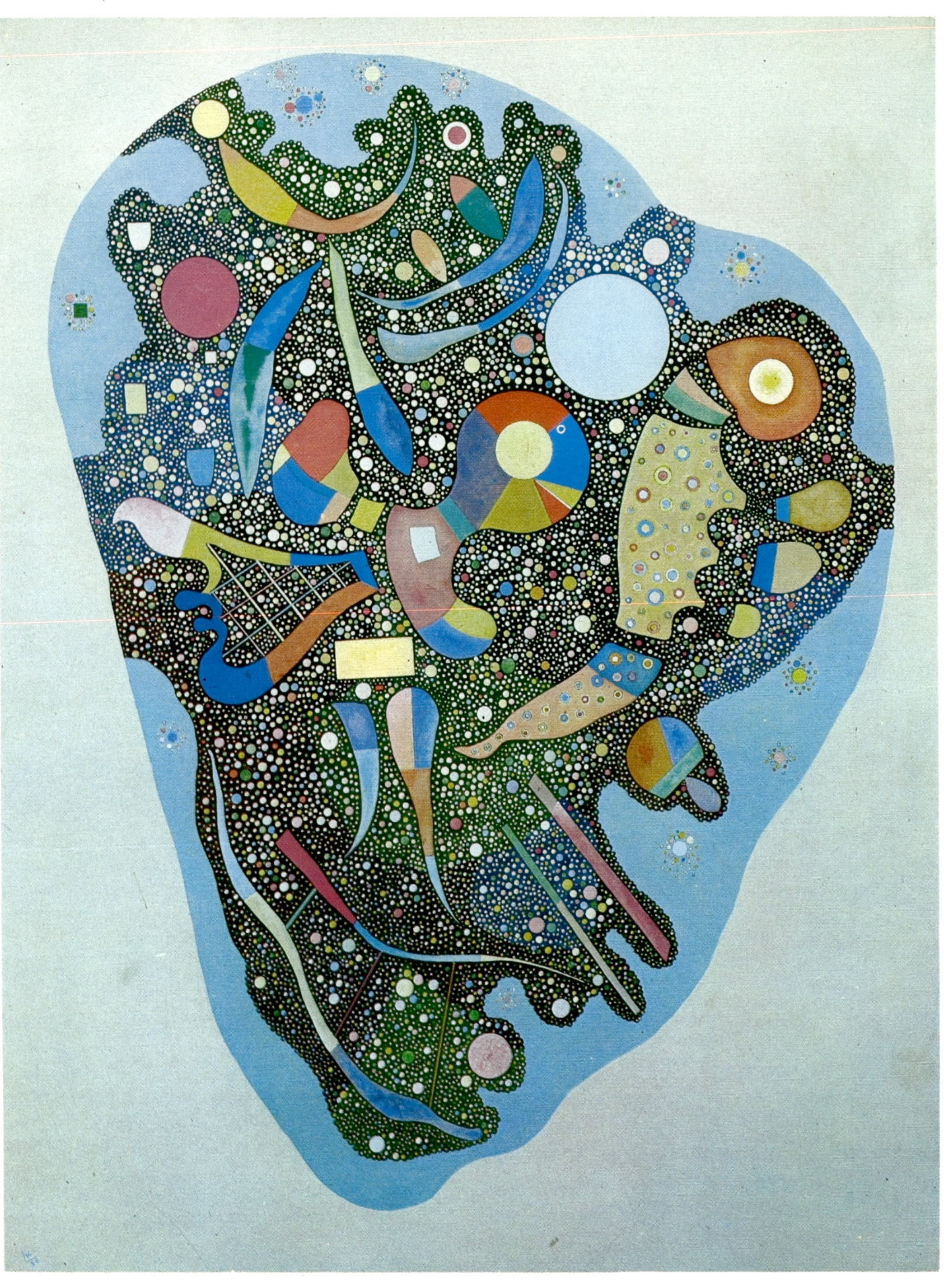

Klee/Kandinsky

Paul Klee

In 1924, Klee delivered a lecture at Jena entitled "On Modern Art" in which he presented a synopsis of his views. Of particular interest is his use of the tree as a metaphor to explain the essence of both art and artist. According to Klee, the artist possesses a singular sense of perception that imposes order on impressions and experiences. This corresponds to the roots of a tree. The roots (perception) absorb various elements (impression and experiences) from the earth and transmit them to the artist, the trunk of the tree. From the trunk grows the crown of the tree (the work of art), spreading in all directions. There is no reason to assume that the crown and roots should take the same form, for the sap, as it is drawn from the roots and passes through the trunk, undergoes many important transformations, and the crown of the tree thus seems to exist autonomously.

The tree analogy expresses many of Klee's convictions about his own art. He believed the artist to be neither servant nor master, but "simply a mediator . . . who assembles that which has risen from the depths and leads it still higher." As they pass through the artist, all things, both visible and invisible, become essential structural elements in a single painting. He viewed art metaphorically as a creative process in a world where creation and formation are constantly taking place.

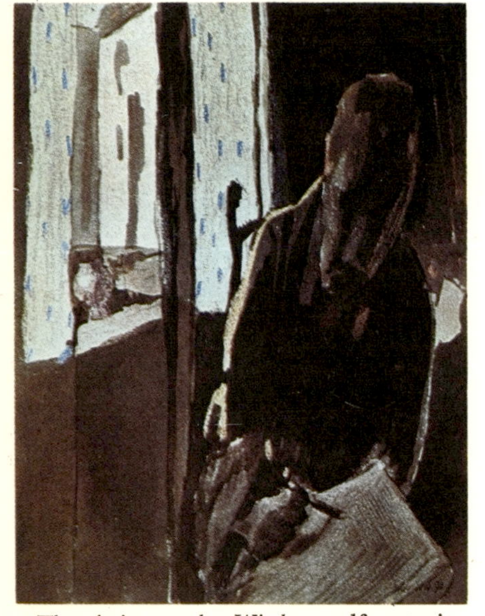

The Artist at the Window, self-portrait (1909). Klee viewed a Van Gogh exhibition in 1908 and a Cézanne in 1909. This work suggests Cézanne influence.

Klee developed these concepts gradually and with effort, but from a very early age he seemed to intuit their fundamental principles. A sensitive child, he was struck by what he perceived as natural law transcending appearance. At the age of nine, he became absorbed in tracing with a pencil a grotesque human face he saw in the mazelike pattern of a marble-topped table in his uncle's restaurant. This episode is noteworthy in that he was later to draw many grotesque faces. He said, "Even then my attraction toward the strange and mysterious had already clearly appeared." A paragraph on "Portraits," written in his diary some fifteen years later, when he had already begun a painting career, further clarifies this early experience.

> There are probably many people who think my mirror is distorted and reflects nothing but lies. However, I do not paint pictures in an attempt to reflect only the surface. . . . I want to penetrate deep within and draw near to truth. I am attempting to shed light on the very depths of the heart in my mirror. When I draw a face, I place ideas in its head and carve words on its mouth. The faces which I draw are closer to truth than reality itself.

The following quotation, written in the same year, vividly reflects the anguish Klee experienced as this "reality" of his, "closer to truth than reality itself," streamed through him like sap through the trunk of a tree. It indicates that visual perceptions did not exist as artistic subjects for him, but as nebulous, confused stirrings at the roots of his being: "My head feels incandescent, as though it were about to fly off. I am trying to give birth to a hidden, unknown world; but until that time comes I must continue to suffer."

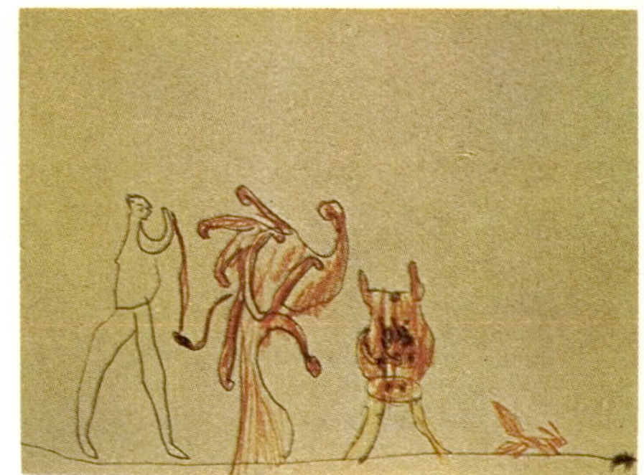

Childhood Drawing: Picture with Hare (1884), drawn when Klee was five.

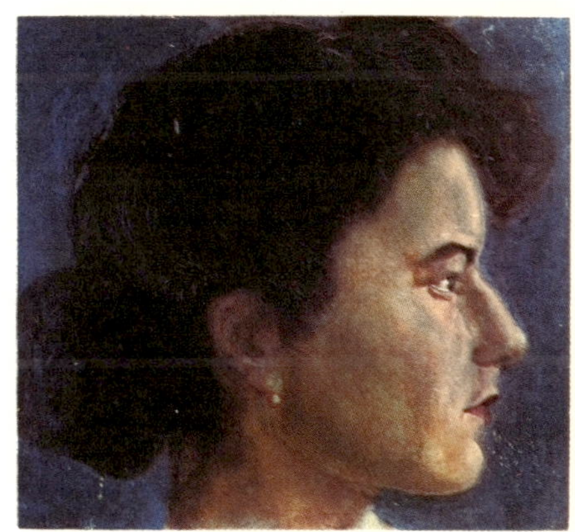

The Artist's Sister (1903). The model was Klee's sister, Matilde, three years his senior. He most likely learned detailed facial expressions, characteristic of the German art tradition, at the Munich Art Academy.

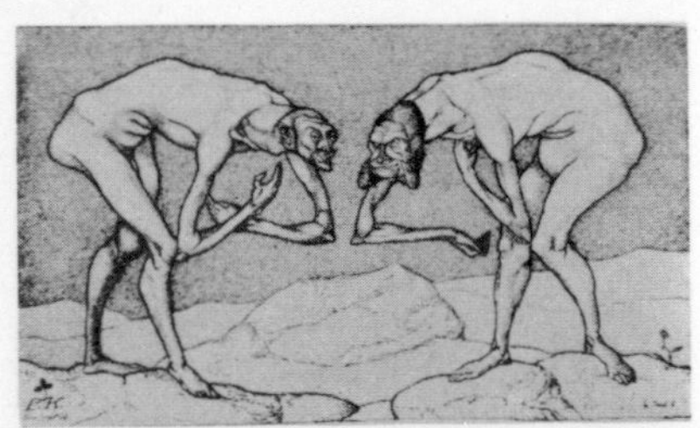

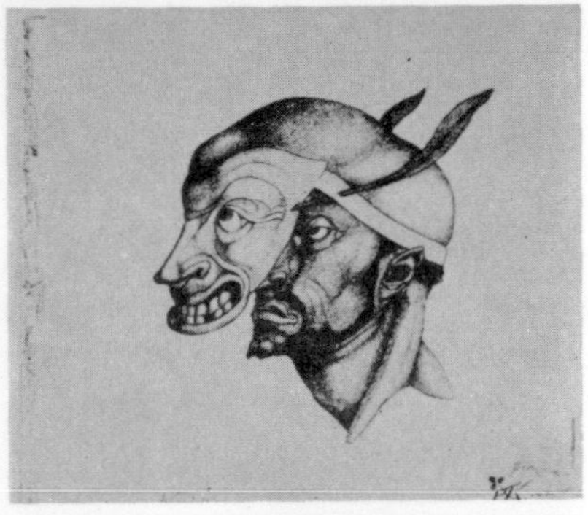

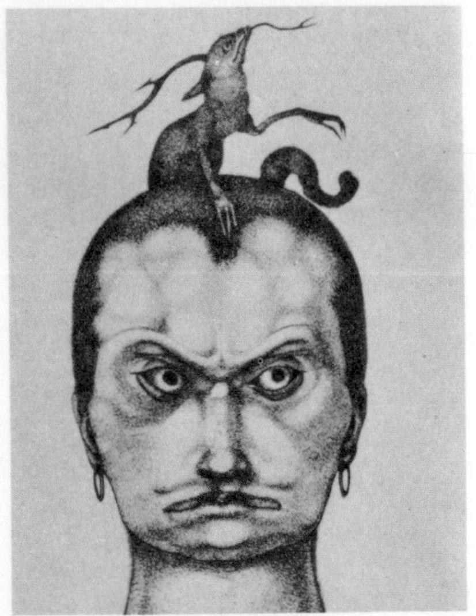

Copperplate etchings by Klee: (top) *Two Men* (1903) (center) *Comedian I* (1904) (bottom) *Menacing Head* (1905)

Such closeness to his art undoubtedly made Klee's path a difficult one.

He was born on December 18, 1879, in the Swiss town of Münchenbuchsee, near Bern. His early growth was influenced by impressionism, a movement that was begun by Parisian painters in the 1860s and was now in its fullest flower of critical and public recognition. But the dominant theme of his later, mature work went beyond mere "impressions" in an attempt to become the medium for the creation of an entire new world.

In a sense, Klee might have been expected to find a more suitable form of self-expression in music, an extremely direct but transcendental art form. Both his parents were musicians and Klee himself was an outstanding violinist. The deep attraction to music never faded. His description of the works of Beethoven is applicable to Klee's own work: "Without moving the interior from the outside, he gives shape to a song which is housed within the interior itself." That music was not a mere pastime for Klee was due, no doubt, to the influence of his parents' musical temperaments.

Then why did he abandon music, his "bewitching lover," and choose painting? On that point Klee has left us nothing but the vague words: "I felt somehow drawn to it." Possibly he realized intuitively that through music, an art form whose elements must possess a certain basic order, he could not give adequate expression to the nebulous, mysterious and contradictory stirrings within him. Klee wanted to portray concepts and the mutual interference of concepts and material objects. His works convey a certain discord between transcendence and sensual directness, as well as a partiality for distortion. Music probably seemed too abstract—or perhaps too self-sufficient—to give life to his ideas. Klee attempted to express himself in copper etchings but, as in music, he experienced a basic conflict of concepts and a cynicism that at times hindered his freedom of expression. So he turned to painting.

That Klee's temperament should lead him first to the linear arts of copper etching and water color on glass was natural. His line is not like that of the naturalist school of painting, a line that he described as "estranging the realms of color and color tone from one another." Rather, it has an independent existence and contains a unique life and dynamism. Sources of Klee's line can be seen in Redon's *Linear Fugue*, and in German art, particularly the works of Dürer, which he admired. The Gothic line influenced his copper etchings, and he showed a definite preference for early Christian mosaics over Italian Renaissance works.

For Klee, as artistic "mediator," a step-by-step progession in using line was necessary for linking cosmic and mundane forces. This linking of forces was a modern trend, one which Heidegger labeled the "Age of the World Image." The artist transformed the world into a creation of his own vision. The spirit of the times penetrated Klee. Nature, once the "setting which refreshes and gives color to the soul," became like a ferocious force ready to engulf him. "The dangerous period has begun. I feel that I am about to be engulfed by nature. When that happens, I am nothing." His aim was

> . . . to be active. Not like the squirming of bacteria scattered all over the face of the earth but linking myself with

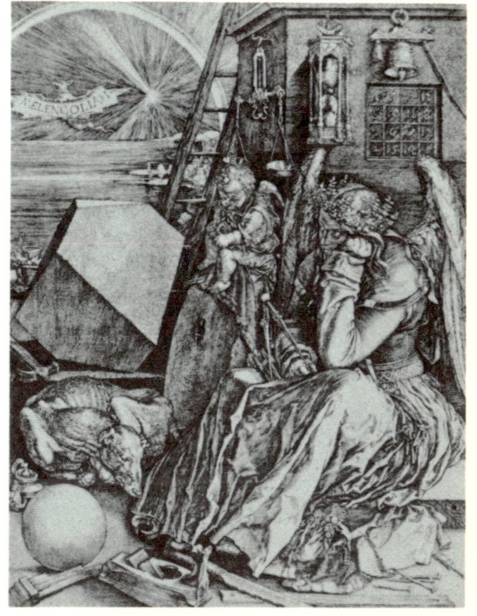

Dürer, *Melancholia* (1514)

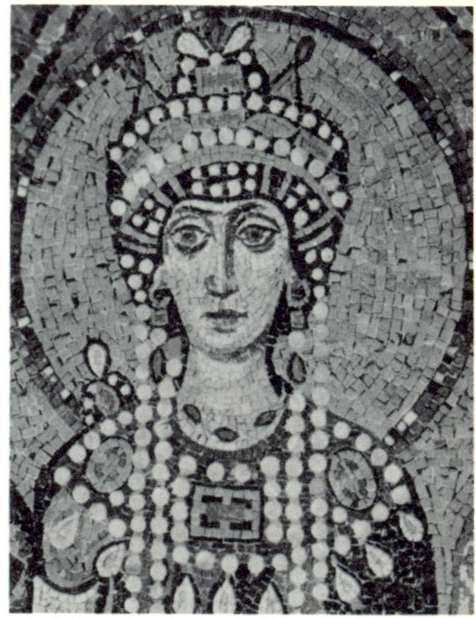

Theodora (c. 547). A famous Byzantine mosaic in the San Vitale cathedral in Italy

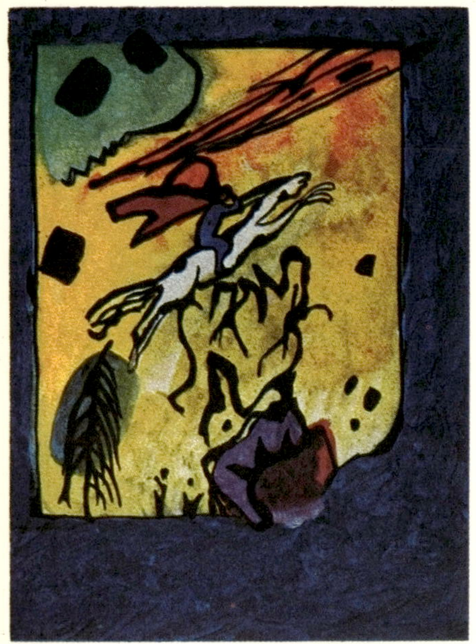

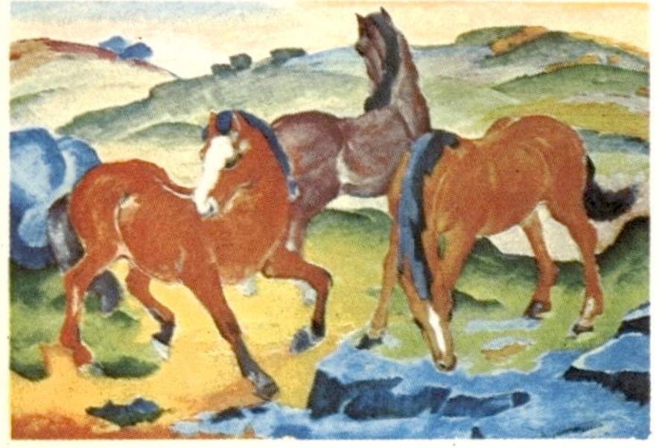

(top) Water-color cover for the annual *The Blue Rider*
(bottom) Marc, *Red Horses* (1911). Franz Marc (1880–1916), born in Munich, approached expressionism by depicting animals.

the world above me—to be active as one man on the earth. To put down an anchor in the earth, and although a stranger in this world, to be strong. This is my goal. But how am I to realize it?

He was speaking of growth and study, and the course was not a simple one. Klee said, "I cannot be understood in this world for I am as much at home with the dead as with those yet to be born. . . ." His was a long and arduous journey in the world of art.

During the course of his development, an exhibition of Van Gogh's paintings in 1908 and of Cézanne's in the following year greatly influenced him. Through the works and letters of Van Gogh he came to understand the significance of discriminatory elements in his own work. The method of "obtaining simplicity through the ability to transform," which Cézanne's works revealed, was a "master par excellence" as he developed his own techniques. His association with the Blaue Reiter (Blue Rider) group of artists, which included Kandinsky, Macke and Marc, strengthened him considerably. The works of Kandinsky impressed Klee as "strange, mysterious paintings without a subject," but Klee was doubtless familiar with the concept of "inner necessity," which Kandinsky repeatedly stressed in "On the Spiritual in Art." The bold works of Delaunay, which developed out of Seurat's neoimpressionism and sought the autonomy and "simultaneous contrast" of color, served as important stimuli, ultimately enabling Klee to make his own discovery of color.

In 1914, Klee traveled with his friends Macke and Moilliet to Kairouan and Tunis, where he had his famous revelation in color. He was overwhelmed by the power of "saturation, intoxication and clarification."

> My work has halted. All kinds of things are penetrating me. There is no longer any need to resist. I am greatly assured. I am entranced by color—I do not need to pursue it. I know that it will possess me until I die. This is the great moment—I and color are one. I am a painter.

This discovery was a personal one, not the result of critical acclaim. It was not due only to the method of color that Cézanne, Delaunay and others showed him, although of course their lessons had an important effect. It was evident that Klee's line now demanded color. A year before his trip he wrote, "I draw with lines only. I draw with lines which symbolize a pure spirit, liberated from the yoke of matter. I have cast away unnecessary analysis and turned boldly and directly toward essentials." But he also wrote, "I am trying to abstractify the world. I am not playing a game. I have an idea which goes beyond mere games. However, I cannot completely destroy my former goals. I am wandering in a state of uncertainty." By comparing these two passages it is possible to gain insight into Klee's feelings at that time. One can picture him standing at the edge of a colorless, abstract, spiritual world of line, waiting expectantly for something. That that something was to be color is revealed in the quiet joy of his statement about his discovery of it. In that passage there is not the slightest implication that an artist whose basic medium was line had suffered an unwarranted attack by color. Rather, he gained a feeling for it that enabled him to inject new life into his works. The basic structural elements of line, tone and color

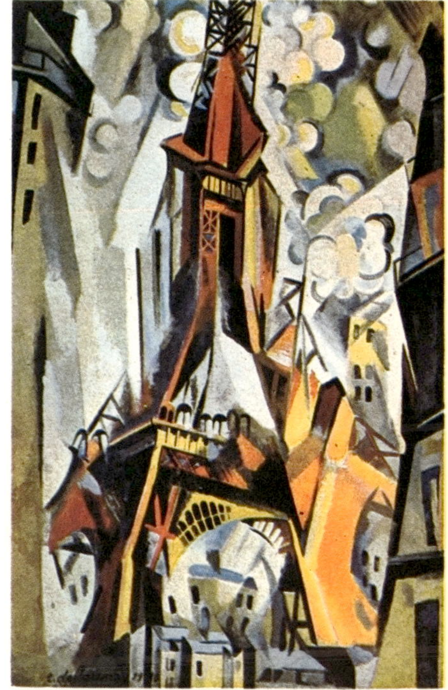

Delaunay, *The Eiffel Tower* (1910). Robert Delaunay (1885–1941), born in Paris, was initially influenced by the neoimpressionists but eventually shifted to cubism.

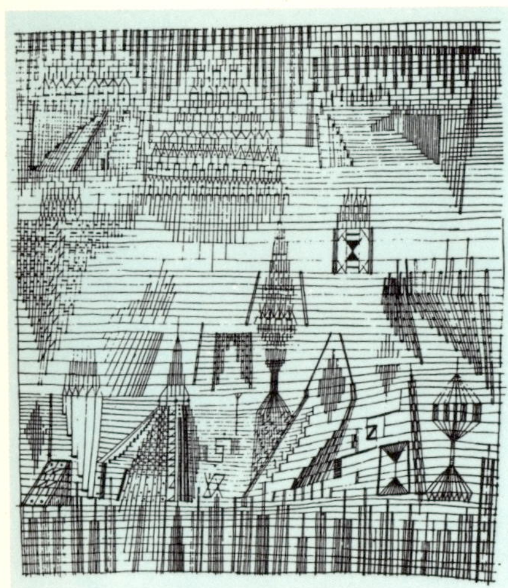

Klee, *Sketch* (1927)

each matured in his work only after a long period of growth. His later compositions possess both solidity and clarity.

In the early twenties, both he and Kandinsky joined the faculty of the Bauhaus, the school of design founded by Walter Gropius in Weimar, Germany. Teaching gave rise to Klee's re-examination of his painting techniques in general and in detail. Because he was a sensitive analyst who always built paintings one step at a time, this undertaking was no doubt extremely beneficial. His introduction of geometrical forms into his works was probably one result of this analysis. His trips to Italy in 1926 and to Egypt in 1928–29 gave rise to further simplification and the use of pointillist techniques in his compositions.

Klee's paintings gradually received the praise and admiration of many, but a dark shadow fell on his career after the Nazis seized power in 1933. His works were removed from German galleries in 1937, and seventeen of them were displayed in an exhibition of "degenerate art." Klee turned toward a simplified style noted for its use of black lines and for a dark loneliness that seems to float on the canvas. It is a style that verifies a phrase from Klee's diary written at the time of the First World War: "The more fearful this world becomes, the more abstract its art."

Klee died near Locarno, Italy, early in 1940, of heart failure.

Wassily Kandinsky

On December 4, 1866, Kandinsky was born to a wealthy merchant family in Moscow. Although his mother was a true Muscovite, his father's family appears to have descended from exiles living in eastern Siberia near the Mongolian border. Some elements in his ideas and works lend credibility to the claim that his great-grandmother was a Mongolian princess. The legend is particularly interesting in view of a similar claim that Klee had Arabian blood. Klee experienced a revelation of color on seeing the Islamic town of Kairouan, and later showed a persistent attraction to Egyptian art; Kandinsky, as if lending support to claims that he had Oriental blood, adopted a style late in life that was reminiscent of the symbolic art of China and Mongolia. His attraction to these art forms may have been atavistic.

Kandinsky's stylistic development could also be attributable to the fact that both he and Klee, the two great artists who introduced the internal and the spiritual into modern art, consistently maintained a clear distinction between cubism and abstract painting. In contrast to artists of the various schools of painting that pushed traditional European composition to an extreme, each of these two men preserved his own concept of art in the deepest roots of his being.

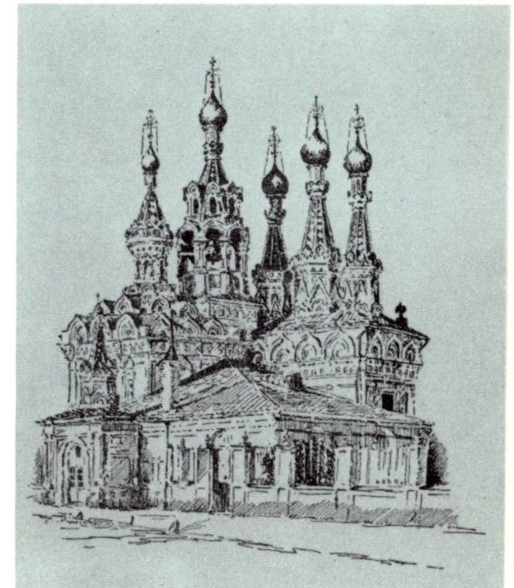

Kandinsky, *Church in Moscow* (1886). Kandinsky was born in Moscow in 1866 and lived there until he went to Munich to study art in 1896.

Kandinsky told of being deeply impressed in his childhood by the fresh, glowing red of Moscow sunsets. This early impression was like music whose echo lingered throughout his life. He said it came vividly back to him upon hearing Wagner's *Lohengrin.* Throughout his career he was able to capture the essence of color—not just use it as an isolated, abstract unit of composition. While displaying an amazing power to refine and purify color, Kandinsky never forgot its emotional origins.

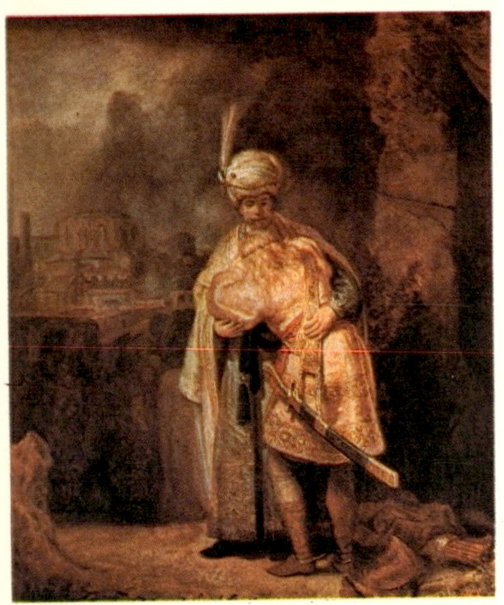

Rembrandt, *David and Jonathan's Farewell* (1642)

His theory of color was developed in his essay "On the Spiritual in Art": yellow, he said, is a "terrestrial color," blue a "celestial color"; white is a "vast silence" full of unlimited possibilities, while black is an "emptiness devoid of all possibility." His colors acquire their fresh independence through the tension between these extremes.

A similar polarity in Russian folk and religious art influenced him. The colors and shapes—chaotic combinations in which the spiritual and the sensual, the mental and the emotional are indistinguishable from one another—take on a mysterious symbolism difficult to define: an arm stretched out toward heaven is both an artistic form and a symbol of prayer. His theories on symbolism in art appear in his book *From Point and Line to Plane*, an extremely detailed and often abstract analysis of those three structural units. One can detect his preference for the delicate mixing of abstraction and essence in the description of a point as "the unity of speech and silence," or of a straight line as "containing the desire to give birth to a surface, that is, the desire to transform itself into a more stable, self-contained being."

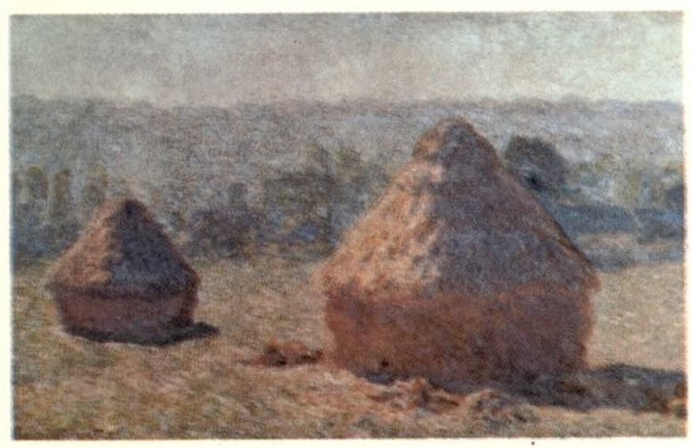

Monet, *Haystacks, End of Summer* (1891). Monet produced about thirty paintings of haystacks, each with a subtly different treatment of light.

Among the impressions he received from other paintings,

the earliest and most important were from a work of Rembrandt that he saw in childhood. He said that from the painting, which seemed to "permeate slowly through the observer," he grasped the key to using sharp contrasts in light and shadow to evoke the painter's emotion in the observer. This doubtless reinforced his impressions of the sunsets and icons of Moscow. That which was awakened in him in Russia was brought to maturity by the work of a single human being.

It is tempting to say that he intuitively sensed the "reality" of paintings at that time, and that later, in studying the paintings of Monet, he became aware of his own potential for becoming a painter. At an exhibition of French impressionists held in Moscow in 1895, he was deeply moved by Monet's *Haystacks*. He claims that from that painting he first came to understand the extent to which an artist is free to separate himself from nature and abandon the use of its subjects. His reaction does show a grasp of the unique and somewhat disturbing aspect of Monet's art in which, through his very closeness to his subject, shape disappears and the entire canvas is transformed into a dream resembling reality. Just as Baudelaire perceived the autonomous music of color in the historical paintings of Delacroix, Kandinsky intuitively sensed those elements in Monet's style that would later be necessary to him. Equally interesting is the fact that Klee, who also moved away from impressionism, praised the impressionists' approach to their subject, saying that it was "the response of the entire being."

Kandinsky's desire to become a painter gradually matured, and in 1896 he abandoned his career as a scholar in

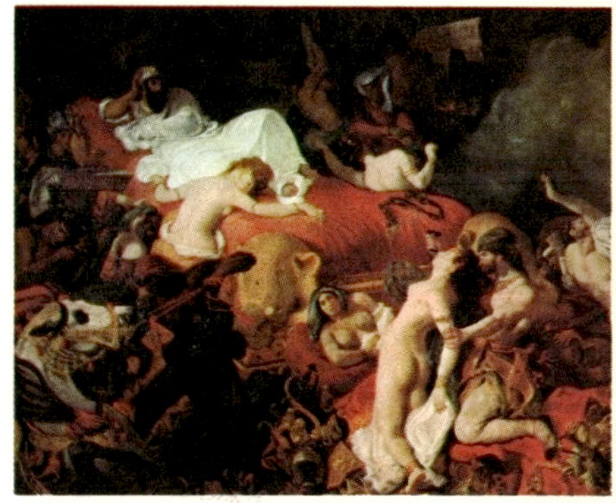

Delacroix, *Death of Balthazar* (1827). Delacroix, flag-bearer for romanticism, was well understood by Baudelaire.

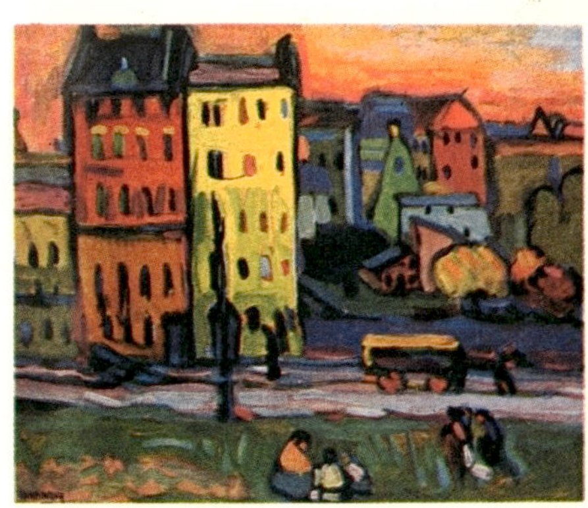

Kandinsky, *Munich Houses* (1908). After moving to Munich in 1896, Kandinsky was introduced to Fauvism; color took on a much more important role in his work.

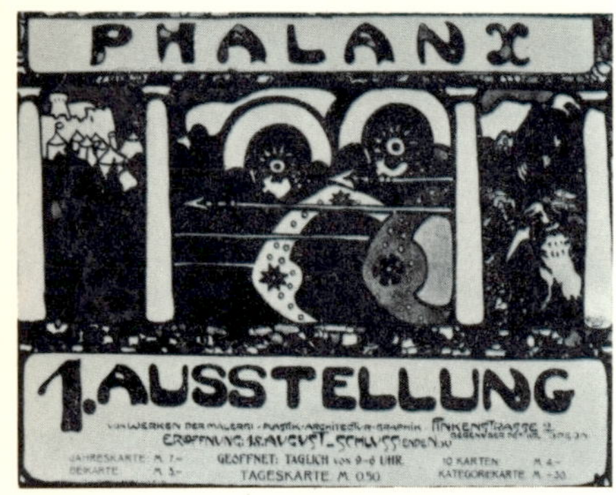

Kandinsky poster, dated 1901, prepared for the First Phalanx group exhibition.

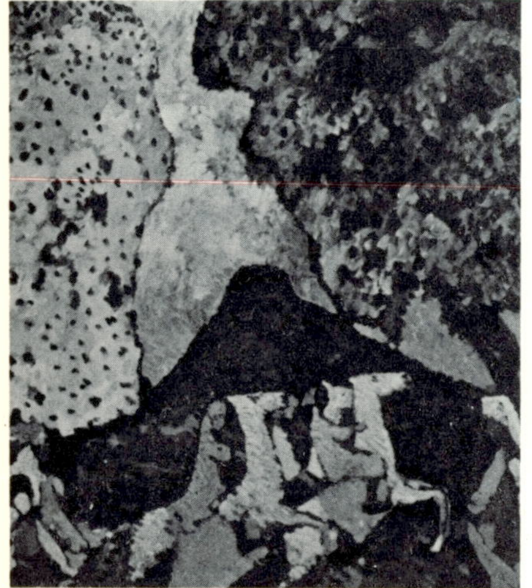

Kandinsky, *Blue Mountain* (1909)

economics and turned to painting. The field of economics itself played an important role in this decision.

> After six years spent studying economics, I now realize that as a result of exposure to both the social sciences and the absolute truths of positivism, the religious faith I had embraced has been completely dissolved. I have resolved to abandon my academic work of the past several years. I feel as though I have lost my entire past. But now, at last, I am able to understand what it is that has been building up within me and sense fully how it has come to be.

Thus for Kandinsky it was necessary that painting, which is capable of breaking down and destroying the positivist method, possess a strong independence and universality in order that it might substitute for his "dissolved" faith. Positivism came to act as a negative force that gave purity to his works. A true artist, Kandinsky was able to make this potential obstacle a structural element for his own work.

Kandinsky headed for Munich, the center of *Jugendstil* (art nouveau), where he studied under Anton Ashe and Franz von Stuck. Although the sumptuous style of *Jugendstil* was no doubt well suited to Kandinsky's own inclinations toward symbolism, it was his contact with impressionism and Fauvism, as well as his travels to Tunisia, Italy and Holland, that most deeply influenced him.

The landscapes of Murnau, which he painted from 1908 to 1909, are extremely interesting as the intermediate stages between his early style and the abstract works of 1910. Overwhelmingly dislocated, concrete shapes sway and move and fissure. Mountains seem to rise up and crumble in the midst of mysterious blues and fresh, vivid, Moscow-sunset reds, while through the gaps men on white horses can be seen riding by. In 1910, after more than a decade of painstaking effort, Kandinsky's individuality as a painter blossomed. *First Abstract Water Color* was completed.

From this point on, Kandinsky's works may be divided into three categories: Impressions, Improvisations, Compositions. Impressions were based on direct, external sense perceptions; Improvisations were motivated by sudden, spontaneous inner motions; Compositions were built from many preliminary studies. The nebulous feeling aroused by the sunsets and icons developed in three directions. Impressions were the indispensable means by which he was made continually aware of fundamental motion. Improvisations, aroused within him by this awareness, gave motion form. In Compositions, by consciously uniting an impression and an improvisation, he constructed a canvas free of any resemblance to nature. This process was a highly personal response to the impressions he gained from the sunsets and icons, and later from the works of Monet, Rembrandt and others. The strength of his individuality is indeed impressive.

In founding the *Blaue Reiter* (Blue Rider) movement with Marc, Kubin, Munter and others, and in writing his epoch-making essay "On the Spiritual in Art," Kandinsky developed his artistic theories and methods with steadiness and precision. Picasso, Braque, Delaunay, Klee, Macke and Kokoschka participated in the Blue Rider group, and musicians such as Schoenberg, Webern and Alban Berg contributed to their magazine. Kandinsky took the role of leader. According to Klee's description of Kandinsky, he

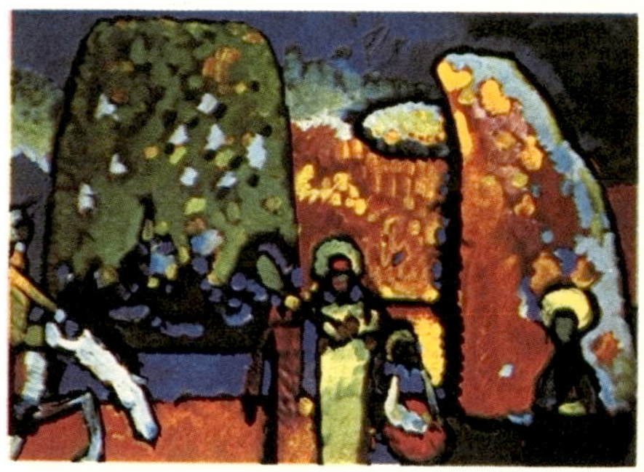

Kandinsky, *Study for Improvisation 2* (1909). Subtitled *April Funeral*, this painting shows Fauvist influences in color and realism.

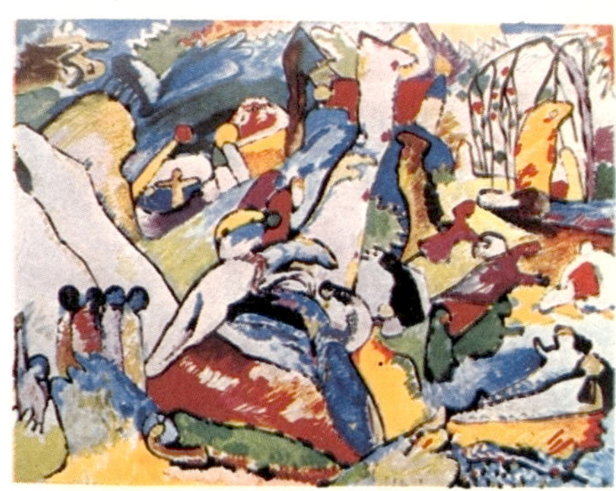

Kandinsky, *Study for Composition 2* (1910). Kandinsky produced his Composition series between 1910 and 1914. Seven works are extant.

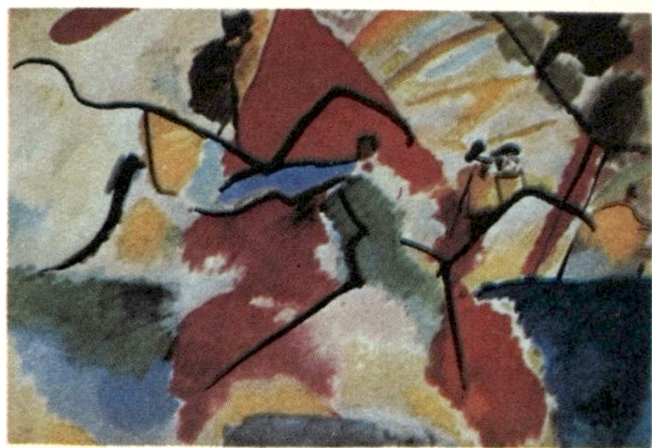

Kandinsky, *Impression 5* (1911). Kandinsky completed all six works in his Impression series in 1911. This painting is subtitled *Park*.

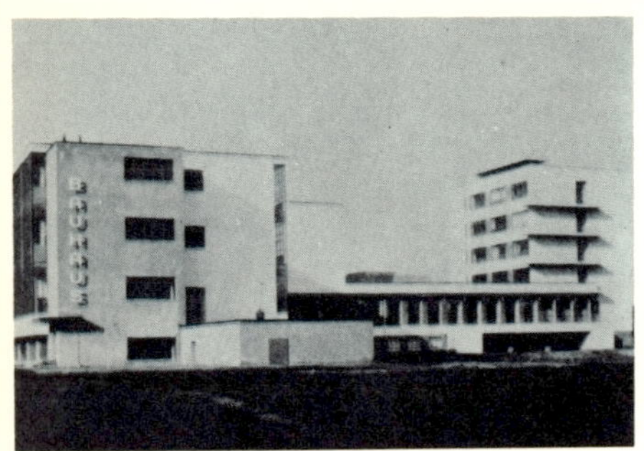

Bauhaus in Dessau. Founded in Weimar in 1919 by the architect Walter Gropius, the Bauhaus was moved to Dessau in 1925 and continued there as a comprehensive school of the formative arts.

was "an extremely charming person . . . possessing an extraordinarily clear mind" for whom a position of leadership was no doubt a necessity.

Although Kandinsky displayed a rich individuality and did not succumb to either cubist or expressionist traditions, he showed remarkable sensitivity to the individuality of others. He described Matisse as "attempting to express the nature of the divine in painting. To achieve that goal he makes use of nothing but the traditional subjects, colors and shapes of painting." Of Picasso he said, "Picasso arrived at the negation of concrete representation by a logical route. However, this negation is not the disintegration of concreteness; it is based on the structural diffusion of specific sections of the canvas." Statements such as these are indicative of his critical insight. His analytical abilities are also pointed up in the close, detailed, methodical *From Point and Line to Plane*, a work in which he does not pose an interference to freedom of movement on the canvas, but, rather, gives one the feeling that transparent tension is stabilized on it. The Compositions consume the Improvisations and Impressions and expand, while the latter discover new freedom within the Compositions.

During the First World War Kandinsky returned to Moscow and was a member of the Fine Arts division of the post-revolutionary Soviet administration. His criticism of nineteenth-century materialism in "On the Spiritual in Art" reflects his view of the revolution as the regeneration of the Russian people. But soon a period of cultural repression caused him to leave his country. He turned to the Bauhaus, where he worked and taught alongside Klee.

Kandinsky continued his activities until the Bauhaus was

finally closed by the Nazis in 1932. He pursued geometrical forms and architectural effects in his work from that time on. Interestingly enough, those traits are also evident in Klee's work of the same period. Kandinsky introduced these forms during experiments with cubism. Either the forms themselves became an "inner necessity" or they emerged out of the influence of the synthetic, collective artistic movement of the Bauhaus. Also, his deep disappointment in Soviet Russia may have caused him to choose more stable, secure shapes. He describes the circle as "uniting

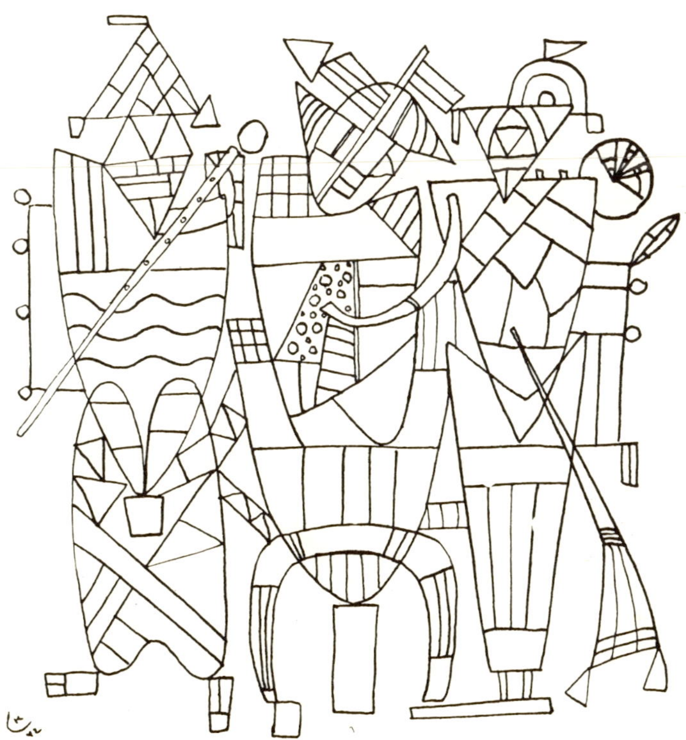

Kandinsky, *Three Piebald Characters* (1942)

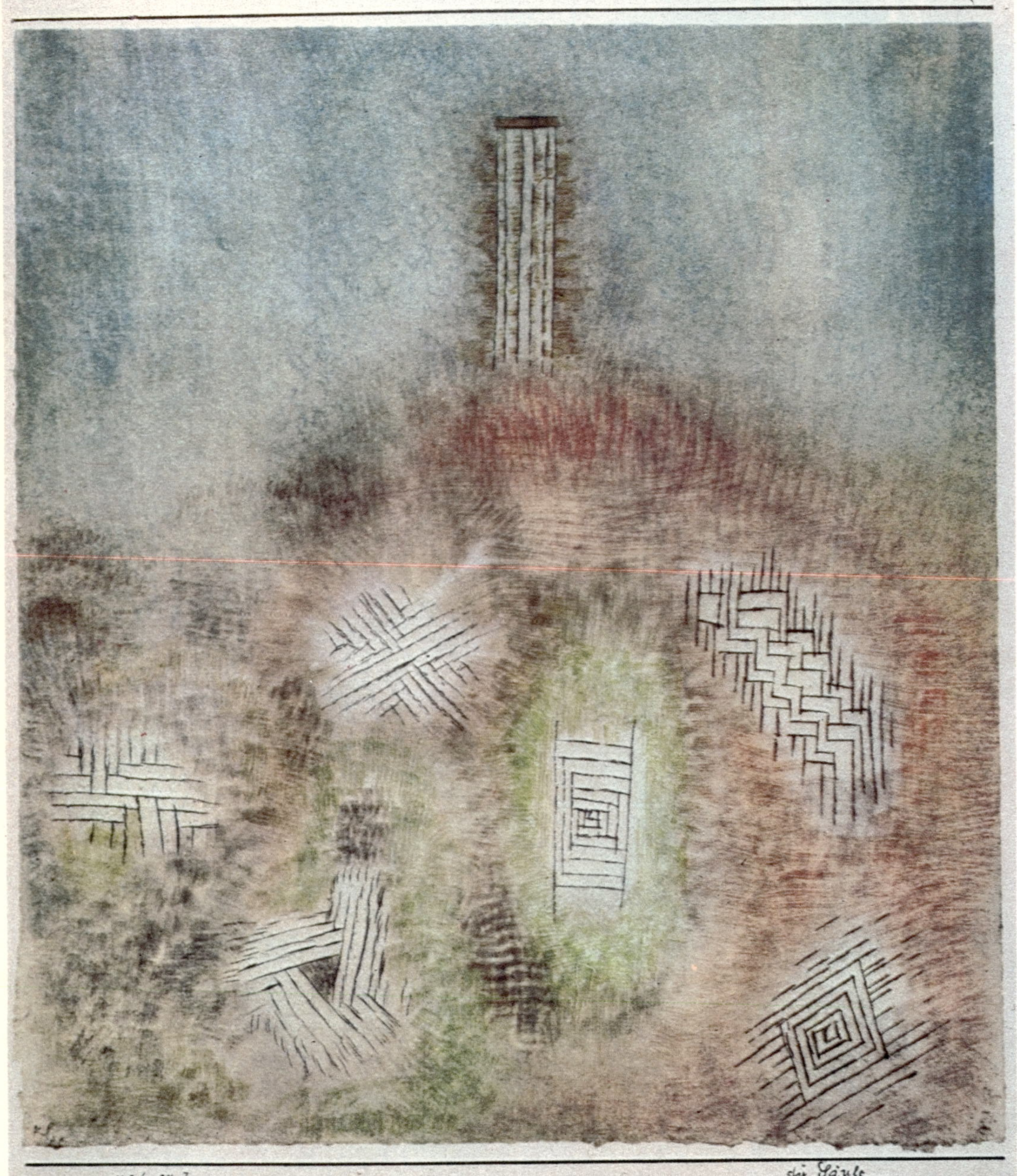

Klee,
A Garden for Orpheus
(1926)

that which is in a state of maximum opposition" and as a form simultaneously stable and unstable, "which maintains a tension between but unites symmetry and asymmetry." Statements such as these tell a great deal about his feelings at that time.

This concept of "unity" was to change. Unity existed not within a circle alone, but upon an entire canvas, and it had to be expressed in a more universal and asymmetrical form. The latter part of Kandinsky's stay at the Bauhaus has been called his "romantic period" by some critics. His next and final period is called the "period of synthesis," during which a strange sensuality in abstract forms and curious shapes resembling microscopic life appeared in his work. In a single painting, the cosmic and the mundane, the macroscopic and the microscopic mutually interact, providing an exquisite balance. These subtle, fresh works, based on ancient styles, seem to convey to the eyes and heart of the observer an explosion of massive proportions.

Kandinsky died in Switzerland in 1944. His paintings, teeming with riddles, will continue to grow ever more important in the history of modern art.

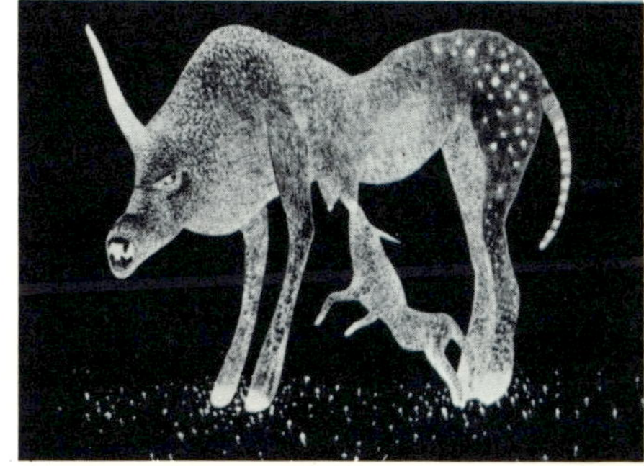

Klee, *Beast Suckling Its Young* (1906). Klee began painting on glass in 1905. One month after marrying in Bern in September 1906, he moved to Munich.

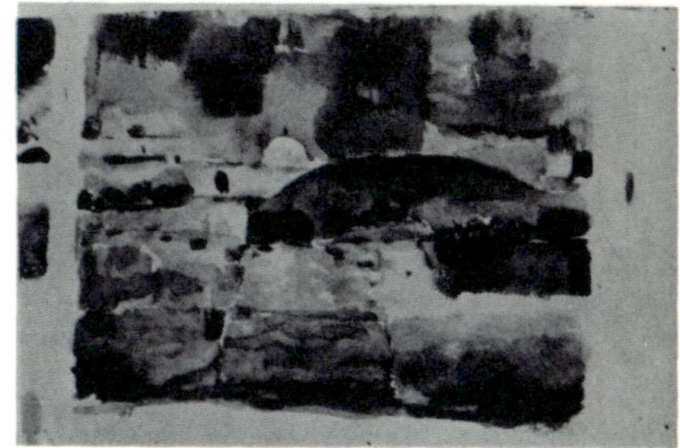

Klee, *Before the Gates of Kairouan* (1914). Klee's trip to Tunisia lasted only twelve days but marked the true beginning of his life as a painter.

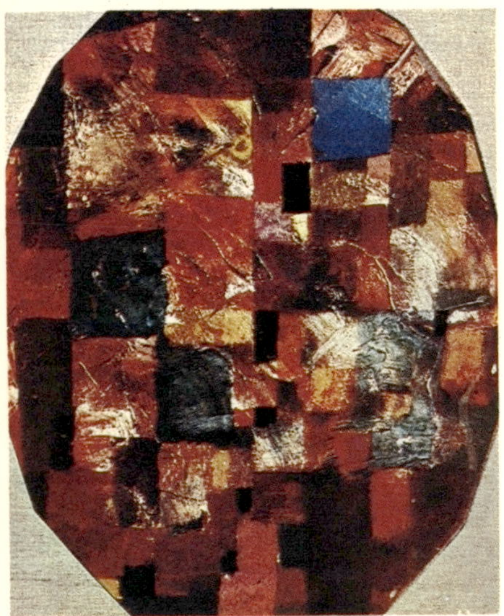

Klee, *Hommage à Picasso* (1914)

NOTES ON COLOR PLATES

Paul Klee (*1879-1940*)

1. *Garden Scene with a Watering Can* 1905

Glass, water color 13 × 18 cm Felix Klee, Bern

1905 marked a turning point for Klee. He was freed from the spell of a type of idealism exemplified in his copperplates, and awoke to a dynamic nature overflowing with vitality and color. Transparent splashes of red and green, suggestive of Matisse, tell of Klee's joy at "separating from a long, hard past."

2. *In the Quarry* 1913

Colored sheet, water color 22.5 × 25 cm Klee Foundation, Bern

Acquaintances of the Klee family owned a stone quarry at Ostermundigen, near Bern. Klee liked the setting and depicted it in glass paintings and water colors. The delicate contrast of grass and trees against the harsh, exposed mountainside was probably particularly attractive to him. The simple forms and bright transparent color tones seem to be waiting for Klee's color revelation the following year.

3. *The Quarry at Ostermundigen* 1915

Colored sheet, water color 20 × 24.5 cm Klee Foundation, Bern

This was painted only two years after *In the Quarry*. Note the surprising stylistic differences, surely indicative of the strong influence of the visit to Kairouan and the color revelation he experienced there. Klee's travels also brought about a synthesis of color and cubistic construction. It might be said that Klee confirmed that synthesis in works depicting this quarry, one of his favorite motifs.

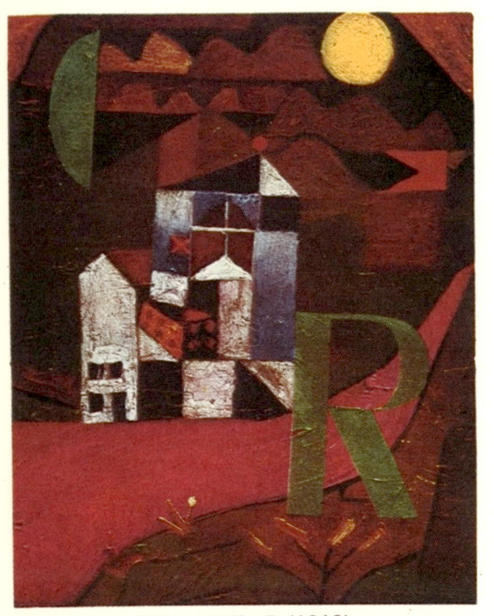

Klee, *Villa R* (1919)

4. *Ab Ovo* 1917

Colored sheet, water color 14.5 × 26 cm Klee Foundation, Bern

Klee translated Robert Delaunay's essay "Uber das Licht" in January 1913; in 1914 he completed the painting *Hommage à Picasso*. That activity reflects the period in his life when he was most strongly influenced by cubism. This painting clearly marks Klee's escape from the cubist influence. The fluidity of form heralds Klee's next period.

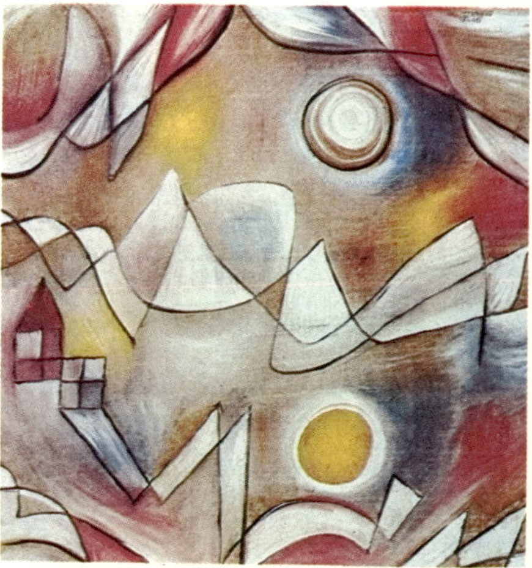

Klee, *Arctic Thaw* (1920). Icebergs and moons in the land of the aurora are done in colors that have mystical powers to excite the viewer's imagination.

5. *Once Emerged from the Gray of Night* 1918

Colored sheet, water color 25 × 15.5 cm Klee Foundation, Bern

Braque and others developed the technique of pasting pieces of newspaper and other material to a canvas. Klee's own feeling about the letters of the alphabet was more subtle; he loved poetry and might have thought of letters as "the soul of language," a metaphor used by the Japanese ancients. Letters rise up from the dark of night like rows of human faces.

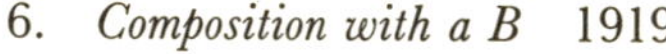

6. *Composition with a B* 1919

Cardboard, oil 51 × 39 cm Klee Foundation, Bern

As in *Villa R* and other works, Klee often placed letters or short phrases at the center of a painting. He might have hoped to restore life and an inner quality to nature by utilizing the evocative powers of these most human of symbols. The letter *B* was possibly meant to suggest an inner music, perhaps in the key of B-flat.

7. *The Bavarian Don Giovanni* 1919

Paper, water color and ink 22.5 × 21 cm Solomon R. Guggenheim Museum, New York

Bright colors and forms Klee might have seen on his Kairouan trip seem to seep through an alien darkness in a work of delicate fusion of Germanic and southern themes. Klee's love of Mozart's music is depicted in this strong impression of *Don Giovanni*. Memories of that opera's mixed musical themes of merriment and gloom perhaps moved Klee to paint his own stage setting.

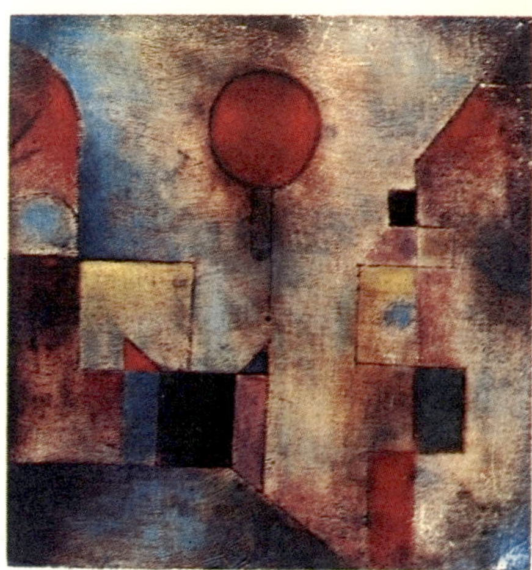

Klee, *Red Balloon* (1922)

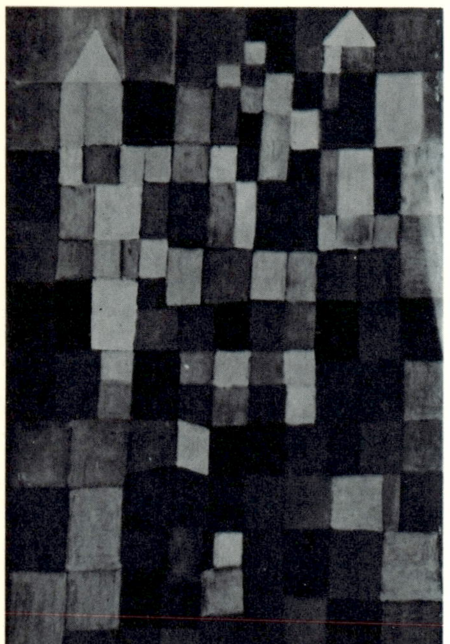

Klee, *Architecture* (1923)

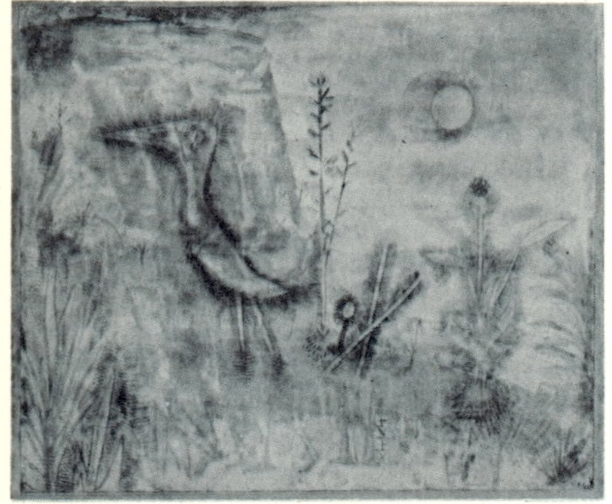

Klee, *The Bird Pep* (1925). Klee loved animals. He mentioned birds in a letter from Dessau to his wife.

8. *Ground Plan for Garden Architecture* 1920

Canvas, oil 43×35 cm Klee Foundation, Bern

Strangely flowing lines move through spaces of pink, yellow and pale green. Objects resembling stone walls and chimneys appear throughout, seeming to recede into the over-all movement. The flow from left to right seems to suggest the march of time.

9. *Perspective of a Room with Occupants* 1921

Colored sheet, water color and oil 48.5×31.5 cm Klee Foundation, Bern

To Klee, who stated that he tried to depict not nature but rather the laws of nature, the lines of perspective were neither cold nor mechanical. In Klee's use of perspective the observer can sense the artist's special attitude toward dimensional lines. Perspective is not simply a way of viewing something, it is also the expression of the act of creating something. The figures at the bottom right of the canvas seem to bear this out.

10. *Stricken Place* 1922

Colored sheet, water color and pen, 33×23 cm Klee Foundation, Bern

Besides letters Klee also liked to use the arrow as a symbol. In contrast to letters, the arrow symbolizes various powers beyond man's limitations: toppling suns, fate or—as in this work—the power of outside darkness. A town, drawn with straight lines to represent human order, is destroyed by the intervention of such powers. Klee uses to advantage the arrow's inhuman effect.

11. *Little Fir Tree* 1922

Cloth, oil 31.5×20 cm Kunstmuseum, Basel

In 1922, Klee was interested in graduated color effects, as this painting shows. One should concentrate first on the delicate nuance between the fragile, transient balloon and fir-tree motifs and the rough architectural compositions with their frugality of line, and next note the elaborate over-all support afforded by the graduated color effects.

12. *God of the Northern Forests* 1922

Canvas, oil 50.5 × 39 cm Klee Foundation, Bern

Klee, who was later to acquire a keen interest in countries to the south, inherited a strong vision of northern Europe. The dominating quality of this work is the dark richness of color reminiscent of northern European forests. One can almost hear flutes sounding faintly through the woods, with the entire forest softly echoing. The square forms blend delicately with the musical effect.

13. *Intensification of Color from the Static to the Dynamic* 1923

Canvas, oil 42 × 28 cm Private collection, Berlin

The seeds of this checkerboard form were planted early in Klee's career. By 1923 the artist was concentrating on such patterns, and he continued working with them until his death in 1940. Klee and Kandinsky were colleagues at the Bauhaus and mutually influenced each other. Although this work shows traces of Kandinsky's abstractions, it is more important as an extreme example of the fusion of musical and architectural elements.

14. *Child in Landscape* 1923

Canvas, oil Museum of Art, Grenoble

A hillside is covered with reddish shrubbery interspersed with blue cryptomeria and other, blossoming trees. A building the same color as trees in the center of the canvas has a window open, like a mouth in the midst of saying something. This is indeed a child's landscape seen through the eyes and heart of an artist who always retained a great affection for children.

15. *Puppet Show* 1923

Colored sheet, water color 51.5 × 37 cm Klee Foundation, Bern

A dog walks where flowers and mushrooms grow. Steps lead to a mysterious tower and buildings. The sun is shining. Is the girl in the center a memory from childhood? At the age of three or four, Klee cried when he thought a monster he drew had moved; he never overcame his fearful fascination. The show's cast of characters is assembled before Klee, the director.

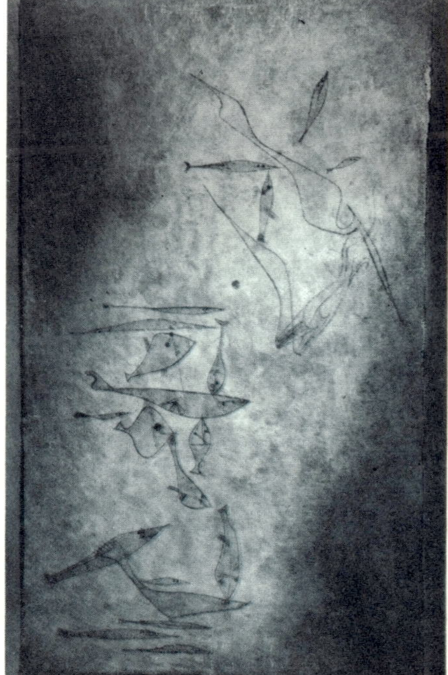

Klee, *Picture of a Fish* (1925). Klee was intrigued by the fluid movements of fish. This painting resembles a mobile.

16. *Villas and Huts* 1923

Canvas, oil 48×55 cm Private collection

This composition features an intricate queue of various buildings arranged in a style favored by cubists. Klee's idea, however, has nothing to do with a formative analysis of cubism. The painting suggests a dreamlike forest landscape with the buildings representing creatures who stretch and jostle each other in the midst of some fantastic drama.

17. *Tears of Blood* 1923

Canvas, oil 17.5×32 cm Klee Foundation, Bern

An organism grows and in the process a face is formed. The organism suffers so much that it weeps tears of blood. In the upper right corner of this painting an eye is in the process of being formed, also with a tear of blood, and at the left, another face. To Klee, nature always existed in such shapes and colors.

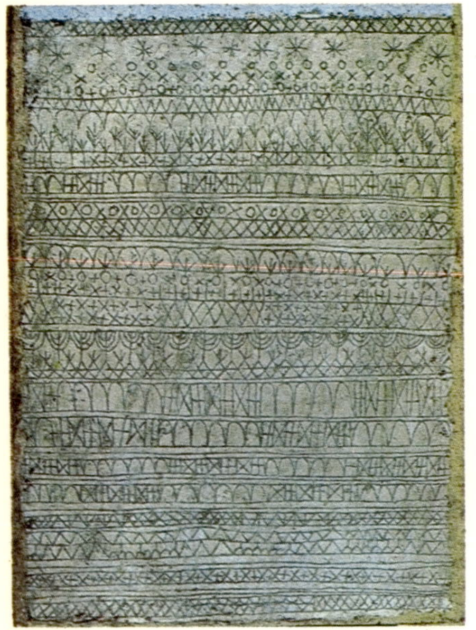

Klee, *Pastoral* (1927)

18. *Ancient Sound* 1925

Cardboard, oil 38×38 cm Kunstmuseum, Basel

This is perhaps the finest of Klee's checkerboard works. Coloring is extremely delicate, and a languorous, clear sound seems to ring through an exquisite color spectrum of dark ambient tones to the bright center, and then to sink back into the darkness.

19. *Fish Magic* 1925

Graphic, oil and water color 77×98 cm Philadelphia Museum of Art

The fish, one of Klee's favorite subjects, live in a dense, fluid world. Perhaps owing to their strangely human expression and their variegated, symbolic shapes, fish first swam in Klee's imagination while he was still young. The observer's world can—indeed as if by magic—easily become that of the fish; suddenly the air about him is permeated with water and he is at the bottom of the sea.

20. *The Ships Depart* 1927

Canvas, oil 50×60 cm Private collection, New York

Embarkation under a blue moon. The land's hue makes it seem like the bottom of the sea, and the contrast with the bright colors of the boats gives this work a fairy-tale quality that joins joy and sorrow. The purple shapes at the bottom right suggest restlessness, a mood that is reinforced by the vivid red arrow running counter to the ships and adding a strange, inauspicious movement.

21. *Mural* 1924

Canvas, tempera 25×54 cm Klee Foundation, Bern

Klee painted a series using this type of lace pattern. It seems clear that he intended to suggest a type of formative music, much as in his fugue technique and his checkerboard compositions. As Grohmann remarked, this form was like a musical score to Klee, with the lace pattern woven by music.

22. *Highways and Byways* 1929

Graphic, oil 83×67 cm Private collection, Munich

Klee visited Egypt from December 17, 1928, to January 17, 1929. The trip had as strong an influence on him as his visit to Tunisia in 1914, and this painting is one of the finest he produced as a result. In the vivid colors that permeate vast space and light, eternal history and time resound like music.

23. *Female Dwarf* 1929

Gouache, water color 31×27 cm Galerie Beyeler, Basel

The image of a female dwarf lost in thought probably was close to Klee from childhood on. The mood is characterized more by enigma than fantasy—an impression is made stronger by the form, which suggests a mushroom rising from the earth, and by the dark red and blue color tones.

24. *Hovering, before the Ascent* 1930

Graphic, oil 84×84 cm Klee Foundation, Bern

In the latter part of the Bauhaus period Klee dabbled in pointillist techniques. This work corresponds to the interval between his pointillism experiments and his earlier checker-

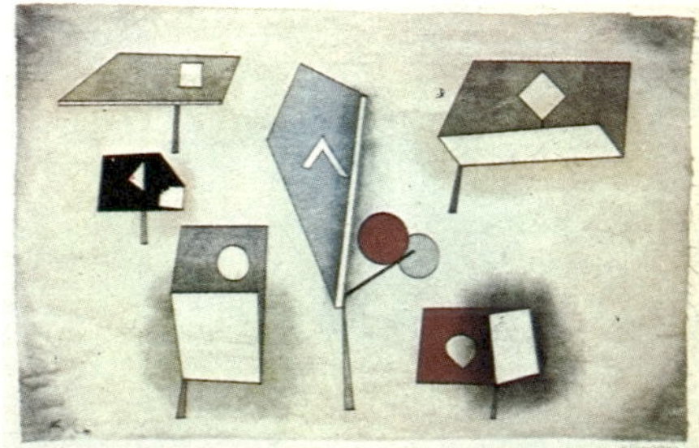

Klee's *Six Systems* (1930) shows geometric forms at play.

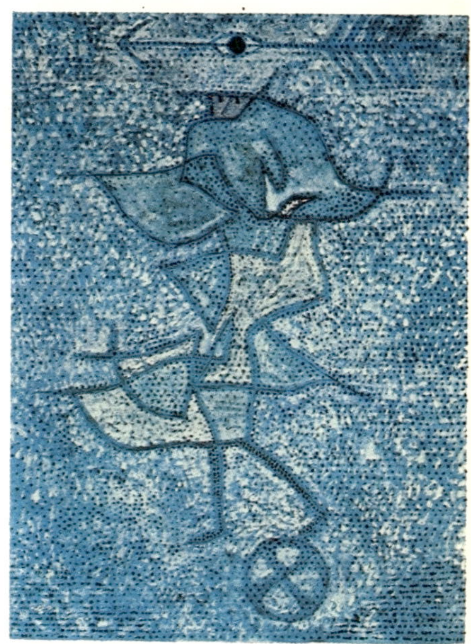

Klee, *Diana* (1931). Diana was the Roman moon goddess. Klee expressed himself here with varicolored points.

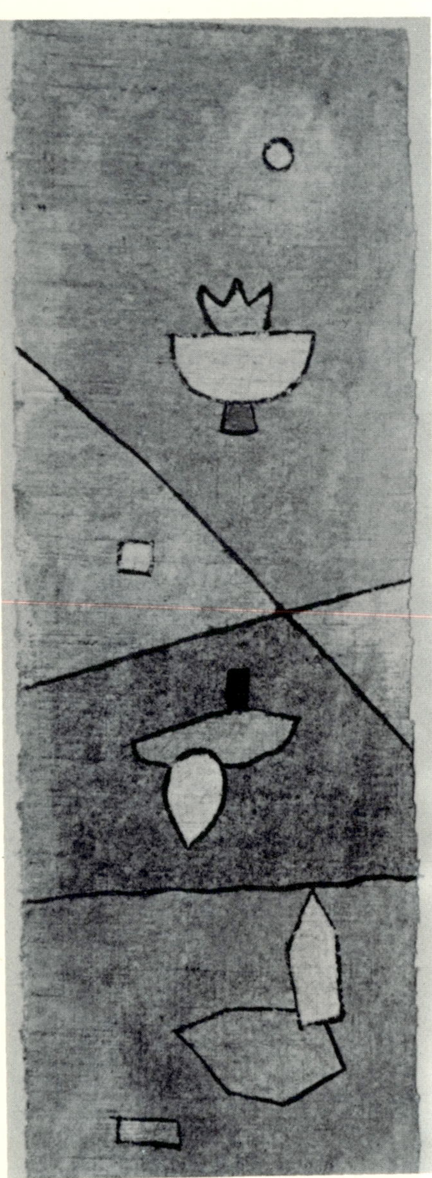

Klee, *Plant—an Analytical Thing* (1932). While pursuing abstract forms and prototypes, Klee presented a unique clarity.

board paintings. His blocks have lost their stability and have begun to float toward a void.

25. *Conqueror* 1930

Colored sheet, water color 41 × 33.5 cm Klee Foundation, Bern

Is the precariously balanced doll-like figure supporting the world? Do the red full and half circles in the overlapping squares represent the sun and moon? In the way that Klee described himself as the balance between yesterday and tomorrow, so might this be a self-portrait set in just such unstable circumstances. One receives from this tersely effective work a strangely bitter impression.

26. *Ad Parnassum* 1932

Canvas, oil 100 × 126 cm Kunstmuseum, Bern

With an orange-yellow sun shining upon a pyramid-shaped mountain, this surely must be the most beautiful of Klee's divisionist pictures; yet the style is not that of Seurat's outside light analysis but more of what can be called an inside light analysis. Each mosaic point of color is not an element of sunshine but a unit of the imagination.

27. *A Nordic Tale* 1930

Gouache, oil 36.2 × 44.8 cm Kunstmuseum, Basel

Does the Nordic story perhaps refer to a fairy tale by Hans Christian Andersen? As in *Female Dwarf*, the principal color tones in this work are dark red and blue. One can almost feel the cold northern air permeating the picture. Against the chilly blueness, children, dogs, sky and sun are daubed with pale red, a color matching the vividness of man's imagination.

28. *At Seven above the Roofs* 1930

Panel, oil and water color 55 × 50 cm Private collection, Paris

Around 1930 Klee was treating mountains and groups of buildings as geometric forms; he produced a series of works that combined the objects rhythmically. The over-all composition is quite stringent, but a strange sense of freedom fills the work and imparts something of early morning's light and freshness. The inlaid black roofs give a particularly unique effect.

29. *Something like a Plant* 1932

Galerie Beyeler, Basel

It is interesting to note that Klee concentrated on various prototypes during this period; two examples are *Hovering, before the Ascent* and *A Rhythmic Object.* His divisionist techniques probably were expressions of the coloring aspects of his search for prototypes. This work is Klee's simplest expression of a plant. The floating, fishlike face is amusing.

30. *Arab Song* 1932

Canvas, oil 91.5 × 64 cm Phillips Collection, Washington

This work most certainly resulted from Klee's time in Egypt. A strange vividness in the simple forms lets us visualize the people he saw on his trip, the molding of mysterious sorrow and joy was probably inspired by the songs he heard.

31. *Rhythms* 1930

Canvas, oil 60 × 50 cm Private collection, Bern

Perhaps this painting prompted further development of Klee's checkerboard works. He seems to be grasping for the basic pattern of rhythm by limiting the number of colors used. A similar work is *Triple Time in a Square.* The black, white and bluish gray in *Rhythms* can be interpreted as representing triple time.

32. *Negro Glance* 1933

Colored sheet, gouache 49.5 × 37 cm Klee Foundation, Bern

As with *Arab Song,* perhaps this composition was also inspired by Klee's trip to Egypt. It is interesting that upon his return Klee gave considerable attention to the structural formation of eyes in his work. Compare the fusion of grotesqueness and humor in this work with Redon's treatment of eyes.

33. *Clown in Bed* 1937

Paper, gouache 27 × 48 cm Klee Foundation, Bern

Klee's search progressed from prototypes, color divisionism and eye forms to a new delineation in which he sought to express his essential nature, shifting to the style of his final period. Klee began his career as a sketcher and engraver,

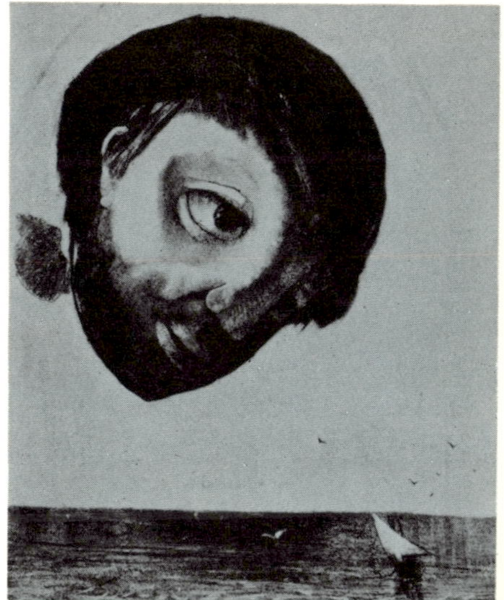

Redon, *Head with Wings Flying over the Water* (1879)

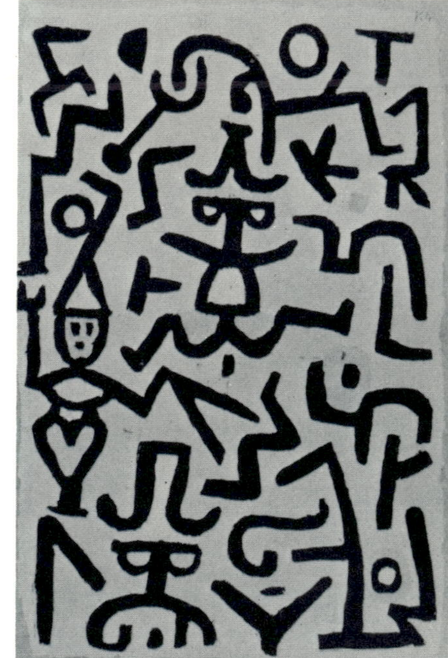

Klee, *Poster for Comedians* (1938)

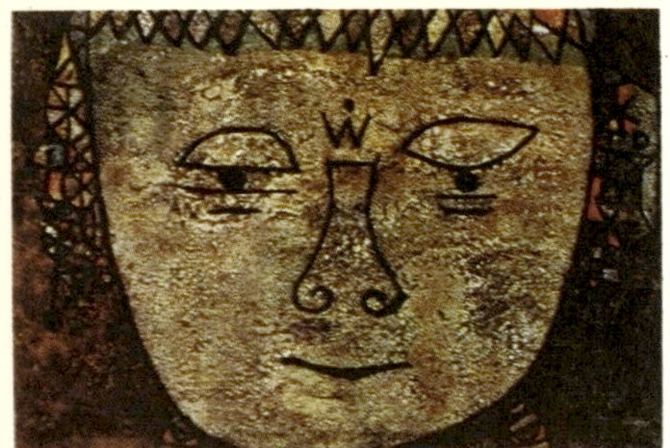

Klee, *Child Consecrated to Woe* (1935). Klee's initial symptoms of sclerosis of the skin appeared in 1935.

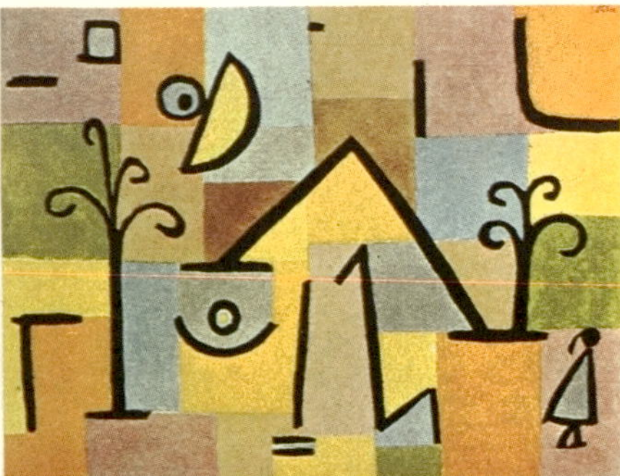

Klee, *Oriental-Sweet* (1938). In 1937 Klee started using thick black lines like those in this work.

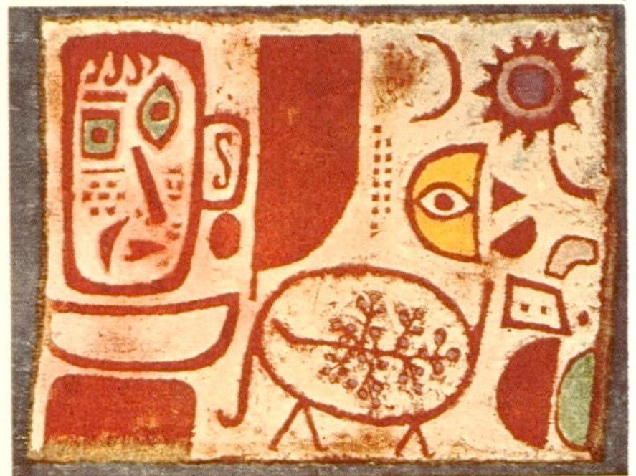

Klee, *Intoxication* (1939). A boat, an *s*-lettered ear, an animal, a flower and a moon make a charming puzzle.

and he seems here to have returned to what he was originally. The transparent space enclosed by the simple, thick lines represents forty years of hard work.

34. *Guarded Plant* 1937

Crayon, gouache 62.5 × 47.5 cm Galerie Beyeler, Basel

A plant resembling some strange sea creature stretches its leaves and branches against an aquamarine background; the figures standing guard look more like octopuses than humans. Klee fused sea and land motifs frequently; this work is the most succinct expression of that fusion. It demonstrates fluidity of movement, yet is as firm as an ancient mural.

35. *Traveling Circus* 1937

Canvas, oil 65 × 50 cm Baltimore Museum of Art

Klee combines color divisionism and a movement of strong lines to create a strangely humorous work overflowing with poetic sentiments. A dancer lifts one leg, a pony is lost in thought, a flag flutters in the breeze; the one-eyed circus leader hurries to find the group's next stopping place.

36. *A Sheet of Pictures* 1937

Canvas, oil 59 × 56 cm Phillips Collection, Washington

Klee obviously retained certain images from Egyptian art. Ancient Egyptians carved pictures on stone that hold a wealth of information about their lives and imaginations. The idea doubtless impressed Klee; the stone surface became the surface of his inner self. A human figure, a fish, the sun and various symbols are placed almost whimsically in open space; yet the whole reveals an exquisite order.

37. *Early Sorrow* 1938

Colored sheet, oil and water color 33.5 × 44.5 cm Klee Foundation, Bern

Klee remarked in his diary that in portraits he depicted internal as well as external elements. The power of his lines no longer has the agonized distortion of earlier years but freely gives shape to agony. One gets the impression that traces of Klee's effort to understand agony have remained in his work.

38. *Park Near L(ucerne)* 1938

Canvas, oil 100.5 × 70.0 cm Klee Foundation, Bern

The briefest movement of thick, black lines surrounded by ultralucent colors is sufficient to prompt us to imagine a park with trees. This period shows a command of evocative powers and the ability to use them with precision.

39. *The Eye* 1938

Felix Klee, Bern

Although identical in style to *Negro Glance*, this work offers not grotesqueness but placidity. The stillness imparts the dark melancholy of people who can only stare with wide-open eyes. Klee's sadness at the time seems to have cast its shadow over this work.

40. *Red Waistcoat* 1938

Canvas, chalk and gouache 65 × 42.5 cm Felix Klee, Bern

Is this perhaps a horse-racing scene with a jockey wearing the red waistcoat? The commanding ocher tones do suggest a racecourse—but what is more deserving of the observer's attention is the intensity created by the strangely vital linear movement.

41. *Twilight Blossoms* 1940

Klee Foundation, Bern

Between 1939 and 1940, coloring seemed to renew its prominence in Klee's work. This painting demonstrates his characteristic premise that linear construction provides the scheme while color adds richness. In the ultimate stage of this style, lines and colors are strengthened and broadened, seemingly in an effort to repel death's incursion.

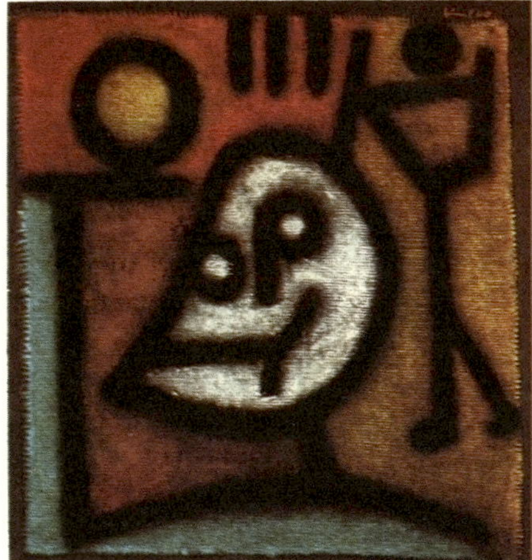

Klee, *Death and Fire* (1940). The title reveals Klee's preoccupation with death late in his life.

42. *Coelin-Fruit* 1938

Colored sheet, gouache 35.5 × 27 cm Klee Foundation, Bern

The fruit, surrounded by bold lines, appears to be growing larger each moment. This work no doubt grew out of Klee's concern with the themes of life and death in his later years. In symbolic terms, the fruit represents the maturation of all of his artistic works. The artist is represented by the tree trunk.

43. *Graveyard* 1939

Colored sheet, paste color 37 × 50 cm Klee Foundation, Bern

Pale blue blankets the painting like cold air while dark trees and crosses stand mute. The atmosphere of death has a blood-chilling coldness that dominates the silence of this scene. Klee once remarked that art was creation, but toward the end of his life he frequently treated death themes.

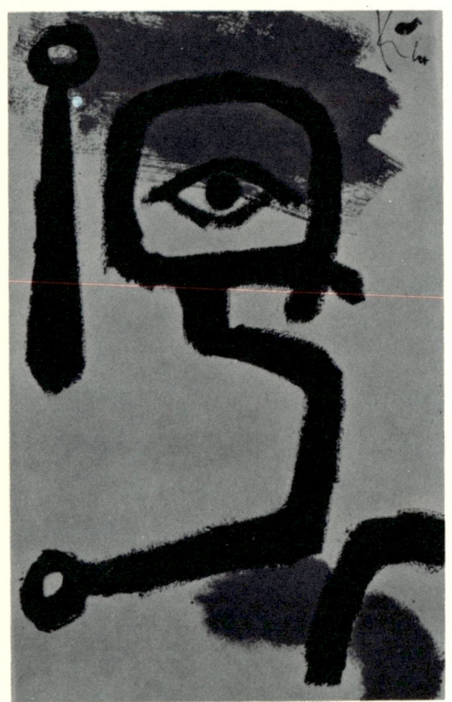

Klee, *Drummer* (1940)

44. *Bastard* 1939

60 × 70 cm Felix Klee, Bern

Klee's father was German; his mother, French-Swiss, reportedly had Arab blood. Perhaps this work betrays Klee's consciousness of his mixed heritage. Could he have modeled this lonely-looking animal after himself? This work is of the period during which he occupied himself with contradictory images.

45. *A Face Yet on the Body* 1939

Felix Klee, Bern

The style of Klee's last period is given its roughest expression in this work. The artist's instinct for line is demonstrated by this painting's linear movement, which seems to have scorched the figure's hair. Spreading out behind the muted passion ruled over by brown tones is the translucent blue of death.

46. *Double* 1940

Paper, gouache 52.0 × 34.5 cm Klee Foundation, Bern

Does the title refer to a double figure or to a departed spirit? The geometric figure is familiar; the surprise is in the

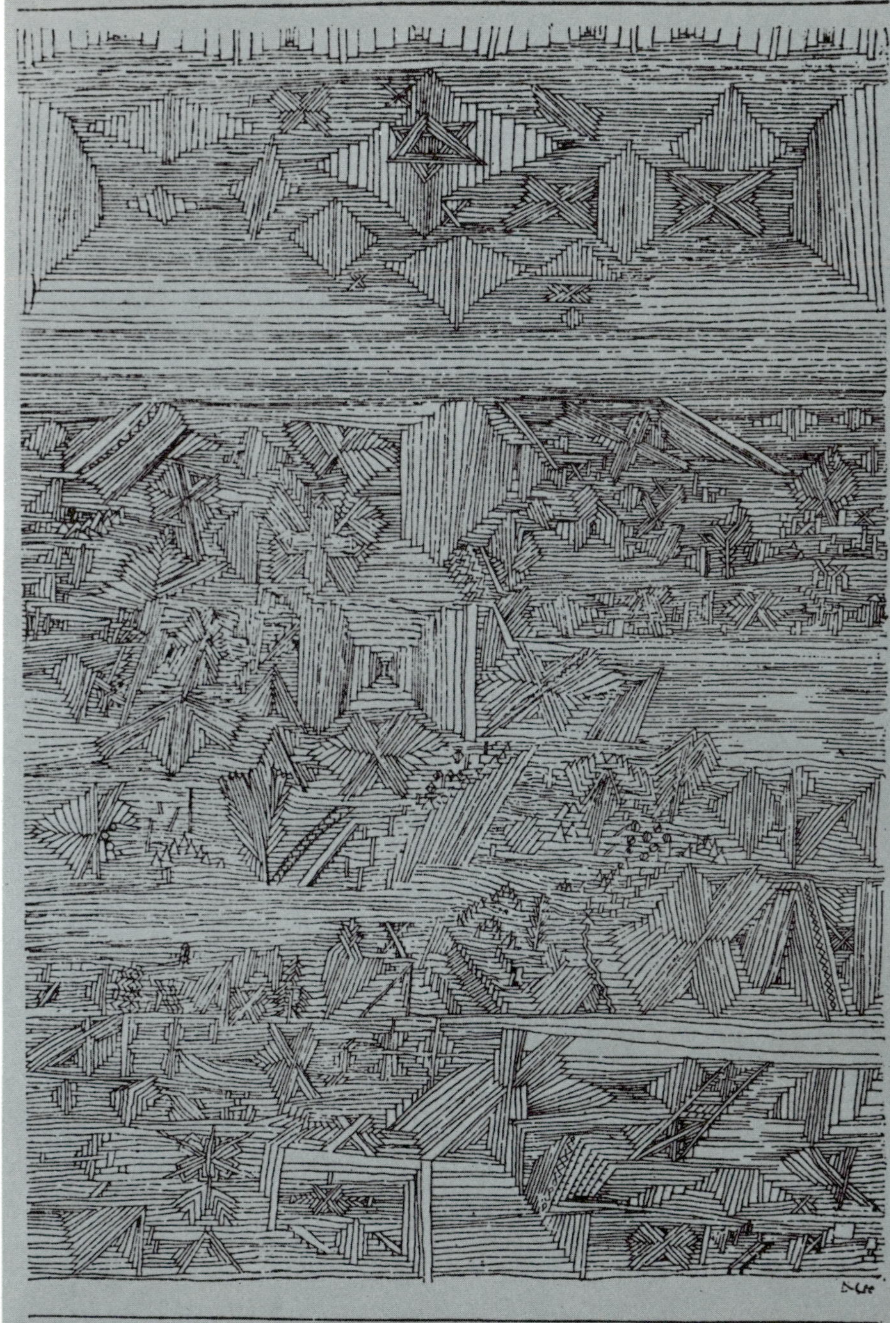

Klee,
Enkei
(Round
Column)
(1926)

way that the over-all form appears to be consumed by flames of death. The work depicts a process of burning and falling back into a type of chaos.

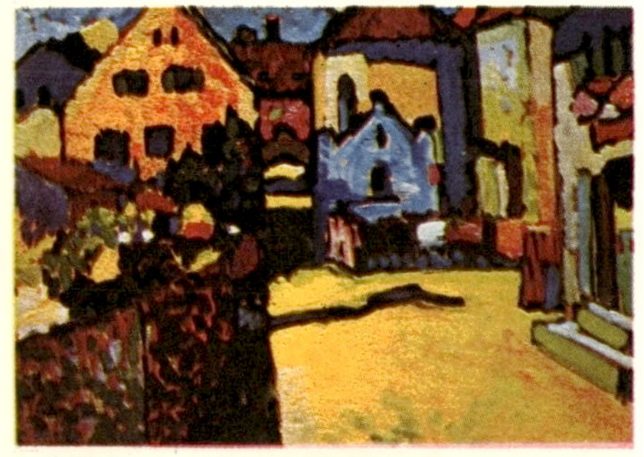

47. *Still Life* 1940

Canvas, oil 100×80 cm Felix Klee, Bern

In this strange still life, a jar and jug raise their "arms" as if alive. They seem to be calling attention to their existence in the darkness. At bottom left is what appears to be a struggle with an angel of death. The flowers scattered on the rug would seem to suggest those the artist used in his works and then cast away . . . or perhaps they symbolize people who died in the dark, final years of Klee's life.

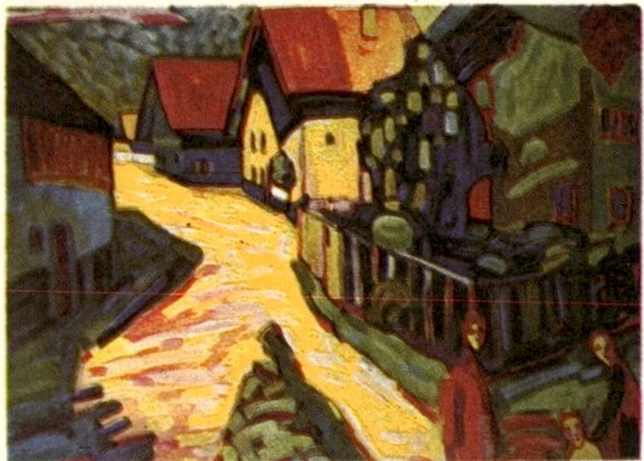

Kandinsky's 1908 *Street in Murnau* (top), and *Green Street in Murnau* (1909)

Wassily Kandinsky (1866-1944)

48. *Landscape with Tree* 1909

Canvas, oil 72.3×97.5 cm Museum of Düsseldorf

This is very likely a scene in Murnau. The composition shows a distinct Cézanne influence; the tree trunk on the right and thicket on the left form a triangle. The branches show brushwork also reminiscent of Cézanne. Kandinsky's use of color, on the other hand, has elements in common with Van Gogh and the Fauvists. By recognizing these influences, we can better appreciate Kandinsky's unique, vivid sense of color.

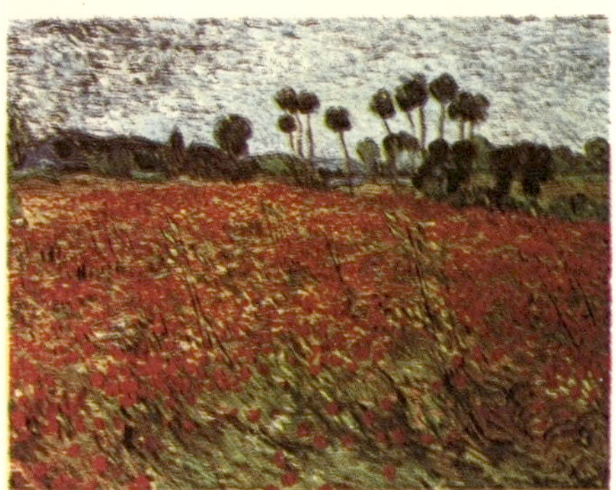

Van Gogh, *Poppyfield* (1889)

49. *First Abstract Water Color* 1910

Paper, water color 47.9×64.9 cm

This work established Kandinsky's individuality as an artist. He tore down the last blocks to a clear vision of his art and created an absolutely free space where the fantasies of his imagination unfold with great speed. Kandinsky gives a mysterious life to blobs of color and to lines, setting them adrift in space.

50. *Nude* 1911

Canvas, oil 147.3 × 99.0 cm Galerie Beyeler, Basel

The lines of the nude barely follow the movement of the artist's eyes; sensual groupings of color seem to run to the foot of the figure. Swiftly moving lines and color overcome various imbalances. Except for the nude, all recognizable forms are split asunder. Cool and warm colors delicately interact; the over-all composition sustains a strong tension.

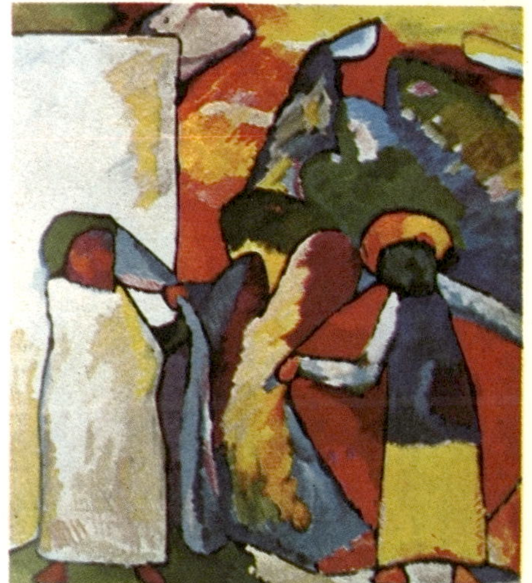

Kandinsky, *Improvisation 6* (1910)

51. *Dreamy Improvisation* 1913

Canvas, oil 130 × 130 cm Private collection, New York

Kandinsky freed colors from their role as cosmetics and seemed to return them to their source. Various lines stretch out like mysterious plants from the artist's imagination, flowering moment by moment and scattering crimson pollen. The black of night at center suggests a Moscow sunset.

52. *Improvisation 30* 1913

Canvas, oil 111 × 111 cm The Art Institute of Chicago

For Kandinsky, improvisation was an expression of an inner, spiritual process—mostly unconscious and formed without previous notice. He painted thirty-five *Improvisations* between 1909 and 1914. In this one, subtitled *Cannon*, one senses the uneasy tension of a warlike atmosphere.

53. *Improvisation 35* 1914

Canvas, oil 110.5 × 120.0 cm Loaned to Kunstmuseum, Basel

This is the last work in Kandinsky's *Improvisation* series, and though it has the same vague quality of the others, there is also a suggestion of the birth of some primitive creature. A shell-like shape in the center, a sea urchin on the right, and various other creatures are recognizable. The circular movement of the painting shows a tendency toward form.

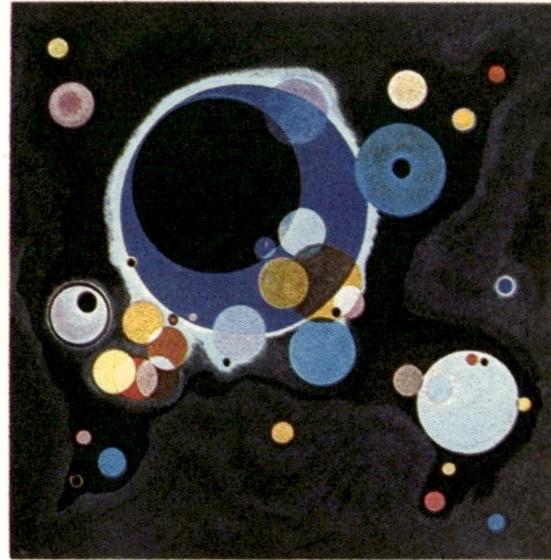

Kandinsky, *Numerous Circles* (1926). Kandinsky published his theoretical *From Point and Line to Plane* in 1926.

54. *Painting on Light Ground* 1916

Canvas, oil 100 × 78.1 cm Nina Kandinsky, Paris

Vague and indeterminate movements of various objects suggest creation in nature and produce an extraordinarily

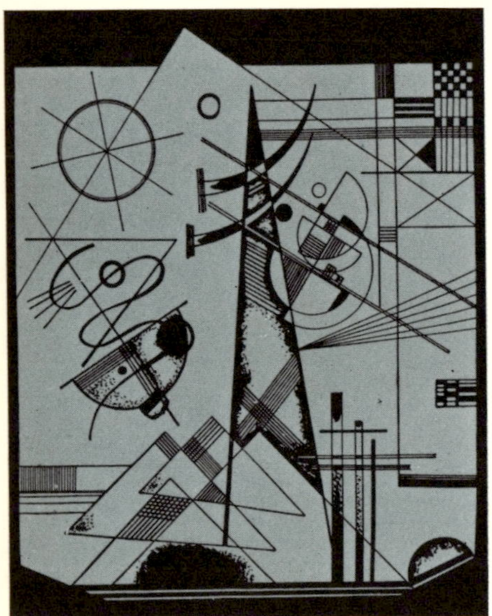

Kandinsky, *Draft Work* (1924)

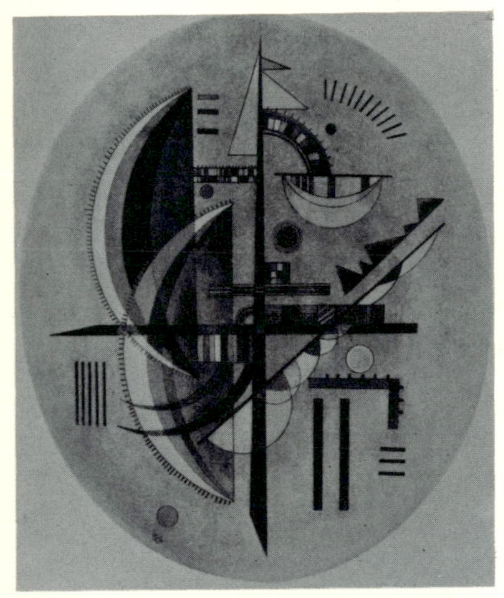

Kandinsky, *A Lyrical Ellipse* (1928). This work reveals a wondrous harmony.

tense and dynamic effect. One feels here the beginning of Kandinsky's pursuit of abstract forms while at the Bauhaus. The over-all composition seems about to become elliptical, while the forms seem ready to become squares and triangles.

55. *Circle within the Circle* 1923

Canvas, oil 97×96 cm Philadelphia Museum of Art

From 1923 to 1926 Kandinsky persistently pursued the circle motif. It was natural that in his effort to fuse image and movement Kandinsky should have turned to the circle, a form that is stable and unstable at one and the same time. Many small circles are here enclosed in a large one; numerous lines cut through the circles and the belts of color crossing them.

56. *Yellow Point* 1924

Canvas, oil 47.0×65.4 cm Private collection

This work has an extraordinarily dramatic tension achieved with basic elements—circles, lines and triangles. Kandinsky gives them precise, individual expression and they affect one another to produce a new form. Against a dark background, this drama of forms seems to be relating an eternal story.

57. *Sharp-Calm Pink* 1924

Cardboard, oil 64×48.3 cm Wallraf-Richartz-Museum, Cologne

Here Kandinsky simultaneously pursues color and basic triangular, quadrangular and circular forms. He expresses the combination not merely as a compositional unit but as an emotional and psychological quantity. This particular union of forms and colors gives the painting a complicated musical effect.

58. Untitled (*Oval No. 2*) 1925

Cardboard, oil 33.9×28.9 cm Nina Kandinsky, Paris

Kandinsky viewed the circle as the "clearest index of the fourth dimension." The ellipse, on the other hand, has strong ties to earthly life. Violently contrasting triangles, lines, half-circles and curved lines impress us with their mysterious harmony. The total effect suggests the germination of form inside an egg.

59. *Mild Hardness* 1927

Wood, oil 50.5 × 37.8 cm Solomon R. Guggenheim Museum, New York

As in *Points in an Arc*, there is here a delicate fusion of softness and hardness; circles and semicircles are placed at random amid the hard lines, and the delicate shifts of color combine to give a mysterious soft quality. Note the interesting eye image in the upper center; the total composition might be an anatomical map of the mechanism that governs the eye's functions.

60. *Points in an Arc* 1927

Canvas, oil 66 × 48.9 cm Private collection, Munich

Kandinsky's intuitive grasp of contradictory elements in a form was exceptional. He found stability and instability in the circle, for example, and in a single color discovered sharpness and softness. The contradictions among these structural elements are essential factors for giving movement to a form.

61. *Two Sides Red* 1928

Canvas, oil 57.8 × 43.5 cm Solomon R. Guggenheim Museum, New York

Various forms between the red faces on either side of the painting give the strange effect of being adrift in a void. This work effectively reveals Kandinsky's extraordinarily keen sensitivity toward form's sympathetic and suggestive qualities.

62. *Jocular Sound* 1929

Cardboard, oil 35 × 49 cm Busch-Reisinger Museum, Harvard

Like Klee, Kandinsky loved music. His concern with musical elements in art shows in his early realistic work as well as in the abstract work of his late years. He seemed always filled with the spirit of music; the simple, limpid compositions he produced around 1929 best crystallized it.

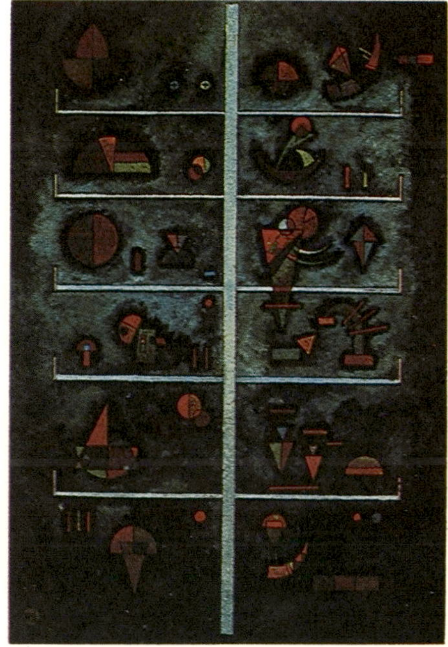

Kandinsky, *Steps* (1929)

63. *Thirteen Rectangles* 1930

Cardboard, oil 70 × 60 cm Nina Kandinsky, Paris

The stable rectangular forms express a light, limpid movement by subtly changing and linking together lines of force produced by diagonals. Stability and instability, stillness and movement, silence and music are in harmony here. Precise calculations fuse into a fresh lyricism, and the listener hears a music of silence.

64. *Brownish* 1931

Cardboard, oil 48.3 × 70.0 cm San Francisco Museum of Art

What Kandinsky called "Something Brownish" might have referred to a shadow of night that had fallen over his clear, bright world. This work's unique melancholic beauty owes much to effective color placement.

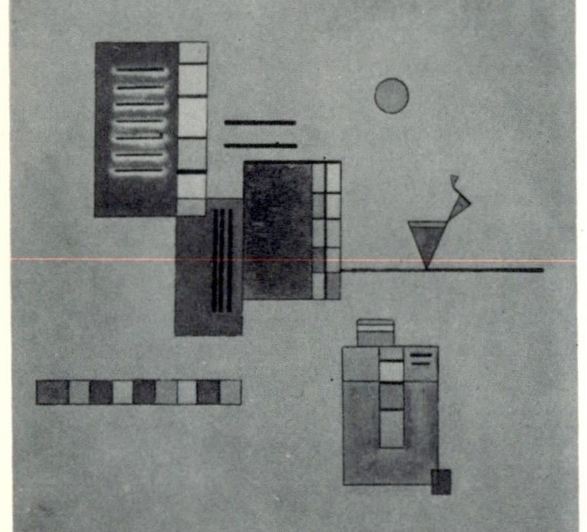
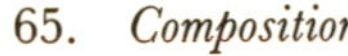

Kandinsky, *Green Steps* (1929)

65. *Composition*

National Museum of Art, Mannheim

Structurally, this work closely resembles *Jocular Sound.* The over-all impression, however, is more complicated. The slightly inclining doll-like images contrast with the stable geometrical forms to maintain a delicate balance. This might be likened to the music of a piano and string or wind instruments playing together; it is an extremely modern work, a kind of capriccio.

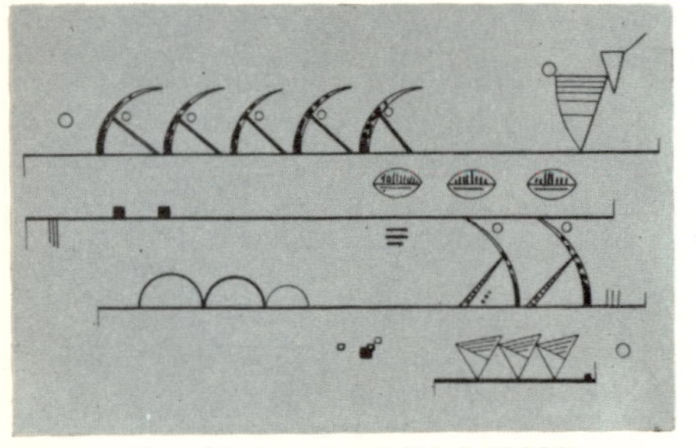

Kandinsky, *Draft Work* (1931)

66. *Gradated Drawing*

Galerie Beyeler, Basel

While at the Bauhaus Klee used diagrammatic techniques in some works. While Klee adopted the movement of lines of perspective, however, Kandinsky concentrated on the relationship among complicated forces produced by flat figures. This work resembles the blueprint of a factory, and could almost be emitting a mysterious sound as it moves forward.

67. *Line of Marks* 1931

Paper, charcoal and tempera 41.5 × 50.5 cm Kunstmuseum, Basel

When this work is compared with *Mural* and other Klee works in which he used a lace pattern, the distinct difference between the two artists is readily apparent. Klee was essentially an artist of the delicate, rhythmical line; Kandinsky was primarily an artist of color, as represented by his musical forms. This work expresses the culmination of his contrapositional technique.

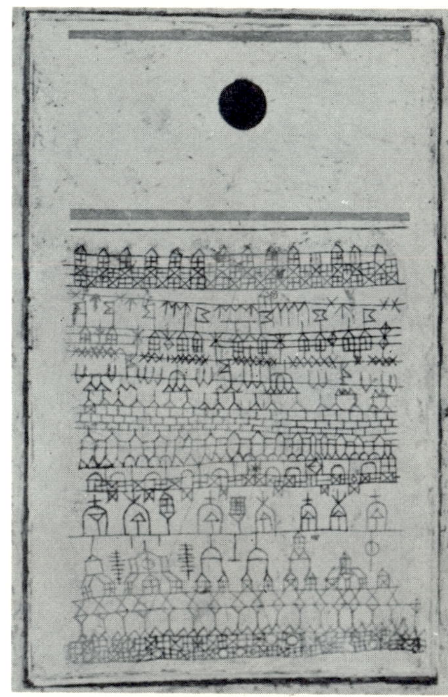

Klee, *A Leaf from a Book of Cities* (1928)

68. *Cool Distance* 1932

Cardboard, oil and tempera 43 × 42 cm Nina Kandinsky, Paris

Various forms float on a delicately colored ground. A strange, isolated atmosphere and a kind of dark humor dominate this picture. The Nazis closed the Bauhaus in 1932, which may account for the painting's sinister quality.

69. *Center with Accompaniment* 1937

Canvas, oil 114 × 146 cm Collection Aimé Maeght, Paris

Static, dynamic, rectangular and stomach-shaped forms, cilia and straight lines are scattered on this canvas with astonishing freedom, almost as if they were performing a musical accompaniment to their creation. The artist's dreams and desires touch and enter every form in this bright space.

70. *Many-colored Ensemble* 1938

Canvas, oil and lacquer 116.0 × 88.9 cm Baltimore Museum of Art

From his late thirties on, Kandinsky frequently utilized a form resembling a deformed African continent. After pursuing abstraction at the Bauhaus, Kandinsky next searched in a different dimension for the essence of life, an effort that carried him from the circle to the ellipse.

71. *Circuit* 1939

Canvas, oil 92.1 × 73.6 cm Nina Kandinsky, Paris

The psychological space with wriggling forms that appeared

in *First Abstract Water Color* seems here to have been enlarged and made more lucid, in accord with the world itself. Numerous germlike creatures pursue abstract floating forms. The only control over their movements is the music of the world.

72. *The Arrow* 1943

Cardboard, oil 42 × 58 cm Kunstmuseum, Basel

Brilliant red, like the rays of a setting sun, falls on rooftops. The geometric forms resemble human bodies heaped together to gain humorous and sensual expression. A large, curved form and an arrow in the center of the picture give the work a strong feeling of motion. In this color ballet Kandinsky gave prominence to his favorites, red and blue.

73. *Moderate Variation* 1941

Canvas, oil 70 × 70 cm Collection Aimé Maeght, Paris

The scene is floating ships and an expanding harbor; a flag is flapping from a tower, and the moon is out. Above this, Kandinsky placed more ships and strange objects. The pleasant contrast between the two parts creates a complicated scheme of motion in the total work, which demonstrates Kandinsky's amazing intuition regarding the movement and weight of color.

74. *Three Ovals* 1942

Cardboard, oil and tempera 49 × 49 cm Collection Aimé Maeght, Paris

The striped pattern in the center may be a chessboard. The painting extends an invitation to the viewer's imagination: a candle flame flutters, and mirrors reflect unrelated scenes. It is already dawn. Birds sing on branches of trees that rather resemble musical scores.

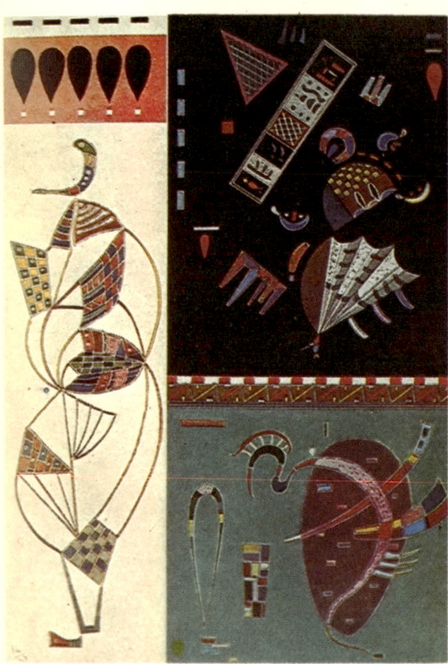

Kandinsky, *Division: Unity* (1943)

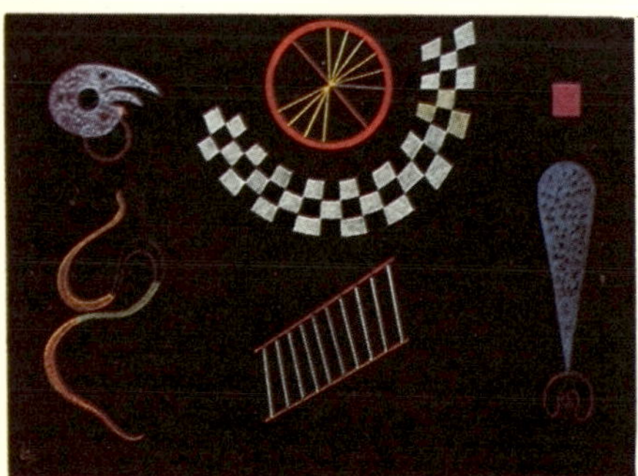

Kandinsky, *Square-shaped Ribbon* (1944). Kandinsky painted this the year he died. The objects set on the dark background make this work strangely impressive.

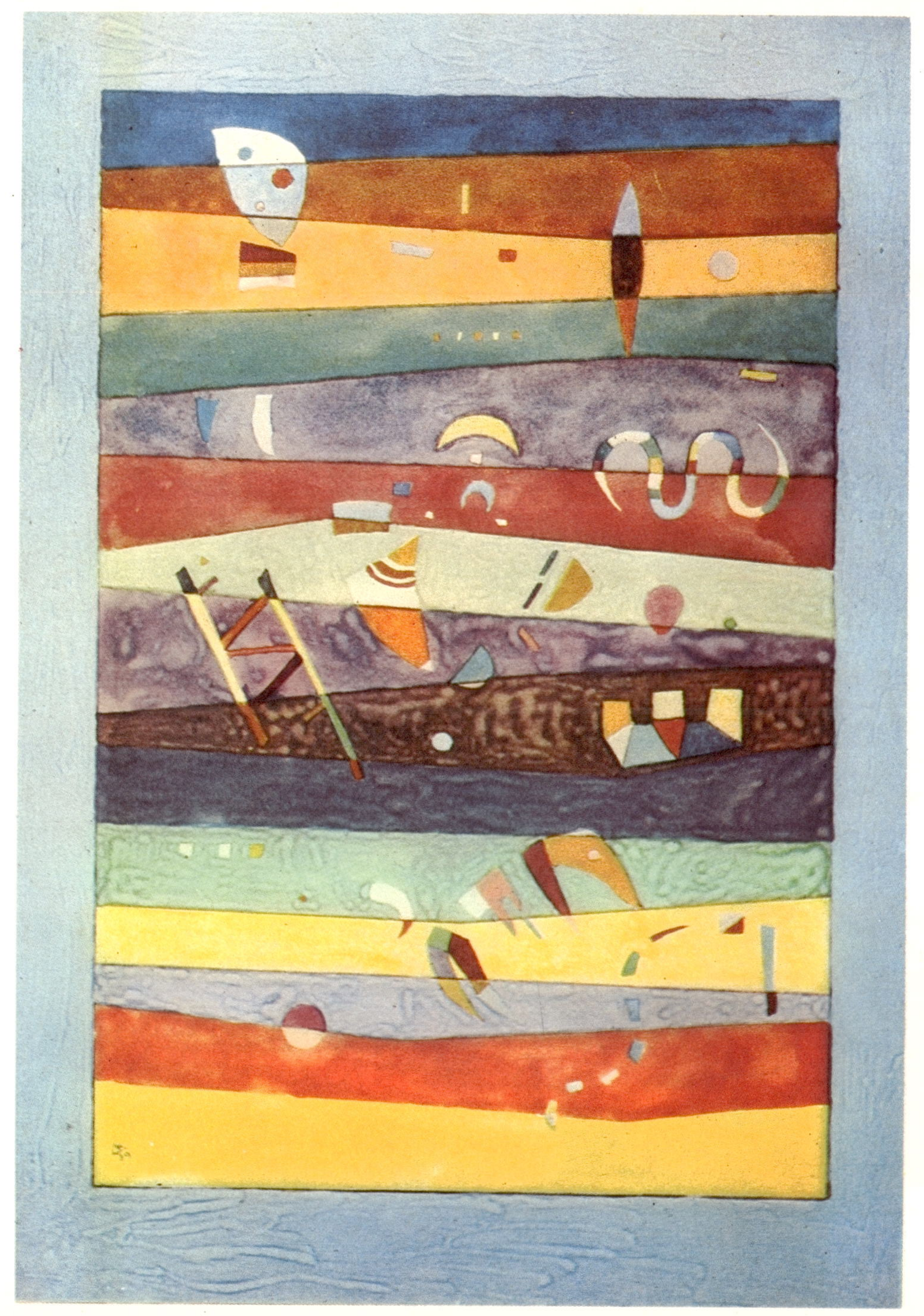

Kandinsky,
Horizon (1939)

CHRONOLOGY

Klee / Kandinsky	*Date*	*General*
Kandinsky born December 4, Moscow.	1866	Manet, Monet and others frequent Café Guerbois.
Klee born December 18, Münchenbuchsee near Bern.	1879	Daumier dies. Fourth impressionist exhibition.
Kandinsky visits Northern Russia as member of team of sociologists. In Saint Petersburg profoundly impressed by Rembrandt exhibition. Visits Paris World Exposition and views newly constructed Eiffel Tower.	1889	
Kandinsky views French impressionist works at Moscow exhibition. Deeply moved by Monet's haystacks series.	1895	Cézanne exhibition opens.
Kandinsky quits university teaching post for art. Moves to Munich.	1896	Verlaine dies.
Klee settles in Munich and studies with Knirr.	1898	Rodin exhibits *Balzac* at Salon.
Kandinsky and Klee study with Frane Stuck at Royal Academy of Art.	1900	Picasso goes to Paris. Tanguy born.
Kandinsky forms Phalanx group. Klee travels with Swiss sculptor Hermann Haller to Italy in September.	1901	Alberto Giacometti born. Toulouse-Lautrec dies.
Kandinsky visits Russia.	1903	
Kandinsky publishes *Poetry without Music*, first collection of woodblock prints.	1904	Dali born.
Klee starts work on glass paintings. Travels to Paris.	1905	Fauvism initiated.
Kandinsky moves to outskirts of Paris in June. Completes *Techniques of Woodprints*. Klee resides in Munich. Exhibits first etchings in *Sezession* exhibition.	1906	Cézanne dies. Modigliani and Juan Gris settle in Paris.
Klee exhibits in Berlin and Munich *Sezession* shows.	1908	Utrillo's white period.
Kandinsky forms New Artists Association of Munich.	1909	Cézanne exhibition at *Sezession.*
Kandinsky publishes *On the Spiritual in Art.* Travels to Russia. Completes *First Abstract Water Color.*	1910	Henri Rousseau dies.
Klee meets Kandinsky, Marc and others. They form *Blaue Reiter* group. Klee's first one-man show held in Munich.	1911	
Kandinsky publishes *Reflections* in Berlin.	1913	Apollinaire's *The Cubist Painters.*
Klee becomes founding member of *Neue Munchner Sezession* group. Trip to Tunis and Kairouan with Moilliet and Macke.	1914	First World War begins.
Klee drafted into German army, serves behind lines.	1916	

Kandinsky appointed administrative adviser for art to Soviet government; becomes professor at National Art Academy.	1918	Apollinaire dies.
Kandinsky appointed professor, Moscow University. Holds one-man show, Moscow. Klee appointed professor at Weimar Bauhaus.	1920	Modigliani dies.
Kandinsky founds Art Academy. Quits Russia at end December for Berlin.	1921	Dada demonstration by Arp, Ernst and Tzara in Tyrol.
Kandinsky appointed professor Weimar Bauhaus. Publishes *Small World*, collection of woodblocks, etchings and lithographs.	1922	Dadaist International Exhibition, Paris.
Founding of *Der Blaue Vier:* Kandinsky, Klee, Feininger and Jawlensky; first exhibition held.	1923	
Klee lectures in Jena on modern art.	1924	André Breton's Surrealism declaration.
Klee publishes *Pedagogical Sketchbook.* Participates in surrealist exhibition, Paris. First one-man show of Klee's works in Paris.	1925	Mondrian publishes *New Plastic Art.* Bauhaus moves to Dessau.
Kandinsky publishes *From Point and Line to Plane* in Munich. On sixtieth birthday holds four exhibitions. Klee travels to Italy.	1926	Monet dies. Ernst publishes *Hakubutsushi* magazine.
Kandinsky produces settings for Moussorgsky's *Pictures at an Exhibition*, staged at Dessau Theatre. Klee travels to Egypt in winter.	1928	Gropius quits Bauhaus.
Kandinsky holds first one-man show in Paris. Travels to Belgium. Large exhibition of Klee works in Berlin commemorating fiftieth birthday.	1929	Museum of Modern Art opens in New York. Bourdelle dies.
Kandinsky paints mural for International Architectural Show, Berlin. Publishes *Contemplations on Abstract Art.* Klee quits Dessau Bauhaus. Appointed professor, Düsseldorf Akademie.	1931	First surrealist exhibition in New York.
Following Nazi shutdown of Bauhaus, Kandinsky quits Germany for France. Klee also forced to flee to Bern.	1933	Nazis purge most of the well-known German artists.
Symptoms of Klee's fatal disease appear.	1935	Signac and Malevich die.
Kandinsky travels to Switzerland, meets Klee. Fifty-seven Kandinsky paintings confiscated by Nazis as "degenerate" art; 102 Klee paintings confiscated; 17 exhibited in Munich show of "degenerate" art.	1937	
Large exhibition of Klee's works in Zurich. Klee dies June 29, Muralto-Locarno, Switzerland.	1940	Nazis invade France, halt activities of artist groups and museums.
Kandinsky falls ill in May and dies December 13.	1944	Mondrian and Marinetti die.

LIST OF COLOR PLATES

Paul Klee 1879–1940

Wassily Kandinsky 1866–1944

48 *Landscape with Tree* 1909 Museum of Düsseldorf
49 *First Abstract Water Color* 1910
50 *Nude* 1911 Galerie Beyeler, Basel
51 *Dreamy Improvisation* 1913 Private Collection, New York
52 *Improvisation 30* 1913 Art Institute of Chicago
53 *Improvisation 35* 1914 Loaned to Kunstmuseum, Basel
54 *Painting on Light Ground* 1916 Nina Kandinsky, Paris
55 *Circle within the Circle* 1923 Philadelphia Museum of Art
56 *Yellow Point* 1924 Private Collection
57 *Sharp-Calm Pink* 1924 Wallraf-Richartz-Museum, Cologne
58 Untitled (*Oval No. 2*) 1925 Nina Kandinsky, Paris
59 *Mild Hardness* 1927 Guggenheim Museum, New York
60 *Points in an Arc* 1927 Private Collection, Munich
61 *Two Sides Red* 1928 Guggenheim Museum, New York
62 *Jocular Sound* 1929 Busch-Reisinger Museum, Harvard
63 *Thirteen Rectangles* 1930 Nina Kandinsky, Paris
64 *Brownish* 1931 San Francisco Museum of Art
65 *Composition* National Museum of Art, Mannheim
66 *Gradated Drawing* Galerie Beyeler, Basel
67 *Line of Marks* 1931 Kunstmuseum, Basel
68 *Cool Distance* 1932 Nina Kandinsky, Paris
69 *Center with Accompaniment* 1937 Collection Aimé Maeght, Paris
70 *Many-colored Ensemble* 1938 Baltimore Museum of Art
71 *Circuit* 1939 Nina Kandinsky, Paris
72 *The Arrow* 1943 Kunstmuseum, Basel
73 *Moderate Variation* 1941 Collection Aimé Maeght, Paris
74 *Three Ovals* 1942 Collection Aimé Maeght, Paris

LIST OF ILLUSTRATIONS

Slip case:
Front *Points in an Arc* (detail), Kandinsky 1927
Back *Twilight Blossoms* (detail), Klee 1940

Front cover:
Insula Dulcamara (detail), Klee 1938